Seven Plays by Women

Female Voices, Fighting Lives.
Edited by Cheryl Robson.

Cheryl Robson studied Drama and French at Bristol University, then worked in film editing and production at the BBC for several years, before freelancing. She has lectured in Higher Education and is currently taking her M.A. in Playwriting at Birmingham University. She was Literary Manager for Bristol Express Theatre Company from 1988-90 and is the founder of the Women Writers' Workshop at the Drill Hall Arts Centre in London.

Her plays include:

Basta Ya - Half Moon Theatre
Scream and Dream Again - Man in the Moon Theatre
O Architect - New End Theatre Hampstead
The Taking of Liberty winner of the South London Playwriting competition at the Croydon Warehouse 1990.

Other publications:

'The Women Writers' Handbook' edited by Robson, Georgeson, Beck.
(Aurora Metro)
'Taking Reality by Surprise' edited by Susan Sellars (The Women's Press)

She lives in London with her husband and two children.

D1081130

Seven Plays by Women

Female Voices, Fighting Lives.
Edited by Cheryl Robson.

AURORA METRO PUBLICATIONS
Copyright © Aurora Metro 1991

FRONT COVER ILLUSTRATION ENTITLED *"Daughters of Minyas."*
Woodcut 48" x 84" a part of "Ovid's Metamorphoses" Series by TSUGUMI OTA

"British Library Cataloguing in Publication Data
Seven Plays by Women
1. English drama
I. Robson, Cheryl
822. 9148092878020
IBSN 0-9515877-1-4.

Caution:

Cover designed by Coda Design. 13 Hercules Street, London N7 6AT

Printed by Polprint
63 Jeddo Rd, London W12 9EE

CONTENTS

The Plays

INTRODUCTION by Cheryl Robson

Plays by women rarely receive publication and if they do, often fail to be reprinted. Many successful plays by women performed each year are forgotten because theatre publishers are not only looking for good plays but also for bankable writers who'll be writing plays in ten years time, so they can recoup their initial publishing investments. Women playwrights are often considered to be unsuitable for long-term investment because they may take time out of their writing career to have children. With more plays by men being published every year, it's not surprising that plays by women fail to be included in courses of dramatic literature, that women's drama is marginalised, treated as an optional extra for women students - who usually comprise over fifty per cent of any theatre studies department.

The financial repercussions of this lack of support from publishers in the early stages of a dramatist's career mean that without the printed text, a play is unlikely to find more than one production, minimising its chances of earning revenue for its author. In addition to this there is the mistaken belief held by theatres around the country that a play by a man is aimed at the general public, whereas a play by a woman is written for a 'specialist' audience of women. This also reduces the number of opportunities for women to be employed as directors, actors, designers, technicians etc., depriving women of the experience of mainstream productions which they need to compete equally for jobs. It drives women theatre practitioners to set up their own small companies where they struggle with a non-existent budget simply to find a way of staging the work. It is hard for women working in this way to gain recognition for their work because they are limited by resources, venue, cast, rehearsal period etc. The belief that women are writing for a 'specialist' audience must be challenged, especially in the light of research which shows that the majority of theatre ticket-buyers are women and that plays which authenticate the lives of women, such as Charlotte Keatley's *"My Mother Said I Never Should"* do well at the box office.

We are all culturally impoverished when we fail to publish or produce the work of women playwrights because women have been at the forefront of experimentation in theatre over the last decade. The most prominent of these, Caryl Churchill is on record as saying that she has earned very little money from her work. Why? When her play *'Top Girls'* was one of the most important plays of the 1980's. It has just been revived at the Royal Court Theatre. Clive Hirschhorn wrote of it in the *Sunday Express*:
"Top Girls...reinforces Caryl Churchill's status as one of the most original and exciting dramatists."

Benedict Nightingale for *The New Statesman* wrote of Churchill: "a playwright of genuine audacity and assurance, able to use her considerable wit and intelligence in ways at once unusual, resonant and dramatically riveting."

Women's plays have disappeared from our stages before because they have failed to be included in the dramatic literary 'canon' that is passed on from generation to generation. There is no doubt that women will continue to create exciting and innovative theatre but it requires a change of attitude on the part of the theatre establishment to ensure that this work can reach a wider audience.

FEMALE VOICES

Is there a difference between a play written by a man and a play written by a woman? Do women perceive the world differently from men? Is there such a thing as female sensibility? If we accept that women are positioned differently from men in society, then we should expect that difference to be reflected in any writing that women undertake.

Women's drama tends to focus on women characters and has been criticised because the plays are often of a domestic nature. Many other playwrights have focused on women and the home such as Ibsen, Chekhov, Shaw but this is not considered to be a flaw in their work but rather they are praised for the way in which they portray the wider society by focusing on a particular group of individuals.

Plays by men have dominated our stages for so long that the male view of life is considered to be representative of the entire human condition. Male heroes change things while passive females only react to change and never initiate it. In this way cultural stereotypes are reinforced and the established view of society can continue, unchallenged.

Since women's perspectives on life differed from the norm, they were inevitably considered to be an attack on the established order. It has always been difficult for women to have their plays accepted by male theatre managements because of the financial risk of producing plays which were considered to be out of step with prevailing notions.

In the tenth century a Saxon nun named Hrostwitha wrote religious comedies in Latin, modelled on the plays of Terence. These were performed by the nuns in the convent but we can only guess at the kind of audience they played to. In this all-female world, Hrostwitha was protected from male authority and allowed the time and space to develop her dramatic craft.

One of the first women to earn a living as a playwright was Aphra Behn. Charles II had been in exile in France where actresses dominated the stage and on his return to England he wanted to see women acting women's roles, instead of the practice of having boys play women. Aphra Behn began writing plays to pay off debts which had landed her in prison. Her plays protested the lack of independence and the scant education that women in the seventeenth century were allowed. She had seventeen plays produced in London although there were only two theatres operating at the time and was so successful that there was talk of her becoming the first 'female laureate.'

Theatre requires collaboration to take place and women playwrights often find themselves in difficulty when their vision of the world is interpreted by male directors, managers and producers. The playwright's ability to manipulate an audience's emotions and to handle all the elements within the play to create an illusory world, has given drama a reputation for subversion which has led to censorship of texts. Women playwrights who are seen to be wielding this power for subversion successfully are often attacked by the authority which feels threatened by it. Micheline Wandor takes up this point in relation to the novel:

"Such control of a multiple set of voices and the public control of an imaginary world...makes the woman playwright a far greater threat than the female novelist to the carefully maintained dominance of men as the custodians of cultural creation." (From *'Impact of Feminism on Theatre'*: *Feminist Review.*)

Why should there be such hostility to female voices? Surely the classics can survive even if women challenge their right to speak for us all? But the effect of women investigating the classics from a feminist viewpoint has led to a reappraisal of those works. The critic Lawrence Lipking wrote:

"Something peculiar has been happening to the classics. Some of them seem less heroic, and some of them less funny." (From the *'Critical Inquiry'* quoted in *"The New Feminist Criticism"* by Elaine Showalter.)

The misogyny at the heart of many of the classics has been understood by many of the actresses involved in playing them. Ellen Terry noted nearly a century ago that there was something missing from Shakespeare's plays:

"How many times Shakespeare draws fathers and daughters and how little stock he takes of mothers!...Of mothers of sons there are plenty of examples...but if there are mothers of daughters at all they are poor examples, like Juliet's mother or Mrs Page." (From *"Ellen Terry: The Story of My Life."* quoted in *"Women in Theatre"* edited by Karen Malpede)

The importance of mother/daughter relationships, central to the lives of women finds little expression in the classics. The Oedipus myth, which is felt to be representative of the human condition refers only to father/son relationships and mother/son relationships. What is being denied by this depiction of women connected to brothers, fathers and sons but not to sisters, mothers and daughters is the fact of female knowledge passed on from generation to generation and the existence of a female tradition. Recently, there has been an attempt to define what it is that characterises women's writing and the mother/daughter relationship was found to be a recurring motif:

"Some critics studied metaphors of childbirth in art and creativity, others asked whether women's writing is characterised by... a 'female poetics of affiliation' dependent on the daughter's relation to the mother."
(From *"The Madwoman in The Attic."* by Gilbert and Gubar.)

In presenting mother/daughter relationships on the stage women playrights are reinstating a female heritage that has been paid scant attention by the majority of male dramatists. But it is also the desire to present women as they really are, demolishing age-old cultural stereotypes, that drives women to claim the very public forum of the theatre so that we can see our own lives authenticated and have confidence in our own ability to speak out and be heard.

FIGHTING LIVES:

All the plays in this collection show women taking action in response to a situation which they find untenable. Some of the women characters use their anger and dissatisfaction to create a different society, or to take political action, others fight on a more personal level against their families, their friends, their employers, against themselves. In this sense, the plays in this collection are feminist plays because they expose injustice, discrimination and inequality affecting the lives of women. They also assert the value of women and their right to human dignity.

Is feminism an essential ingredient in plays by women or are we living in the age of post-feminist theatre?

A male journalist on *'The Sunday Times'* was recently given several pages to complain that women in the nineties have achieved too much equality and that it's now up to men to fight for their rights, especially with regard to paternity.

This backlash against women fails to acknowledge 'the glass ceiling' of discrimination which prevents women from being promoted into top jobs in many companies and the more obvious discrimination in salaries where women earn only seventy-five per cent of the wage men get for equal work.

Men habitually pay lip-service to notions of anti-sexism at work but in an all-male group, misogynist jokes and sexist language flourish. Women not only need men to genuinely change their attitudes, they also need men to stand aside and let them share in authority and decision-making processes. This lack of power-sharing is as true in the theatre industry as it is elsewhere in Britain today.

If women's theatre is to address itself to the discrimination and disadvantage that persists in our society then it is allying itself with the feminist movement. But feminism has failed to appeal to working class women in particular because they are often more accepting of their role in caring for children and the home, believing that men have more right to full-time work than they do.

This acceptance of unpaid childcare work and domestic labour, underpins the present economic system, although the current recession has meant many unemployed men taking on the domestic role while their partners go out to work. The effect of role-reversal has been documented. The loss of status, the lack of income and the decline in self-esteem all induce considerable stress which is only increased by childcare and household responsibilities that are not even acknowledged as 'real' work. Women are usually expected to tolerate these conditions without complaint and make way for men in a shrinking job market.

Feminism needs to ally itself with other marginalised groups, including working class women to fight for equal representation. It needs to acknowledge that issues of class, race and sexuality are potentially divisive. At the same time, the past successes of the women's movement should be remembered - who else managed to get questions of equal pay and opportunities on the political agenda, alongside those of abortion, rape, sexual harassment and domestic violence?

There are those who argue that women no longer need their own theatre to express the particular nature of women's lives and experiences. Women have won the right to vote, to education, to work an eight hour day and to control their own biology. What more can women have to say? There is a generation of young women now who want the gains made by feminism, without having to align themselves with a movement which they regard as unfashionable. They think the fight is over because some women have achieved a little power. They are ambitious, but only for themselves. They fear that by associating themselves with feminism their chances of promotion will be harmed. If they fail, they may blame themselves for not being smart enough, tough enough, dynamic enough - or they may ask whether all the doors are really open to them, whether power is really being shared, whether it is possible to change social positioning based on gender in so short a time?

Unless women work to keep the issues of women's representation in society alive and firmly on the agenda we may see the erosion of women's rights in favour of the rights of men. Women's theatre has an important part to play in providing a forum for challenging and exposing the continuing discrimination against women in our society and in doing this, it makes a lasting contribution to the cultural and political life of the nation.

All the plays in this collection are by writers who have been either members or tutors of The Women Writers' Workshop at The Drill Hall Arts Centre in London.

LOOKING THROUGH, LOOKING BEYOND...
Sian Evans

Look Back In Anger and the movement it spawned -'The Angry Young Men' have entered theatrical mythology. According to literary reference books *Look Back In Anger* was a play which:
'Voiced postwar feelings of frustration, class consciousness and disillusionment among the young.' (*Oxford Companion to English Literature*, ed. Margaret Drabble 1987)

'It proved a landmark in the history of the theatre, a focus for reaction against a previous generation.' (*Dictionary of Theatre*, ed. David Pickering 1988)

'His (Osbourne's) outbursts of rage against comtemporary society are frequently exhilarating, for the anger that made him known as an Angry Young Man remains one of his strongest theatrical weapons.' (*Oxford Companion to English Literature*)

But whilst *Look Back In Anger* describes the moral and political confusion of an educated working class man in post-war Britain, there is no coherent political argument. Jimmy Porter lashes out indiscriminately at the Welfare State and the Ruling Elite; he even expresses nostalgia for Britain's colonial past. Yet his anger is tangible if unfocused and whilst much of his rhetoric against Alison's middle class family seems tame now, in 1956 it was both exhilarating and shocking for audiences numbed by polite drawing-room drama.

The reaction to the play fell into two camps; those who were outraged by the upstart Porter but thought the playwright showed promise and those who saw the play, though flawed, as a vital piece of dramatic writing, the mouthpiece for the anger of a new generation of dramatists.

The first camp revealed deep-seated snobbery. How dare this young man, housed and educated by the Welfare State turn and bite the hand that blessed him; how dare he not want to use that education to improve himself, how dare he presume to marry into the middle classes. The *Daily Express* referred contemptuously to Jimmy Porter as 'A university chap of working class background who lives in a filthy attic.' The *Birmingham Post* called Jimmy 'self pitying, uncouth, deeply vulgar.' The reviewer of *Punch* commented 'He bullies and humiliates his wife, whose parents have not unnaturally opposed the marriage...he has chosen to... live in an animal way in an abysmally sordid one bedroom flat.' They were obviously deeply affected by the sight of Alison and Helena doing their own ironing.

Other critics realised they might be out of touch with the anger of the young and jumped at the chance to hail Osbourne as their spokesman. He speaks 'The authentic new tone of the nineteen fifties, desperate, savage, resentful and...funny.' He is 'the modern romantic' his voice is 'the genuinely modern accent - one can hear no doubt in every other Expresso bar, witty, relentless, pitiless and utterly without belief.'
No doubt.

The shocking thing about these reviews is not their ignorance of working class life nor their elitism but the fact that they fail to notice what is now recognised as one of the play's main features - its misogyny. Jimmy's anger is partly directed against Alison as a person, partly against her family and the establishment but women are the main target of his tirades. This angle wasn't explored for many years and is still something many male academics either refuse to acknowledge or tacitly accept. It is chilling to consider that before the Women's Movement began to expose misogyny and its many forms, the views expressed by Jimmy Porter were so acceptable as to be not worth mentioning.

Not that the reviewers didn't rush to the rescue of Alison - they almost fell over themselves in their attempt to sweep her onto their metaphorical white chargers, they were ecstatic in their chivalrous outrage - 'his wretched little wife'; 'his pretty wife'; 'the pathetic little wife'; 'the insulted, quivering wife, Mary Ure, gave an exquisitely moving performance'; 'long passages of pain and silence'; 'the battered, brow beaten and trampled on girl who says nothing and does nothing in reply.' Kenneth Tynan said 'it is her endurance, her futile endeavour to escape and her final breakdown which are the truly moving part of the play', 'the sympathy goes to his wife...dumbly taking it.' (*New Statesman*)

Jimmy's anti-women speeches with their images of death and decay show profound fear of the female; Helena's 'Cup of blood'; men are 'butchered by the women'; 'Thank God they don't have many women surgeons! Those primitive hands would have your guts out in no time...I say she ought to be dead. My God those worms will need a good dose of salts the day they get through her! ...She will pass away, my friends, leaving a trail of worms gasping for laxatives behind her - from purgatives to purgatory.' Women are 'sweet and sticky on the outside, and sink your teeth in it, inside, all white messy and disgusting.'

Neither group of reviewers examined the confusion between class and gender in *Look Back In Anger*. It is more than a mere co-incidence that all the female characters are middle class and all the men working class. (The one exception, Alison's father, is treated with grudging respect; he and Jimmy are linked by their maleness which transcends class boundaries. The Colonel, unlike Alison's mother, can be calm and reasonable, he can be magnanimous and understanding.) As soon as Jimmy begins his assault on Alison gender and class become almost indivisible.

'They're either militant like her Mummy and Daddy. Militant, arrogant and full of malice. Or vague. She's somewhere between the two.' Women exploit men just as the middle classes exploit the working classes. They 'bleed us to death.' The middle classes (and women) are essentially passionless 'Oh it's not that she hasn't her own kind of passion. She has the passion of a python. She just devours me whole everytime.' But what about working class womanhood? Two women are mentioned briefly though never seen. One is Hugh's mum, a stereotyped picture of maternal suffering and sacrifice, the other Madeleine, a former girlfriend of Jimmy's (ten years his senior) a cross between mother and scoutmaster, ' Just to be with her was an adventure. Even to sit on the top of a bus with her was like setting out with Ulysses.'

Even middle class women can redeem themselves through suffering and motherhood it seems. Those who dare reject Jimmy and his world view are frosty and virginal but Jimmy can tame them; he instructs them in passion. Helena 'looks more attractive than before, for the setting of her face is more relaxed' and of course like Alison before her she's soon cooking their meals and washing and ironing their clothes (one wonders whether it's the sex or the ironing that's helped her relax!) There are no passionate or angry young women then in Jimmy Porter's world, women are frustrating and ultimately pathetic creatures whose redemption lies in their losing their separate identity and assuming the identity of their man.

The most commonly quoted passage of *Look Back In Anger*, possibly seen as the heart of Jimmy's confusion is the one which contains the phrase 'There are no good brave causes left.' The paragraph begins with the words: 'Why, why, why, why do we let these women bleed us to death? and ends with the sentence: 'No, there's nothing left for it, me boy, but to let yourself be slaughtered by the women.' Porter is expressing here a direct opposition of politics, bravery, a cause and the female, not just middle class women but 'All the women of the world.'

It's not surprising then that the angry brave voices of working class women took so long to surface in the theatre. (Although the very title Angry Young Men effectively rendered women in the movement, such as Ann Jellicoe, invisible). If women were not allowed a separate identity, how could they express their anger? Jimmy Porter was supposedly speaking for his generation; one might be presumptuous enough to assume that meant young working class men and women. But by using misogyny as a tool to appeal to the audience (he speaks of men to men) Osbourne could only alienate women. When women did emerge in the 70's and 80's, nurtured not by the theatre establishment but by the Women's Movement the reception was less than friendly. This time reviewers were not shocked by glimpses of working class life (they knew the layout of a council flat better than the tenants themselves); it was the subject matter that startled. Whereas the misogyny of *Look Back In Anger* was taken for granted by critics the condemnation or even criticism of male attitudes towards women provoked responses ranging from out and out dismissal to rabid anger.

Sarah Daniels' play *Masterpieces* was one such case. Produced at The Royal Court Theatre Upstairs in 1983, twenty six years after John Osbourne's play, the anger that fuelled *Masterpieces* focused on the link between pornography and violence against women. One common response to this 'Angry Young Woman' was a refusal to take her work seriously. *The Standard* headed its review 'Wailing Women.' Even those critics who disliked *Look Back In Anger* used the following vocabulary to describe John Osborne's anger. 'He writes with searing passion, a fine flow of savage talk, a virtuoso display of passionate overwriting, a dazzling aptitude for provoking and stimulating dialogue, an obvious turn for forceful writing, intense, angry, feverish, undisciplined, blazing vitality, savage, abounding with life and vitality, savage humour, powerful, his wild and whirling words.'

Daniels' anger is described as 'A scream of outrage, strident overkill.' Irving Wardle was mightily offended that after encouraging Daniels' first play he was not rewarded with less political plays thereafter: 'After seeing *Ripen Our Darkness* I bestowed some patronisingly masculine compliments on Sarah Daniels as a gifted feminist playwright with much to offer the general public. But after her return to Sloane Square ... with *The Devil's Gateway* and now this new piece, I think I got Ms Daniels wrong, as she seems less interested in writing good plays than in staging consciousness raising seances.'

In many of the reviews the playwright is attacked more than the play: Sarah Daniels was labelled one of the 'man-hating batallions', the *Standard's* reviewer went on to comment on her 'obvious loathing of men.' In the *Financial Times* Michael Coveny praised the writing with one provider 'Now all she has to do is write a good man's role.' (It's difficult to imagine someone commenting on Osbourne or any other male playwright - All he has to do now is write a good part for a woman.)

Reviewers praised Alison's stoic silence in the first half of *Look Back In Anger*, her dumb endurance. Dumb endurance is one thing, coherent anger is obviously quite another. Many critics and academics have reinforced the idea that male anger is virile, passionate, just - female anger is petty, ignoble, and unjust.

Aphra Behn of course said it all 300 years ago. After her play *'Sir Patient Fancy'* was slammed by the critics, despite a successful run, she wrote: 'the play had no other misfortune but that of coming out for a woman's' and 'had it been owned by a man, though the most dull unthinking rascally scribbler in town, it had been a most admirable play.' When Behn managed against all the odds to carve out a successful career as a writer it was left to male reviewers and subsequent generations of academics to destroy her reputation. They were very successful; Aphra Behn's work remained hidden from her descendants for hundreds of years.

Within months of the first production of *Look Back in Anger*, *'Declaration'* was published, a book in which members of the Angry Young Man movement were invited to express their vision of the world. By 1961 *'The Writer and Commitment'* by John Mander was putting The Angry Young Men into a political and artistic context by comparing them to socialist thinkers of the 1930's. And so it continued, 1962 *'Contemporary Theatre'* by Edward Arnold, 1963 *'Anger and After - A Guide to New British Drama'* by John Russell Taylor. The work of these young men entered academic discourse almost immediately, and subsequently, of course, the school and college curriculum. This has not happened with Women's Theatre. In 1988 a study of GCSE English set text by Heather Morris revealed that of 50 dramatists, 49 are men.

Even recent academic studies by men of texts such as *Look Back In Anger* show little progress. Some now feel obliged to explain Jimmy Porter's misogyny but in doing so reveal attitudes as damaging as those expressed by Osbourne, if not more so, couched as they are in pseudo-scientific language and promoted as 'the truth' by 'an expert'; Dr. Gareth Griffiths, wrote in 1981: 'It is to this primitiveness in woman that Jimmy's attacks are directed.' Hence, says Dr. Griffiths, 'his image of Alison as a python, a reptilian snake swallowing him alive when he makes love to her. Jimmy sees the struggle between man and woman ...as the struggle between creative sensitivity and the blind instinctive forces that swallow up the future a stifling obsession with the biological urges of the present.' All the references (to homosexuality) here serve two purposes. First they establish that Jimmy is rejecting women. He is not homosexual; the speech makes this quite clear; but', says Gareth Griffiths, his main point is 'that women and domesticity, children and social responsibilities often stifle creativity. Therefore many homosexuals have been deeply creative, since they are not so burdened.' He draws parallels with Shaw's *Man and Superman*, as there: 'is a struggle between man's desire to create artistically and to dare new things and women's desire to hold and nurture what exists, protecting the biological life force on which the continuance of the species depends.'

So apart from the physical obstacles facing women who wish to use theatre as a public arena in which to voice their anger (damning reviews, lack of funding etc) they face a minefield of 'psychological' obstacles according to Dr Griffiths. If righteous anger is seen by critics and academics as essentially male, Dr Griffiths goes one further and says that women cannot be creators, they can only stifle the creativity of the men around them; they are locked by their biology into the present, incapable of either standing back from their subject or passionate involvement.

Writer Dale Spender has written at length on the inbuilt male perspective among teachers and academics. It applies equally to theatre critics and male directors. Dorothy Smith wrote in 1978: The circle of men whose writing and talk was significant to each other extends backwards as far as ... records reach. What men were doing was relevant to men, was written by men about men for men. Men listened and listen to what one another said.' (*Women's Studies International Quarterly* Vol I)

Although the percentage of women's plays being produced is still very small, (see Caroline Gardiner's report '*What share of the cake?*) it is increasing. This is largely the result of committed women working for greater representation in the theatre and a growing confidence among women writers (as well as the growing realisation by the theatrical establishment that women can be as commercially successful as men). But it is important that the work of women in the theatre becomes part of our theatrical heritage, that it passes on to future generations of women. In order to do this we have to challenge the male bias among critics, academics and teachers; we must continue to express ourselves on our own terms and insist on our right to be heard, our right to be angry.

Look Back in Anger by John Osborne published by Faber & Faber.
Masterpieces by Sarah Daniels published by Methuen.
'*What Share of the Cake*' The Employment of Women in the English Theatre from The Women's Playhouse Trust.

ZOFIA KALINSKA and the DEMONIC WOMAN:
Work in Progress
Betty Caplan

A nun crouches over a dead body in prayer, silently mouthing words which disfigure her face. A young woman in a long, frilled white dress carries the train bunched up in front of her belly like a foetus. A tall vampire with a red tulle skirt draped round her head like an ostrich on fire hisses and spits. This gallery of "rogues" is part of the improvisatory first stage of Zofia Kalinska's *The Sale of the Demonic Woman*. An enterprising young Nottingham-based company called Meeting Ground have chosen to use their Arts Council development subsidy to enable Kalinska to devise the project. Founded in 1985 by Tanya Myers and Stephen Lowe, Meeting Ground aims to bring together people working in different aspects of the theatre, to discover new roles for women and explore new ways of working. The actresses involved are an international group, some of whom (Tanya Myers and Celia West) first worked with Kalinska on *Nominatae Filiae* in 1987-8 as part of the Magdalena International Theatre Project, others having been drawn to Nottingham by Kalinska's reputation as an exciting and innovative director.

The material is drawn from the works of the Polish playwright and painter Stanlislaw Ignacy Witkiewicz, also known as Witkacy, a title he fashioned for himself, Dada style, out of two of his names. Although little known in the west, Witkacy was very close to Artaud in his thinking. He lived through the trauma of the 1917 revolution, but as Hitler's armies approached, he refused to witness a second apocalypse. In 1939, a week after the German troops had begun shelling the outskirts of Warsaw, he slashed his wrists and took poison. Like Artaud, the theatre of his life was not bound by the perimeters of any stage. 'When choosing my destiny I chose insanity' he wrote, quoting Micinski for the motto of his novel *Insatiability*. It is the insatiable quality of the women in his work which has inspired his compatriot Kalinska to put together a piece which will be finalised and shown in the late autumn of 1990. Why use a man to shatter patriarchal stereotypes of womanhood though, I asked her? In *Nominatae Filiae* which she devised as part of the Magdalena project and which toured the country in 1988, what text there was evolved largely out of the actresses' own input. Could she not have done the same again? 'He is a great playwright' Kalinska insists. 'He employs many figures of demonic women which are strong, grotesque, funny and deformed all at the same time. He seemed to hit on the truth about eternal woman. And he dealt with the femme fatale at the turn of the century, a period which saw the beginning of women's emancipation. I want to strip this figure naked, to see the connections between her and contemporary women. We may put on trousers, but there is still a difference. We must find our power as women.'

Kalinska comes from an older generation than the women she directs; a veteran of Tadeusz Kantor's Cricot 2 company, she was also a colleague of Grotowski's. Her working methods were gleaned from her experience with Kantor - long, intense improvisations, sparing use of language, a lot of play with costumes and make-up, and a strong emphasis on the visual and musical elements of performance.'I was educated as an artist by Kantor. He is a genius, he has his own way, of course, but I also work from intuition, from the subconscious, not only through the intellect.' Like Kantor and Grotowski, she is searching for primal rituals, for the freshness and simplicity of the child, something hard to find in actors nowadays.

'They use tricks,' she complains. In the end the cheating fools no-one. 'The most important thing in theatre is to be surprised, to be moved.'

In her book on the Magdalena Project, Susan Bassnett describes the rules Kalinska laid down during the preparations for *Nominatae Filiae*:
'all performers had to change into clothing in the three basic colours of the performance, red, white and black and casual clothes were not allowed in the rehearsal room... The second basic rule was the requirement of all performers to begin whatever actions they later developed by walking in a circle, moving progressively past six objects: a bed, a chair, a mirror, a window, a bowl of water and a broom, again to establish a sense of ritual in physical terms.'

In Nottingham, in order to achieve her aim, to find the "inner person", she set up improvisatory meetings between Witkacy's protagonists which engender conflict - a femme fatale and a pregnant fiancé, for example - or the whole group improvising a scene in a graveyard with an empty suit acting as the dead male lover who is the centre piece. Sometimes the room comes to resemble a bizarre cabaret or kindergarten - the exaggerated, swaggering figures having been copied from paintings by Witkacy, who, like Blake, was able to mould his visions into two distinct forms. The work with costumes is extraordinarily evocative; even the limp suit takes on a life of its own as the various "archetypes" fight, like Hamlet and Laertes, over who loved most. All of this work will be used in some way for the performance, but for now, Kalinska is content to simply let it happen. 'There is a danger of closing something off at this stage.' The shaping and editing will come later.

The group has read and studied the relevant Witkacy texts, but they are used only as a hanger for the frock, not as the entire wardrobe. A proper language for the theatre is one of Kalinska's chief concerns. The work on *Nominatae Filiae* used bits of text that were meaningful for the actresses - Euripedes' *Medea* for Celia West, Wilde's *Salomé* spoken in Adele Saleem's mother tongue of Farsi. The Magdalena Project has itself been deeply preoccupied with the task of finding a special language for women's theatre. In her manifesto, Jill Greenhalgh wrote: 'There's something new and vital and female that is lying latent and untapped, trapped under thousands of years of patriarchal art, and you just can't quite grasp it.'

Kalinska believes it is an international language to which we can gain access through a study of myths, symbols and archetypes. Words are not central. She cites the fact that she directed Genet's *The Maids* in Marseille in 1986 in Polish, and received critical acclaim. She finds much of western feminist theatre lacking, too verbal and intellectual in its mode of expression.

'It's too policital,' she says. 'It has nothing to do with art.' It is significant that the closest thing to her ideal is Pina Bausch's Wuppertal Dance Theatre. Her next move is a piece which links Heloise and Abelard with Salomé and John the Baptist who are unlikely to be able to converse in the Queen's English.

The "magic circle" which bound women throughout history, the cycle of birth and death, has affected her very personally. When Grotowski asked her to join his company, she was a single parent with a young child and was forced to decline. 'We always have the responsibility for the children', she says.'Even when the

16

husband is helpful, we are the ones who are thinking about them.' Would the coming generation of women be able to break that magic circle? These concerns feed into her work; *Nominatae Filiae* showed the meeting of archetypes like Medea and Salomé. Held up to us as mythical incarnations of the demonic, we have come to see them as evil because of their insatiable desires, but Kalinska does not visualise them in that way: 'For me demonic means strength, the power of will, not evil. It means to want fulfilment in everything. Women have always been circling, biting their own tails. Medea killed her children, but she became empty. Many modern women have become successful but they have lost something in the process, their self-realisation happening in one direction only. We must be careful not to lose our warmth and our feeling.'

How do these notions of femininity relate to her own work as director? 'Women work in a different way. I try to encourage them to be more open, to find the truth about themselves. To express the things they have never been allowed to express before - power, anger, love. To break the stereotypes. To find their own creativity. It's no fun being a mere figure on a chess board, is it?' Were there particular stresses and strains on someone in her position? 'Actresses are used to a male director. When they don't feel well they hide it. But with a woman director they are like children.' And watching her at work, it strikes me that she is utilising a lot of the qualities associated with motherhood, and not necessarily always the gentle, caring ones. She can be very demanding: 'Don't think! Don't discuss! Just come and work!' she exhorts her offspring. The women, being younger and, with one exception, from the west are confused. They are used to talking things through in order to understand. The problematical role of the director in a company of women striving for genuine quality is something Susan Bassnett takes up in her book. In Nottingham, these difficulties are compounded by differences of generation, language and culture. Despite her commitment to the idea of a women's theatre free from the kinds of hierarchical obsessions which characterise patriarchal ventures, Kalinska feels that in the end democracy can't rule: 'I must make a decision. I don't believe in collective direction.' Yet she admits it is a delicate balance to maintain, especially if one doesn't wish to become "man-womanly".

In her account of *Nominatae Filiae*, Susan Bassnett focuses on the contradictions inherent in the female directorial role:
'During the three months of work, Zofia Kalinska complained at being constantly pushed back into what she termed a "masculine" directorial position' where the performers demanded to be told what to do. She...kept insisting that they follow their own working pattern in exploring their relationships with the chosen archetypes, instead of having a series of demands placed on them by another person. These two very different perspectives... led to clashes, and in the moments of conflict the terminology used by both director and performers was that of the mother-daughter relationship.'

The "magic circle" at work again? Bassnett concluded that "for the most part the performance was the expression of the director's concepts and ideas, in the tradition of director's theatre.' Perhaps women's theatre needs to address itself for a time to exploring the roles of mother and daughter which may otherwise bedevil (!) the working relationship. Interestingly enough, though myths like Salomé and Antigone and Electra abound, there is a real paucity of material dealing directly with the mother-daughter bond. To my knowledge, the Greek story of Demeter and Core is the only example, but I am willing to be corrected. Surely if the work on mythology is to mean anything, we must make it part of our own practice?

It seems to me that these trials highlight some of the problems which constantly beset the roles of actor and directors generally, and are perhaps seen in more acute form in an all-female group because women are currently so preoccupied with issues of power in a male-dominated society. What personal motives drive someone to become a director? What are the psychological features of those who wish to be actors and to leave the responsibility for final decisions to others? It must inevitably be an uneasy compromise that is reached, and this, surely, explains many recent moves to blur the distinctions between the two.

In the best theatre, there is often a kind of regression to childishness - indeed, Kalinska speaks for others in her tradition of "poor theatre" when she claims to be searching precisely for that very "simplicity." Yet Celia West who has had a wide variety of experience as an actress, and who played Medea in *Nominatae Filiae* has said that there is a tendency for actors to want to abdicate responsibility, to stay in that charmed kindergarten. They want to be able to trust someone else to take an overview of the situation. How necessary is it for the actor to have this freedom in order to fulfil his/her potential? At what point does the creative child become the sullen baby? How does the dominating "mother" ensure that she allows space for the "child's" individuality, when she herself has had so little opportunity to develop her own powers?

A great deal must hang upon the status of the text; when you think about it, a text can act as a buffer between actor and director, performers and audience, a kind of "safe house." When in doubt, refer to line 64. Where there is no fixed text, and the material is the stuff of women's most traumatic experiences, there is considerable danger. The "poor" theatre calls upon the performer's most profound resources, and the dividing line between some of the work and madness is a fine one. Indeed Kalinska herself admits she is using "psycho-drama, hysteria, trance."

Very Artaud, but very risky. How is the actor to be protected? Does the director require some therapeutic understanding to be able to handle such material? I would have thought so. In the end, one can perhaps only conclude that these are truly fascinating questions, ones which, if pursued, may allow women's theatre to herald a regeneration in what is rapidly becoming an exhausted art form.

Bibliography: Bassnett, Susan (1989) *Magdalena International Women's Experimental Theatre*, Berg Oxford, New York, Munich £12.95.
(Reprinted by permission of *M.T.D.* Issue 2 Middlesex Polytechnic)

THE NEXT STAGE: DEVALUATION, REVALUATION, AND AFTER
Diane Speakman

Cardiff Laboratory Theatre, the company responsible for initiating Magdalena '86, has created some seventy experimental theatre pieces for special events in and out of doors, as well as more formal productions for theatre spaces, over the past twelve years. Many of the projects have toured throughout Europe. As early as 1977, Cardiff Laboratory Theatre was invited to an international meeting of theatre groups in Bergamo, instigated by Eugenio Barba, the director of Odin Teatret, Holstebro, Denmark, and former disciple of Jerzy Grotowski. This was crucial to the group's development in several ways. For example, on their return, members negotiated to put down roots in an extension of Chapter Arts Centre's Edwardian school building, and the gymnasium became the group's base. Another important outcome was the growth of collaborative work with individuals and companies from home and abroad, including Odin Teatret (1980), and Grotowski's Teatr Laboratorium from Wroclaw (1982). Their example and that of Artaud have informed the work of many of the individual women and women's groups taking part in Magdalena '86 - in the emphases on dream and trance and the creation of a special kind of energy, anthropological 'fishing' for revitalizing material with which to improvise and the dedicated training of the body and voice as instruments.

The ideal of having, for the first time in Europe, an international festival of women in experimental theatre was conceived in 1983 at another festival in Trevignano by Jill Greenhalgh, who became the project's director, Julia Varley of Odin Teatret, Geddy Aniksdal of Grenland Friteater, and others. They were concerned on one hand about experimental theatre's increasing struggles to combat inertia and create and develop into the unknown, while receiving less and less funding and public interest; on the other, they were curious about the nature of women's creativity and keen that these actors, with their own artistic strengths and presence, should be given more opportunity to devise their own art, if it is distinct; explore their own experience, fully bring to life their own vision and culture, exert their rightful influence in male-dominated companies and open up new directions for their work. The festival's title, 'Magdalena', established early on, derived from the cult of Mary Magdalen, a powerful, independent spirit exuding sexual energy, relegated to the margins of society rather like women's art.

The festival was funded by the Welsh Arts Council, the Calouste Gulbenkian Foundation, Chapter Arts, the British Council and various private sponsors; it was organized by a team of more than twenty-eight women and men. Greenhalgh worked on the project more or less continuously for three years. Using personal contacts made during her work with Cardiff Laboratory Theatre, she invited up to thirty women, each on the basis of her contribution to experimental theatre in her own country either in a group or solo, from about fifteen countries, including South and North America, Europe, but not the Third World, to participate as workshop leaders, performers, visual artists, technical staff. Each woman invited had to find her own funding.

Magdalena was planned in two phases, covering nearly three weeks. Phase I, from 11-17 August, comprised morning workshops, afternoon discussions and other events, and at least three sequential evening performances. From 18-28 August the practitioners collaborated in an unstructured female process, and in Phase II 29-30

August, showed their work-in-progress to the public. All the events were open to men and only two workshops - Kozana Lucca's and Maria Consagra's - were for people with previous experience of vocal or physical theatre work.

In launching this first festival in Wales the aims of the organizers were: to open up discussion of women's role in new theatre forms and to encourage the public to appreciate women's artistic power and the validity of female interpretations of life; to provide a forum for women from different cultures to exchange ideas about their work in experimental theatre in a variety of companies; to explore the nature and different aspects of women's creativity and perhaps attempt to define its components; to bring strong talented women artists together that they might share and develop their work, to allow something to take root organically from that collaboration; to produce a record of the festival's work and process; to break down all sorts of barriers - between theatre and life; performers and designers; artists and audience - to reduce physical tensions and linguistic misunderstandings.

On the morning of 11 August, about 120 women and a handful of men crowded into Cardiff Laboratory Theatre's gym to register for workshops. In the company of about twenty-five other women, I began working on sense-perception techniques with Graciela Serra, a Mapuche Indian from Argentina. Serra met Gerda Alexander (no relation to the Alexander of the Alexander technique) thirteen years ago and has been developing her own approach to body work on Alexander's principles - of, for instance, the flexible use of correct amounts of energy for each action - since then. Serra specializes in building up intuitive physical awareness and working on tensions all over the body, accumulated in daily and theatrical life: children's perception of the contradiction between their parents' words and their body language, which affects their own behaviour, relaxation techniques for pregnant women who have opted for natural childbirth; actors' chronic stress points. Her aim is to unblock, to encourage healing creative energy to flow once more as it did in our first months of life.

Akne Theatre's production, in Polish, of Genet's *Maids* was disturbingly powerful. The venue, a cellar under the CPR, was an essential ingredient in the evening's success: smells of corruption, damp stone, rotting woodwork, something indefinable; thick motes of dust floating through the light beams; bench seating arranged to induce claustrophobia - truly, 'the darkness is dangerous'. In Zofia De Inez-Lewczuk's set design, Madame's bedroom was draped with black and white dresses, some upside-down like bats or hanged people. And then there were the mirrors, literal and metaphorical, layers of them. The sisters, narcissistically and incestuously reflected their own ambivalence and self-loathing (Claire: 'I'm sick of seeing my image thrown back at me by a mirror, like a bad smell. You're my bad smell'); through their ceremonial role reversal, mirroring the class struggle, they play out servants as 'rich people, distorting mirrors'; the text as a whole reflects the audience's, society's, secret fantasies and impulses. Appropriately but ironically, a large portrait of Saint Genet, actor and martyr, was triumphantly shown to the audience at the end.

Anna Lica, formerly of The Theatre Marquez, Arhus, Denmark, constructed her show, *Madame Bovary - Downtown* (given in English), with Tage Larsen from Odin Teatret, who also directed. Lica gave a varied and polished performance; she has a strong presence and a distinctive quality of contained stillness. She and Larsen offer Sally as a contemporary reflection of Emma Bovary's self-indulgent yearnings for that 'marvellous world where all was passion, ecstasy, delirium'; Sally is installed in poverty in a downtown Parisian garage after being spurned by her husband George. (In Lica's skilful impersonation, George is so emotionally impoverished he can only spout from the *Wall Street Journal* or *The New York Times* before sending Sally his rejection letter.) In the garage, from a crate marked 'Do not tilt', Sally flamboyantly re-runs her life, enacting her compulsive image-making of our time, always starting from a base-line of masochistic self-loathing, invalidation and distrust. So we see the woman whose husband and children have left, forced to choose between days of dutiful housework or driving maniacally round Paris, long blonde hair streaming in the wind; or, in the thick alcoholic haze of the party our culture has constructed for male heroes - Jagger, Newman, Bogart - Sally, the hostess with the leastest, feverishly welcomes guests to the ironic strains of Sinatra's '*My Way*'. There were some stunning visual images; Sally winding the tape of George's rejection letter round the neck of his suit hanging from a stand; the slices of lemon the woman abandoned fitted inside her glasses before her bitter drive round Paris, Lica's dance, in a long white slipper-satin dress whose sleeves extended until they became a straitjacket into which she fastened herself (this was so powerful a climax for me that I had difficulty attending as the sequence moved on); and the last image as Sally lies dead across the crate, surrounded by blue standard lights flashing crazily.

Netta Plotzky, from Israel, gave a performance remarkable for its visual inventiveness, its generosity - many needs and fears are revealed - and its swiftly-flowing transformations in movement and emotion, from pathos to laughter, curiosity to menace, to sexual invitation...She was also the only performer to establish an explicit relationship with the audience: she started playing among us, eating an apple, tearing our tickets, making noises, evoking laughter. Thereafter, the show, *The Happiness of the Pre-form*, was split into three parts. The first was '*Variations on Ophelia*', the 'mad' woman validating the non-rational - we feel on the whole 'comfortable with her madness'. To flute music Netta, dressed in an all-embracing white plastic mac, with an umbrella that suddenly turned on her and one enormous, one normal-size shoe, that reminded me of Little Titch or Chaplin, drank from the umbrella, attempted to stuff up the flute, brought mid-stage an object wrapped in red cloth (what was it? a baby? a stone?)... A figure in black enters (Anna Lica) -Hamlet, Death, Fate - Ophelia dons an absurd small black net hat, complete with squeaky squid attachment, to lure him. At this point she is speared by a butterfly (memories of love, happier days...) Squeaking, on the attack, Ophelia hesitates and then collapses into a waiting wheelbarrow (pram, coffin, refuse carrier); the mood changes yet again, and after a moving and pathetic sexual invitation, in which she opens her self, her legs, to the black unresponsive figure, mad Ophelia is wheeled off, butterfly still flapping.

Part two offered us an ageing, perhaps senile woman, a Polish Jew in wartime, wearing glasses, who mumbles, sings, potters, dreams of her youth, is suddenly distracted by the audience and goes to sit on a chair surrounded by toys on the floor. Then comes the most powerful image in the show, for me: after half-heartedly uttering 'Heil Hitler', she mimes eating a rose and, standing on the chair, vomits it up all over the playing area. Later, in yet another change of mood, the old woman gives us a wonderful knowing wink.

The third part was called '*Young mask searching for a love*' and was full of sadness and ambiguity: the woman mask becomes a young male mask; her back becomes his front, all the usual clues of facial expressiveness are lost to us and we must look afresh at the body's language and focus on the significance of the props used - here, hats.

Appropriately, the most overtly political piece in the Festival was *8961: Caneuon Galar a Gobaith (Songs of Grief and Hope)*, constructed and performed by Lis Hughes Jones and directed by Mike Pearson, both directors of Brith Gof, a theatre company dedicated to performing in a language spoken by only 500,000 people, a minority confronted by the threat of cultural takeover and suffocation. In a scaffolded cube of light and dark, cell, cellar, square, against a 'backdrop' of corrugated iron used for the shanties in which so many of the world's poor have to exist, Hughes Jones became in turn, through her body, one of 8961 desaparecidos in Argentina undergoing torture, one of the oppressors, one of the women - mother, daughter, sister, wife - waiting in dread and in hope for news, for confirmation, for the loved one.

The first part of the piece, the torture sequence, electrified me - the guard's torch probing the dark cell to transfix the prison, the crash as the hurtling body hit the corrugated iron... Some people were angered and moved by the material and left feeling powerless because they didn't know what to do to help, others questioned whether it was appropriate for non-Argentinians to do the piece at all - yet I know that Graciela Serra, herself one of those threatened with 'disappearance', was very moved by it. Whatever the reaction, Hughes Jones's performance was strong, haunting and powerfully imaginative. At one point, the waiting woman washes and hangs out a shirt belonging to her lost love - and suddenly hurls blood at it; the drips continue to punctuate the action. Victor Jara sings and Hughes Jones sings, in a voice that comes from the belly, to John Hardy's piano music, songs from fiesta and songs of lament; and she dances the tango. She feels, smells, the suit of the man who has gone, places it on a chair and sits on his 'knee', his 'arms' around her once more...

In their solo performance Sandra Salmaso and Cinzia Mascherin (Italy), Geddy Aniksdal (Norway) and Helen Chadwick (England) all used text by Sylvia Plath.

The Stars are No Nearer, 'a journey in the poetical world of Sylvia Plath', directed by Tor Arne Ursin, was Geddy Aniksdal's first solo performance and she gave (in English) a tensely dramatic and subtly expressive interpretation of five poems: *'Thalidomide'*,*'Mirror'*,*'Death & Co'*,*'Lady Lazarus'*, and *'Edge'*. The recurring images of these poems are the moon and stars, flowers, mirrors and stretches of water, and the human body in various stages of corruption; the colours black, silver, shadow, ash, white and red. Aniksdal appeared before us in a longish wine-red dress virutally concealing her pregnancy, and the *'Thalidomide'*, for instance, proceeded to croon and cradle her ideal baby in her arms before suddenly dashing the bundle to the floor to maniacal cackles of laughter, her shadow clawing its way down the white back wall of the play area as she slumped to her knees. Aniksdal did indeed make 'each word a physical event', and the blood run cold.

A Gift for Burning has been constructed from poems, essays and letters by Sylvia Plath, Frances Bellerby, Stevie Smith, Anne Sexton, Marina Tsvetayeva, Susan Griffin and H.D., with additional poems and music by Chadwick herself. No fewer than three of these seven poets committed suicide. The undoubted appeal of the piece lies in its simplicity, clarity, luminosity - the 'staging' consists of a piano, several wicker chairs for the women makers and sharers, and a set of lamps - and the haunting quality of some of the melodies. Chadwick presents, in the material she has selected, a range of emotion, from rage at the rape of an eighty-three year old woman, to enjoyment in pointing Smith's surreal text; but for me (and the basic subject matter is near the top of my emotional agenda), the performance was curiously muted and I feel there is even more pain to find. It may be plumbed in her next solo show, for which she plans to write as well as compose her own material.

Several women led workshops but did not perform in their own shows. Maris Consagra (USA/Italy) who teaches in New York University's Experimental Theatre Wing, worked along the lines of her current research to channel energy through an 'object' to produce a piece of theatre.

Andrea Dishy and Stacy Klein (USA), the artistic director of Double Edge Theatre, Boston, who has collaborated with Rena Mirecka from Grotowski's Teatr Laboratorium, led a two-day workshop using physical, psycho-physical and vocal training, texts, and musical instruments, to encourage participants to find a new source of energy and theatrical invention.

Kozana Lucca (Argentina/France), for fourteen years one of the forty members of the Roy Hart Theatre community, whose work is founded on the study of the human voice, led a workshop directed towards musical and theatrical expression.

In the afternoon of the week of Phase I, in addition to other events, there were discussions, all except the opening and closing ones suggested by participants. No product was forthcoming, or pat answers, nor was consensus arrived at, but the process of voicing questions such as these was important and may be far-reaching:

- What is the nature of women's inspiration and creativity?
- Is there a feminine or feminist aesthetic? Should there be? - Is there a feminist style of acting, directing?
- Why aren't there women theatre theorists as influential as Barba and Grotowski? Are they essential?
- Women often have to rear as well as bear children. If women feel these experiences are creative, can they be combined with their creativity as artists in processes of cross - fertilization?
- What is theatre? Simply 'what takes place between spectator and actor? Every room; everywhere? What is experimental theatre?
- Have we, as spectators, the right to say a 'performance' is not theatre? Do there have to be professional standards of singing, dancing, acting, before 'theatre' can be said to take place?
- Do we have to 'understand' a performance for it to be valid? Does it matter to the creators that people see different meanings and significance in the same performance?
- Are collages, fragments, episodes, cycles, the natural structures for women?
- How can women 'go public', gain more confidence as artists in a patriarchal world?
- Do women speak a different language at work? Have we learned to speak in two modes? Can we develop our own language?
- How important are class as well as gender differences in art?

- Should women artists encourage the use of tapes rather than books and radio phone-ins, where possible, instead of theatre, for wider accessibility and participation?

The final discussion, before the performers started collaborating on their piece, exposed some sharp divisions between women who felt too many shows had been constructed with too many men in the traditional hierarchical patriarchal way, and that even where men weren't involved, there had often been an 'authoritative' text -in three instances, by Plath - and an absence of women's own truly experimental text; and those who felt that the performers were being devalued as puppets by these remarks, that there was no difference between male and female creativity and that more communication was needed between the sexes, not less.

Out of the discussion emerged the concept of a ceremonial 'enactment' rather than a conventional performance, and we were asked to help the performers by meditating on an object or idea or a feeling we'd been close to or thought of or had during the week, and to feed our images to the group. Among those put forward were recurring circles, broken or breaking and rejoining, jumping butterflies (me); a volcano of tears; a flower and snake; Mary Magdalen; fire; bronze; audience involvement; softness, sexuality, ritual and fun. The performers had also been sent extracts from Susan Griffin's *Woman and Nature*, as possible sources of inspiration.

Then we left the twenty or so actors, three musicians, four artists and four technicians for ten days to their unstructured, undirected collaboration, assailed by risk, reliant on individual strengths, skills and talent, but also facing differences in personality, politics, religion, language, culture and theatrical tradition.

In the morning the performers worked in the gym, with different facilitators. The rest of the day they worked in their eventual (and very cold) playing area, entitled, rich in irony, *'Edward England's Potato Factory'*. As expected, the women ran through most of the emotional range in their collaboration and alliances shifted, broke, got refocused. One woman left and several, including, to my regret, Serra and Lucca, scarcely particpated. It was time that pressured content in the end - something had to be put before the public on Friday 29 August.

I saw the work-in-progress (for which the public was not charged) on both nights and this proved to be essential, for spectators were split up and saw different things each night. I hadn't known this the first evening and had interesting if bemusing discussions with other spectators afterwards. The area outside and the whole ground floor of the factory were given over to a promenade production in twelve scenes. The structure, particularly the first night, resembled a patchwork of different pieces of material woven - an image floated by Greenhalgh to practitioners at planning stage - into a loose whole. There were changes to the content the second night, with the result that the piece cohered much more, and was seen to be a time piece - no one actually took an alarm clock apart, but we had to wade through a sea of them on the way out...

Several sequences did work or begin to work, for me. The opening was haunting. Set in an industrial urban wasteland fit for washer-queens, and to bell-peal and gulls' cry, Hughes Jones and Krukowska shared a work song (if not the work), as Hughes Jones thwacked and washed and hung out sheets by the canal. Lica walked perilously along a parapet, in her potent slipper-satin dress, luna-tic, and beat the water with a long straitjacket sleeves before rescuing a baby from it (Moses? the Divine Child of Eleusis?) while the other women whispered together looking righteously askance...

Then, inside, the group of six demonic women working with Kalinska, who want to continue their collaboration, in symbolic white, black and red evening dresses, circled around a clock face, looking, as women have had to, through another medium - here, a bandaged mirror/window - into worlds within and without, playing with ritual objects and fighting, loving, despairing, hating, to climax and reprieve, as Kalinska tightened one thread -'Remember the circle' - and Susan Bassnett the other, with her improvised archetypal narrative.

I was very shocked and moved, the first night, by Brigitte Kaquet's appearance, naked, as the mad Ophelia with weeds entangled in her hair and flowing down her (and our) beautiful and vulnerable female body. She slowly advanced along the sand, writhed, turned, and retreated, to a speech pre-recorded: 'I always thought that I loved you so much, Daddy, but sometimes I have to beg your pardon because I am so happy without you. I am so happy because you are dead.' After a tender and farcical meeting, mid-stream, between an ageing Mary (Ambrova) and a heavily-pregnant Joseph (Aniksdal), presenting as Andy Capp at the seaside, we were ushered back into the first arena for the final re-enactment: *The Last Supper*. Hughes Jones sang us out, the second night, simply, fittingly, in Welsh.

So the Festival ended. For me, Magdalena '86 was a rich and varied learning process, in theatrical and personal terms. Further, it seems to me that a number of the organizers' aims have been realized, at least in part: an exchange of ideas and attitudes among participants began, albeit more often in private than in public; something organic and exciting did start to emerge from the 'work-in-progress' and I think spectators recognized there, and in the Phase I shows, the validity of women's creative contribution and certainly their artistic strengths.

AFTERWORD

The Magdalena Project, as Magdalena Conferences (UK) has now been established as a permanent networking, research and work-development organization, an associated project of Chapter, Cardiff, funded by the Welsh Arts Council.

To find out more, contact:
Mary Mumford, Magdalena Project, Chapter Arts Centre, Market Road, Canton, Cardiff CF5 1QE, Wales, Tel: 0222 220552

(Reprinted by permission from *'Themes in Drama II'* edited by James Redmond (Cambridge University Press)

THE SALON AT PAINES PLOUGH
Anna Furse and April de Angelis.

"Oral drive, anal drive, vocal drive, all drives are good forces, and among them the gestational drive - just like wanting to write: a desire to live oneself within, wanting the belly, the tongue, the blood" Hélène Cixous *La Jeune Née*

Anna Furse :

I was appointed Artistic Director of Paines Plough in January 1990, inheriting a company which, during its 16 years in existence, has built itself into a forceful catalyst for New Writing on a national scale. The company not only tours new plays, but is constantly active in high profile training work-script panels responding to unsolicited scripts, writers' workshops, special courses and residencies.

I felt it was becoming pressing for this work - jargoned theatre 'process' - to be harnessed to the specific artistic direction of the company as a whole. This artistic direction is concerned with strong theatricality, experimentation and an international outlook both in style and concerns as well as literally vis touring abroad. Alongside more generalised Writers' Workshops therefore, a range of courses, forums, discussion groups, seminars to stimulate writers to this end became imperative. I sought, together with members of the company, to identify needs and provide workshops accordingly, workshops of a specific theme - writing with music in mind, writing for black theatre etc. Also, to offer what I call 'provocations' - talks, groups, arguments, stimuli for debate about our theatre culture and the place of a writer in it.

The British Playwright as a traditional institution is white, male, and a promoter of firmly held convictions of 'what makes theatre', 'the well made play', and the role of the writer in the company who must 'serve the text'. I wanted to question some of these safe assumptions. I wanted writers to examine other 'softer' (i.e. less verbose) theatre forms which tend to get packaged into the label 'performance art' simply because they aren't packaged plays-as-we-know-them. I wanted to urge reading and debate into some of the new critical theories which haven't yet touched theatre making or reviewing in this country and yet have had an impact on film and dance.

Also, what was becoming remarkable, is that a young breed of academics are coming up through some of the more interesting cultural studies courses in British colleges who were not only conversant with the work of more radical theatre makers, but were armed with BOOKS and new theoretical perspectives which validated our work as speaking for a COLLECTIVE (and international) non-mainstream voice in our culture. What we deplore most is our missing history as women and as artists. It leaves us without a language, apparently, with which to communicate our investigations. What is a 'feminist aesthetic'? What is 'feminine' theatre language? Why do so many women writers experience a natural impulse to de-construct and break down traditional forms of playwrighting? Why are those plays not having an influence? Why are they not being seen? Do the more radical voices operate a self-censorship for fear of not getting commissioned? Isn't theatre supposed to be iconoclastic?

At The Lyric Studio early Spring in 1990, we ran a forum called Women Writing and the Poetry of the Theatre. The event was sold out. Women there were discussing just these issues. Meanwhile I had been reading Hélène Cixous 'La Jeune Née' and reeling from her inspiring and uncompromising exhortations on women to write in order to complete themselves, language being the 'masculine' in our culture. I felt this text might be an excellent starting point for discussion. Our writer-in-residence April de Angelis was excited by the idea of THE SALON and agreed to co-ordinate it. We called it THE SALON half ironically, with visions of lively debates albeit not on chaises longues but in our offices after hours. We have had two blocks of SALONS and will soon be running a third.

Meanwhile, Paines Plough continues to place the issue of women writing high on the agenda. Following *How the Story's Told* - a weekend workshop festival on women playwriting - at Riverside Studios in November 1990, we will be running a sequel festival in the Spring of 1991 to concentrate on women who make/write experimental theatre.

I have changed the company sub-titles from 'The Writers' Theatre' to 'New Theatre, New Writing'. I believe women writers contribute vitally to telling what such new theatre might be. I look forward to reading them.

April de Angelis:
The Salon met once fortnightly at the Paines Plough offices. It was attended by a varied group of women united by a common interest in writing for theatre and aware that a whole canon of difficult but potentially thrilling literary criticism, which had grown out of some of the major philosophic movements of the twentieth century (Marxism, Psychoanalysis, Feminism and Saussurian Linguistics), awaited them and was ready to revolutionise the way they wrote for theatre. Film theory, we reflected, had already got there, so why couldn't we?

The thing about modern critical theory and its corollaries is, it's bloody hard to grasp and often brutally disregarding of feminist sensibilities. The group was alert, intense and apprehensive. While Hélène Cixous was discussed with rigour and appreciated with soul what were we to make of Lacan's theory that women do not exist or Kristeva's that women should not write because it brings us too close to the edge (i.e. Plath, Woolf). If the symbolic is phallic and language a toxification what clues should we ascertain for scene structure? Quite simply, none.

Truth, the group dwindled a bit. But this was often due to births and attendance of first nights of plays that would be written without any reference to Derrida or Irigaray whatsoever. Still, us that were left were stubbornly excited by this prospect of something, something...afterwards in the pub over packets of cheese and onion crisps we burbled about theories of the imaginary, patriarchal binaries, why men had to be trained at sex and how wonderful it was to feel your brain hurtling along a series of premises and not daring to stop unless you lost the thread. Surely something must come out of all this. Surely...

The speakers that visited the group all seemed pleased with the prospect that normal folk outside of the environs of academia wanted to know more of their territory. These varied theories and approaches were out and getting an airing. Why aren't they more widely acknowledged? Because they are complex, difficult? Dangerous? All three, especially the last. Very dangerous and challenging to how we see the world. Contentious, tending to tip the world on its head, not packagable under neat ideological labels, these theories felt 'hot'. Perhaps that gives an intimation to the theatre that might take seed from THE SALON. Perhaps each of us will go away, and alone, start shaping something new, with a new core, a new shape, and dangerous.

For information about Paines Plough's THE SALON or other courses, workshops, events, or to join the mailing list please call 071-284 4483.

SPEAKING IN TONGUES BUT IN WHOSE LANGUAGE?
IN SEARCH OF A FEMALE AESTHETICS.
Nina Rapi

Do women write in a language specific to themselves? Is there such a thing as 'Womanspeak' or women's aesthetics and if so, where does it come from? Trying to define women's aesthetics is as slippery as trying to define woman. The moment you arrive at a reasonably satisying definition, its meaning has already shifted to somewhere else. I shall here tread this tricky ground and in the process scan some of the various theories on this elusive entity called 'feminine écriture' (feminine writing).

What then is 'woman'? As Simone de Beauvoir first pointed out in her *'Second Sex'*, despite the definite fact that females inhabit this planet and constitute at least half of its population, we are continuously being exhorted to 'be women, remain women, become women'. It follows then that female and woman are two entirely different qualities/species. One is born female, but without 'that mysterious and threatened reality known as femininity', one is not a woman.

Monique Wittig, following on from de Beauvoir, differentiates between 'women' (the class within which we fight) and 'woman', the myth, (based on the naturalization of socially constructed differences of masculine and feminine) and insists that both 'woman' and 'man' are political and economic categories and not eternal ones. I believe that if there is any ground for a women's aesthetics, then it would be this one, and not any mysterious, 'essence' or 'mothermilk' shared by all females.

Feminine / Women's / Feminist Aesthetics
The debate over aesthetics has raged amongst feminists over the past twenty years or so and it will probably continue for a long time, as any discussion of it is intrinsically linked to notions of 'womanhood', the self, the subject, language, sexuality, history and representation, all under constant re-definition. Largely, we can distinguish two dominant schools: the French and the American, their names refering not to geographical origins per se but rather to intellectual traditions. The French school (e.g. Hélène Cixous, Luce Irigaray, Julia Kristeva), grounded in a linguistic and psychoanalytic tradition, understands the 'feminine' as a disruption, by either males or females, of a phallocratic symbolic order; and the subject as having a phallic place in language, which must therefore be broken and decentered. The American school (e.g. Elaine Showalter, Nancy Chodorow), following a largely humanist tradition, believes in building 'a strong core of self', apparently inherent in human beings, and proposes a feminist aesthetics based on a distinctly female consciousness and experience of reality. Both schools emphasize the liberating aspects of female difference and associate the feminine with fluidity, multiplicity and openess.

There is a third critical voice, of a materialist feminist position which criticizes both the above schools as 'essentialist', i.e. reducing women to their biology and ignoring the class, race and sexuality differences between them. The materialists reject a 'feminine' morphology, that is an aesthetics largely formed around analogies to women's sexuality and consisting of multiple moments of rupture rather than heading to one big climax; of unfocused, ambiguous fragments, characterized by 'nearness' and being without closure. Materialists dismiss this 'feminine' aesthetics as assigning women to the ghetto of gender and propose a non-gendered aesthetics (i.e. Monique Wittig and Zande Zeig, more of whom later), where women are free to experiment with whichever forms and structures they choose. The above position is not a unified body as there are distinct differences between the various writers identifying themselves as materialist feminists. Monique Wittig, for instance, considers it a historical necessity that women constitute ourselves 'as the individual subjects of our history' and develop our identity but emphasises that what is crucial in terms of aesthetics, is 'to shift the axis of categorization', i.e. to create universal art but from a specific point of view, be that of 'woman', black or lesbian.

bell hooks, although she acknowledges the necessity of an identity, pinpoints the dangers of 'identity politics' and of 'personalizing' everything, thus negating the structures of domination that shape identity. For hooks, gender is one of many interlocking structures of domination. She views the self 'not as signifier of one 'I' but the coming together of many 'I's, the self as embodying collective reality past and present, family and community'. hooks believes in women finding their own voice but focuses on the difference between black women's 'changing speech' and white women's 'breaking the silence'. Critically naming the point of difference and marginality one occupies, through language, is for hooks 'a gesture that deeply shapes and influences the social construction of the self'.

Sue Ellen Case, in agreement with semiotics, rejects the 'outmoded' belief in self as a biological and natural entity, and identifies the subject as 'an intersection of cultural codes and practices'. The subject has traditionally been male and 'constructing women as subject' on stage is the very basis of a 'new feminist poetics'. Case embraces both materialist and 'feminine' viewpoints and proposes that women use 'guerilla action' and swing from 'feminine' to materialist aesthetics positions depending on which is most effective at provoking and focusing on the 'feminist critique'.

Finally, Rita Felski argues against feminist aesthetics altogether, defined by her as 'any theoretical position which argues a necessary or privileged relationship between female gender and a particular kind of literary structure, style or form'. She holds that a text can be defined as feminist 'only in so far as its content or the context of its reception promote such a reading'. Michelene Wandor too, asserts that women's theatre can only be differentiated from men's in terms of content rather than form, since 'emotional, aesthetic and structural styles are very varied among women writers'.

Seizing the occasion to speak
Let us now look in some more detail at the 'culprits' of 'feminine écriture' i.e. French Feminists, a school of thought as powerful and influential as it is inaccessible and controversial. Their ideas have obviously filtered through or are simply shared by an increasing number of women who generally adopt a 'feminine morphology' stance and way of looking at art, politics and everyday life. Hélène Cixous is the very woman who originated the concept of 'feminine écriture', in the mid-seventies. Writing in a form that combines essay, poetry, autobiographical and prophetic prose, Cixous urges women to write themselves, with their bodies, 'working the in-between', springing forth the subconscious, where both the masculine and the feminine exist, non-hierarchized. Women must write, express their desire to 'live self from within', fight against a living death, phallocracy,

never let it hold them back. Even though Cixous believes that there is such a thing as 'marked' i.e. gender specific writing, she asserts that it is impossible to define a feminine practice of writing. This practice can never be 'theorized, enclosed, encoded' (masculine practices) and will only be conceived by subjects/peripheral figures (biologically male or female), who can never be subjugated by authority. Against Freud's 'biology is destiny' and Lacan's constitution of the subject, in terms of a drama reinstating the religion of the father (and woman's Lack), Cixous locates sexual difference at the level of sexual pleasure (jouissance). Jouissance is inscribed on the body and the subconscious through the 'other bisexuality' i.e. a state of being and writing in 'exclusion of neither difference nor of one sex'. This view of the formation of 'I' is particularly exhilarating for a lesbian writer like myself, striving to both be and write in a way that defies gender restrictions. But where Cixous disappoints is in ultimately reinstating Freud's 'biology is destiny', despite her stated intentions to the opposite.

For her, woman's libido can produce radical political and social change, through language, 'the very possibility of change'. Woman enters history by 'seizing the occasion to speak', breaking the snare of silence, ecstatically expressing herself through writing in 'white milk'. It is this emphasis on 'white milk' and libido that reduces Cixous' otherwise inspirational writings to biological determinism. Women's writing and resistance is ultimately determined by the secretions of their bodies! And as Rita Felski points out, the problem with theories that '...locate resistance in every micropolitical strategy, in every libidinal impulse, is that subversion is located everywhere and nowhere'. And valorizing the feminine as a site of resistance 'fails to acknowledge that women's assignment to a distinctive 'feminine' sphere has throughout history been a major cause of their marginalization and disempowerment.'

Woman's 'other meaning'
Biological determinism is a trap that Luce Irigaray also falls into, again against her stated intentions. For Irigaray, 'in her statements - at least when she dares to speak out - woman retouches herself constantly'. Having sex organs everywhere, she can experience pleasure almost everywhere, can be autoerotic, can be double, plural within herself. Woman can express this pleasure through her speech and thus preserve her autoeroticism and homo-sexuality, bringing her freedom from the state of being an object. Woman's language must be heard differently in order to hear 'an "other meaning" which is constantly in the process of weaving itself, at the same time ceaselessly embracing words and casting them off to avoid becoming fixed, immobilized.' Women's pleasure and language is complex, subtle, diffuse and distinguished by 'contiguity', a nearness, a 'touching upon'. Woman's sexuality is tactile but western sexuality is scopophilic (i.e. voyeuristic, and based on the male gaze). Therefore woman's entrance into the dominant scopic economy signifies her relegation to passivity and negativity: to the beautiful object, there to excite the instincts of the 'subject' on the one hand (or to become "goods" of exchange value) but also representing the fear of having nothing to see (i.e. no phallus). In this system of representation and desire, woman's sexual organs are absent: Woman, in this culture, is outside representation. The interplay of desire among women's bodies, sexes and speech is inconceivable in the dominant socio-cultural economy.

Irigaray bases her theories on the concept of 'specularization' which doesn't only suggest the mirror image from the visual penetration of the vagina with the speculum but also hints at a fundamental assumption of Western philosophy, i.e. "the necessity of postulating a subject that is capable of reflecting its own being". The philosophers' speculations, argues Irigaray, are essentially narcissistic, based on the logic of the same. The entire male imaginary is based on the same. Freud for example casts the little girl the same as the little boy. She is not a little girl but a little man. Man consitutes himself as subject by delegating woman as the object. The pleasure of self-representation, of desiring the same, is denied to Woman. Woman can defend her desire, notably through her speech and 'by refusing to go to the market'.

The Female Gaze
I disagree with Irigaray's assertion that woman's sexuality is only tactile. Women experience pleasure in 'the gaze' as well as in touching. It is the nature of the gaze that is different. For instance, I, the female playwright, explore woman not as a mirror image of me but as a separate being, from the inside out. When this character is shaped and performed on stage by an actor, I experience intense pleasure in looking at her, while she is looking back at me. This interlocking of gazes, this 'female gaze' allows a mutual dynamic to take place, becomes a space for creative conflict and ascribes subjectivity to the 'object of exploration' i.e. the stage character. My desire for creating a theatrical representation of a woman is neither scopophilic nor tactile per se but rather based on the pleasure of building a space, in this case a theatrical one, where 'self-representation' can occur. This 'female gaze' is determined not by any inherent 'nearness', like the folding of our labia, but by how we, as women, are positioned socioculturally.

Breaking language and the revolutionary subject
The above view is in some agreement with Julia Kristeva's writings which locate the repression of the feminine in terms of positioning rather than essences. Kristeva doesn't have a theory of femininity per se but rather one of marginality, subversion and dissidence. If 'femininity' has any definition at all in her terms, it is 'that which is marginalized by the patriarchal symbolic order'. This then includes men. Kristeva argues that "a woman cannot 'be'; it is something which does not even belong in the order of being. It follows that a feminist practice can only be negative, at odds with what already exists so that we may say 'that's not it' and 'that's still not it'. In 'women' I see something that cannot be represented, something that is not said...". For Kristeva, revolutionary writing, the kind that challenges phallocracy, is that which introduces 'ruptures, blank spaces and holes into language' as for example that of avant garde writers like Joyce and Artaud. But all speaking subjects are bisexual to a degree, which means they 'can explore all sources of signification'. Therefore woman who is 'a subject-in-the-making, a subject on trial', is also beginning to break language. Only just. Kristeva here specifically refers to Sophie Podolski as a single example of this practice, while remaining dismissive of most of 'women's' writing as over-concerned with identity and the family rather than with breaking language.

It is rather ironic that Kristeva's theory on the 'revolutionary subject' and writing is based largely on a few white males, once avant-garde but currently widely canonized in the West. Her faith in their ability to 'overthrow phallocracy' is remarkable. It is approaching the theatre of the absurd to be presented with an elaborate and sophisticated theory of the 'revolutionary subject' that excludes ninety-nine, point nine per cent of the world population as possible participants. As Toril Moi points out: 'It is still not clear why it is so important to show that certain literary practices break up the structures of language, when they seem to break up little else'.

Changing speech

French Feminists' over-estimation of the importance of breaking up language does not negate the fact that language is an important site of struggle for women. But 'speech' and 'coming to voice' have different meanings for different groups of women. bell hooks, for instance, as already mentioned, counterposes 'changing speech' to 'coming to speech from silence', which has been the main concern of W.A.S.P. feminists. bell hooks argues that black women and women from diverse ethnic communities have not been silent but have used a different kind of 'womanspeak', i.e. the soliloquy, which was not being listened to. It is the nature of this therefore that has to be changed, so that women's speech can actually be heard. bell hooks has developed what she calls a 'politic of domination', where patriarchy is viewed as only one of a number of interlocking structures of domination. hooks posits that those who dominate are seen as subjects whereas those who are dominated are seen as objects. Subjects have a right "...to define their own reality, establish their own identities, name their history. As objects, one's reality is defined by others, one's identity is created by others, one's history named only in ways that define one's relationship to those who are subject". Language is one place for struggle, where women can assert their subjectivity. hooks advocates women 'coming to voice' in a context of risk as opposed to one of nurturance usually favoured by white feminists. And emphasizes the importance of linking that 'voice' to history, culture and politics.

Lesbian Aesthetics

What then of lesbian aesthetics? Could lesbian not be said to be the same as 'woman'? For me, as for many other lesbians, 'woman' equals heterosexual. And in the theatre, whenever 'woman' supposedly assumes the lesbian what often happens is that the lesbian simply disappears. Here, as with women's aesthetics, definitions can be as restricting as they can be liberating. As Bonnie Zimmerman points out, the difficulties in locating a lesbian text are not small. For instance, one has to 'consider whether a lesbian text is one written by a lesbian (and if so, how do we determine who is a lesbian?), one written about lesbians (which might be by a heterosexual woman or man), or one that expresses a lesbian 'vision' (which has yet to be satisfactorily outlined)'. Despite the difficulties, a number of lesbians have in the past few years attempted to define and develop a lesbian aesthetics in literature, film and theatre. I shall here concentrate on work done in the theatre.

Again, a brief pause on 'what is a lesbian' is called for. Beyond the obvious 'a woman who desires another woman', I hold that a lesbian is someone who out of necessity invents herself, continuously constructing and deconstructing boundaries in the process. Likewise with Lesbian Theatre. And I agree with Monique Wittig who points out that the refusal to become or remain heterosexual 'always meant to refuse to become a man or a woman, consciously or not'. Thus a lesbian has to be something else, 'a not-woman, a not-man, a product of society, not a product of nature, for there is no nature in society. 'Man' and 'woman', as social constructs, are nothing but costume, gesture and ways of claiming or lacking space in the world. The costume and gestures of the man are to do with open spaces and freedom; those of the woman are to do with restrictions and confinement. The lesbian, caught between these two fixed ways of being, has to construct a self and a stance out of both. Sometimes she leans more towards the costume of the man, the 'mannish' lesbian, the butch, sometimes she leans more towards the costume of the woman, the 'womanish' lesbian, the femme. She sometimes transcends both and creates a truly androgynous way of being.

Zande Zeig, with Monique Wittig, developed the above ideas into a theory and practice of a distinctly lesbian aesthetics, based on 'the pursuit of androgyny', through gestures. Zeig's performance of Wittig's 'The Constant Journey' was widely acclaimed for its unique blend of femininity and masculinity. Zeig, in her article the 'Actor as Activator', articulates an approach to gestures 'as a particular aspect of the oppression of women' and focuses on the body of the actor, since without 'the body of the actor there is no theatre'. Lesbians, both as social actors and as actors on stage, are 'forced to look at their physical selves in a political context'. Zeig regards gestures as an essential theatre language, the production of which can be controlled. She asserts that by changing our movements and gestures we can change our perceptions and ourselves. Lesbian actors have a special role to play in that: 'Through gestures, lesbians are able to radically influence the direction of contemporary theatre'. Their aesthetics is rather different from the one located by Sue-Ellen Case who argues that 'the butch/femme dynamic is at the heart of a Lesbian Aesthetics'. Her theory is largely based on the work of Split Britches, who indeed 'play' with the butch/femme dynamic in almost all their productions, both erotically and hilariously 'stripping' femininity and masculinity on stage. But in a recent interview for Rouge Magazine, Split Britches' Lois Weaver placed their Butch and Femme dynamic as only part of what they do: 'we often pull from popular culture and popular culture is defined as man and woman. And rather than dealing with it in this way, which we find limiting, we take it one step further, which is Butch and Femme and then we play with it... we are theatricalizing that part of ourselves, to over blow it, to go past the stereotypes and claim it...it is not something that defines us'. Further, she described their aesthetics as very much a 'feminine' one, i.e. 'moment to moment... non-linear... coming from image and impulse rather than a cognitive process'.

Like Split Britches, Siren, the longest-running lesbian theatre company in Britain, have also largely delved into popular genres to subvert traditional images of women. And so, together with other lesbian theatre companies that emerged in the eighties, like 'Hard Corps', 'Character Ladies' and 'Shameful Practice', established burlesque, often of dark undertones, as the dominant form of popular lesbian theatre in the eighties. But in terms of individual playwrights and text, the picture is somewhat different. While recently doing a study of lesbian aesthetics, based on the following four lesbian plays, i.e., 'More' by Maro Green and Caroline Griffins; 'Neaptide' by Sarah Daniels; 'Dressed Suits to Hire' by Holly Hughes; 'Chiaroscuro' by Jackie Kay, I discovered that these plays could in no way be said to share the same aesthetics or even a similar content. They varied from the experimental, tragi-comic exploration of body, space and hidden disabilities in 'More', to the social realist study of lesbian motherhood, class conflict and male bigotry in 'Neaptide'; from the 'dykenoir' of intense, claustrophobic, sexual relationships in 'Dressed Suits to Hire' to the 'choreopoem' of naming and identity in 'Chiaroscuro'. Still, there was one common element to all of them - the freedom / confinement dynamic, something which, I am aware, also runs through my own work. Perhaps then, I was looking for it?

Interestingly, Bonnie Zimmerman in her search for a lesbian aesthetics in literature came to a similar conclusion. She wonders: 'might lesbian writing, because of the lesbian's position in the boundaries, be characterized by a particular sense of freedom and flexibility or rather by images of violently imposed barriers, the closet? Or, in fact, is there a dialectic between freedom and imprisonment unique to lesbian writing?'

Kate Davy, on the other hand, maintains that lesbian theatre can be distinguished by how it positions itself in relation to its audience. (Davy here specifically refers to the work of theatre artists performing at the New York WOW Cafe, a women-only space.) By implying a spectator who is neither the generic, universal male nor the social construct 'woman' but lesbian, lesbian theatre undercuts the dominant heterosexual model of performance. And, Davy argues, as it is generally accepted that representation is grounded in the dynamics of sexual difference and as heterosexuality is the socio-cultural institution where this difference is played out, dropping it from the performance address, could be a step to bringing radical change.

A new language?

The above, necessarily selective, overview of the diverse theories and practices of women's/feminine/feminist and lesbian aesthetics reveals that there is no one single female aesthetics, true to all women. Rather, there is a multiplicity of them, influenced by the sociocultural positioning of the particular women developing it. Still, the search for a new language for women will never cease and it is I believe a far from futile effort. It is instead a crucial aspect of the historical necessity of women becoming subjects.

Bibliography:

- De Beauvoir, Simone *'The Second Sex'* (Picador Classics 1988).
- Marks and Courtivron eds. *'New French Feminisms'* (Harvester Wheatsheaf, 1981).
- Case, Sue Ellen *'Feminism and Theatre'* (MacMillan, 1988).
- Felski, Rita *'Beyond Feminist Aesthetcs'* (Hutchinson Radius 1989)
- hooks, bell *'Talking Back, Thinking Feminist, Thinking Black'* (Sheba, 1989).
- Moi, Toril *'Sexual, Textual Politics'* (Routledge, 1987).
- Wandor, Micheline *'Carry on Understudies'* (Routledge & Kegan Paul, 1986).

Articles:

- Wittig, Monique *'One is not born a Woman'* (Feminist Issues, Winter 1981, USA). *'The Point of View: Universal or Particular?'* (Feminist Issues, Fall 1983).
- Zimmerman, Bonnie *'What has never been; An Overview of Lesbian Feminist Literary Criticism'* (Feminist Studies 7, No.3, Fall 1981).
- Zeig, Zande *'The Actor as Activator; Deconstructing Gender through Gestures'* (Woman and Performance Vol 2,Part 2 1985).
- Rapi, Nina *'Theatre of Moments: Nina Rapi interviews Split Britches'* (Rouge Magazine, issue 6 Spring 1991)
- Davy, Kate *'Constructing the Spectator'* (Performing Arts Journal 29, Vol 10, Part 2, 1986).

DIRECTOR TRAINING FOR WOMEN
Anna Birch

I founded Sensible Footwear in 1981 to give voice to female experience through theatre. Since then I have directed first productions by women writers which led to a formal period of training at the Royal Court Theatre.

Many female directors have created their own on the job training by setting up small companies and producing shows for fringe venues and community tours. This desire to experiment and to find new forms of theatre, executed on a shoe-string budget, leads to a limited directing experience because venues, productions, tours and cast are likely to be small scale. The possibility of reasonable production budgets is increased for the director working in mainstream theatre. One way of making the transition into mainstream theatre is through the director training schemes offered by some theatres e.g. The Royal Court, R.S.C., Battersea Arts Centre and the Regional Young Theatre Directors Scheme. This is a usual route for young men straight from college. Women are likely to be more experienced and older when they seek director training opportunities. Training opportunities need to be advertised properly as women in particular may be excluded from useful networks. Women trainees often find themselves working in an environment where the power is in the hands of the men running the theatre. This can work against the director as the concerns of her work may be different from those of the people taking the budget and programming decisions.

In my experience a trainee director can expect to be offered a wide variety of training experiences. She can observe rehearsals, run workshops, work with writers and publishers, direct rehearsals, direct rehearsed readings, direct her own production in a studio space, monitor shows in the director's absence, give notes to the actors for the director and be responsible for the technical rehearsals of a show on tour. Trainee directors need to know how much they will be expected to do and for women this is particularly important as their availability may be restricted by childcare considerations.

The representation of women in the theatre can be improved by changes in training. The ad hoc nature of director training means male assumptions are bound to prevail. This imbalance can be redressed by developing a method for training. A method offers a starting point for discussion between the host theatre and the trainee and offers a systematic way for the training to operate. By using a method the training that is on offer becomes clear and accessible to all trainees irrespective of gender and this promotes healthy cultural development in the theatre. An open approach to director training will help those who are under-represented in the profession to get an equal share of the cake and eventually to apply for jobs directing main stage productions or as Artistic Directors with regional theatres and larger companies. A method for director training can provide the trainee with something to respond to and helps to ensure that the person offering training fulfils their responsibility to see that the trainee is gaining from the experience.

For director training to work the trainee needs a negotiated approach to her training, good role models and feedback offered to her about the training process. A method can help the trainee to take an active role and not be put in the passive position of accepting whatever is on offer.

Negotiation

Director training needs to be a negotiated process. As a skill negotiating is crucial to the director because she works in a public setting. Convincing the theatre that she needs training and negotiating her training with the theatre are the first steps she will need to take. A negotiated approach to learning facilitates good learning. Learning how to ask for what she wants from her company is the single most important skill for a director.

Role Modelling

Through the process of role modelling trainees can learn many aspects of the job. It is important for female trainees to be given the opportunity of working with women directors. This experience may be limited precisely because women are under represented in the theatre. Without female role models to follow the trainee receives a distorted experience because she needs to understand what it is to be a director working from a female perspective. Women directors working only with men may come to question their approach and lack the confidence to pursue their particular female vision of a play. Women need to bring each other along to strengthen networks and facilitate exciting and creative enterprises. Through a commitment to this kind of nurturing our theatre work can be empowered. The best way forward is through the experience of doing and not telling and trusting new directors with responsibility. The traditional role model identified with theatre directors of a solitary genius is male and therefore inadequate for the multiplicity of roles women enact during their lives.

Feedback

Time needs to be set aside for feedback to be given to the trainee director. Through the process of receiving feedback she can take more control over her attainment and gain confidence in her skill as a director. A regular meeting with the director responsible for her training offers continuity and the opportunity for the trainee to sustain a central professional relationship.

As a trainee director I learnt the most when I was made to think about the needs of the production. Learning takes place when the trainee is trusted by the director and given responsibility to improve the production.The director offering training needs to have insight into their own work process and the desire to pass this on to new directors.

Anna Birch is a freelance director who specialises in directing new writing by women. She received the first Gerald Chapman Trainee Director Award from the Royal Court and Leicester Haymarket and was invited by the Academie Experimentale des Théâtres to participate in 'Le Secret de L'Acteur et Les Jeunes Metteurs en Scène' at the Odéon, Paris a symposium for new European theatre directors.

Director Training for Women - telephone Anna Birch 071-249 4528.

THE STATUS OF WOMEN IN THEATRE
Caroline Gardiner

In 1987, Jules Wright of the Women's Playhouse Trust approached me with the suggestion that it was time for an update of the Standing Conference of Women Theatre Directors and Administrators' influential 1984 report on the status of women in theatre. Their report had shown that women held fewer than 50% of the senior artistic and administrative posts in theatre, and that only 11% of the playwrights being produced were women. The three year gap since the publication of the report had led some theatre workers and commentators to suppose that the situation for women must have improved in the interim. Increasingly, when commenting on the position of women in theatre in the light of the 1984 report, one met with responses such as that of the 1986 Cork Enquiry into Professional Theatre in England (sub-title *"Theatre is for All"*). On women in theatre, the report had this to say. 'There have been encouraging developments in the last 15 years, like the founding of women's theatre companies, and the Women's Playhouse Trust ... as the present younger generation of women is developing its career, there are signs that the situation may be improving.'(1)

Such comments are indicative of how easily complacency can set in when some time has elapsed since the publication of figures. Given enough time, things would improve for women, wouldn't they? The situation may have been bad in 1984, but theatre had moved on since then, hadn't it? We suspected that in fact the situation would have changed very little since 1984. If that proved to be the case, then it would be essential to alert the theatre world, and especially the women working in it, to the fact that complacency was not justified.

Ironically, the one women's group singled out for a specific mention by the Arts Council sponsored report as "an encouraging development" did not receive any revenue funding from the Arts Council, and this important group was not accorded the status of Arts Council "client".

In April 1987, I undertook the up-date of the 1984 study. The research was carried out by telephone interview with all the 62 theatre companies in receipt of revenue funding from the Arts Council of Great Britain in the most recent financial year. The twelve month period preceding the interviews was covered. The position of women as artistic directors; general managers or senior administrators; members of boards of management; finance directors; production managers and chief electricians; heads of design; associate, freelance and assistant directors; and as writers was researched. Not only the positions held by women, but also the distribution of funding according to sex was included in the research.

The results showed that not much had in fact changed since 1984. For almost every level of appointment that might be expected to have a significant impact on theatre policy, women were disadvantaged financially, and therefore artistically, compared with men. Even when women held the decision-making posts, the amount of money they had access to was less than that of men in the same jobs. Women were more likely than men to be working in small companies with low levels of funding, with small scale touring companies without a permanent building base, or in theatres with small auditoria. Women were much less likely to get the top jobs in theatres outside London than they were in the capital.

Women accounted for fewer than 50% of artistic, associate and freelance directors, members of boards of management, finance directors and production managers. 34% of all artistic directors were women. The only posts in which women accounted for more than 50% of those working in the field were head of design (58%), assistant director (53%), and general manager (51%). Interviews with male artistic directors during the research suggested that assistant directors and even general managers were sometimes seen primarily as "helpers and supporters" of the artistic director. The "handmaiden" role is a familiar one to many women, and its persistence may have accounted for the small majority of women in these posts.

At first sight, there might seem to have been some improvements on the 1984 study. In 1984, 12% of artistic directors were women, and 44% of general managers. However, the practice of working in collectives, where several people shared the role of artistic director and / or company administrator, accounted for many of the women surveyed in 1987. If collectives were excluded from the results, then only 15% of artistic directors and 42% of general managers in 1987 were women. Both figures were very close to the result in 1984.

The 1987 results probably reflected an increase in the number of collectively-run companies over the intervening three years, rather than any real increase in the numbers of women in charge of well-funded companies. 82% of women artistic directors in 1987 were running companies with Arts Council funding of less than £100,000. Only 43% of male artistic directors worked with such a small amount of funding. 60% of women administrators ran companies with funding of less than £100,000. Only 31% of male administrators ran companies with this amount of funding.

A similar pattern was found throughout the research. Where there were apparent small improvements in the position of women, this could usually be traced to an increased number of collectively and co-operatively run companies. Such companies appeared to offer greater opportunities for women. Many had an actively enforced equal opportunities policy. For example, several collectively run companies deliberately sought an equal balance between the sexes in the freelance directors and company members they employed.

It might be thought that many women found a collective structure more congenial than a hierarchical one. Perhaps it was the conscious choice of women to work in such companies, because of the nature of their management, rather than their being excluded from the larger companies. But it must be remembered that the collectively run companies tended to be those functioning on small amounts of funding. Women working in theatre were therefore likely to be offered less ambitious projects, with smaller casts and fewer resources, than was the case with men. The opportunities for women to extend their skills and experience must by the same token have been less than those of men. Nor were the limitations on women solely artistic. Women administrators were less likely to gain experience of handling large budgets and large number of staff than men were. Women working on the production side were less likely to be exposed to new technical developments and equipment. If it really is the case that women generally prefer to work with collectively run companies, then this is an argument for funding such companies on a more generous basis.

The situation of women writers showed that here was an area in which women might be disadvantaged even before they began. Only 11% of the plays produced during 1986/7 were original works by women playwrights. This is exactly the same figure as in 1984. Many of the plays which theatres initially classified as original works by women were in fact dramatisations of novels by women, often adapted for the stage by men. Novels by Agatha Christie, Jane Austen, the Bronte Sisters, and Flora Thompson were often dramatised. Among contemporary women playwrights, only Pam Gems, Caryl Churchill and Sue Townsend received more than a couple of productions in that year. Women writers were much less likely than men to be produced outside London, or to be given a main house production.

None of this is likely to offer much encouragement to the aspiring woman writer. Following the same pattern as in other areas of theatre, the larger the likely audience and the greater the production budget, the more likely the writer was to be male. Perhaps women writers now limit themselves in choice of subject and style, because of their low expectations for the type of production they are likely to receive. Much is being heard about the financial peril of theatre in Britain in the 1990's, with playwrights of both sexes being forced to write for small casts. The limitations placed on all playwrights during a period of financial stringency should not be allowed to obscure the fact that plays by women are much less likely to be produced than plays by men. It is not just a question of fewer plays by women being produced. When they do get produced, plays by women are given lower budgets and smaller auditoria than plays by men.

The theory that women's position would improve given time was proven incorrect by the 1987 study. The 1986 Cork Report implied that one of the possible reasons for the poor representation of women was that theatre was a relatively new career for women. The Department of Arts Policy and Management at City University, London, where I teach and research, has been training arts administrators for 16 years. At the time of the 1987 research, 68% of those who had received the Diploma in Arts Administration were female. It is true that not all students go on to work in theatre administration, nor is the Diploma a necessary or an automatic route to senior posts in theatre. It might be argued that women are more likely than men to take such a course because they find it more difficult than men to get practical experience. Or that women tend to take time off to have children. But the fact that the majority of the Diploma holders were women does suggest that the majority of theatre administrators nationally would be women. The fact that the course has been running for so many years would mean that women qualifying early on could, even if they took time off to have children, be well advanced by now in their arts administration careers. Yet only 29% of the general managers of theatre companies receiving more than £250,000 in funding from the Arts Council were women. Even though more than half of all the theatre general managers surveyed were women.

The survey also showed that women were more likely than men to employ other women. 100% of the theatre companies which had a woman as artistic director had performed work by women writers. Only 67% of the companies with a male artistic director had performed work by women writers. In all the companies run by women, women were more likely to have opportunities in the senior artistic, managerial and technical roles in theatre than was the case in companies run by men. If fewer companies were being run by women than by men, and if the companies that were run by women were still under-resourced compared with those run by men, then where were women to find the opportunities to train for the senior posts in larger and better-funded theatres?

Like its predecessor, the 1987 report, entitled *"What Share of the Cake?"*, and published by the Women's Playhouse Trust, created considerable media interest, thanks to the campaigning work of Jules Wright. It was taken up by the Shadow Spokesman for the Arts, Mark Fisher, and used in his deliberations on Labour Party Policy on women in the arts. A Press Conference held by Mark Fisher at the House of Commons in October 1987 highlighted the WPT report and others, such as Nicola Lefanu's work on women composers and musicians. The *Sunday Times, The New Statesman,* and *The Stage* printed articles about the research. The general awareness of women's disadvantaged position in theatre may now be greater than it was prior to 1987. But although a number of individual women have had considerable success as directors and general managers since then, I am not aware of major improvements in the situation for women in theatre overall as a result of that increased awareness.

Now at the beginning of 1991, the same kind of objection can be raised to the 1987 study as was raised to the 1984 study. 'Time has passed. The situation for women must have improved. The research is out-of-date. It no longer reflects the real position of women in theatre'. Theatre in the UK is generally seen as being under threat. The danger is that any attempt to improve the position of women may be seen as a distraction from the "real" issue - keeping the theatre alive.

An up-date of the research is planned for 1991. At the time of the 1987 project, I had seen my role as purely that of researcher. My part in promoting women's interests in theatre was to be that of providing the ammunition which others would use in their campaigns for better representation of women in theatre. The ability to demonstrate what otherwise may be only assumed to be the case is certainly an important benefit of any statistical survey of women. But in the current climate, any new research must become more than a collection of figures. It must attempt to address the issues raised by the previous studies, to examine practical ways in which the position of women in theatre might be improved. This will probably mean a change of focus from the purely statistical approach. It is time to explore in more detail the reasons for the results that have been found. What is it that is apparently holding women back from senior theatre jobs? What can be done to improve the situation? Statistical research will only show what the situation is, not why it exists. In-depth interviews with women working in theatre, with theatre companies, and with those running theatres, will be necessary. Research also needs to be done more frequently, probably on an annual basis. The argument that things will improve for women, given time, has not proved correct in the past. This argument can be, and has been, used to support a tendency to inaction, and it needs to be resisted. The statistics must always be up-to-date. When action is taken, the effects of it need to be monitored. If women's position does begin to improve, we need to see how and where, so that we know what kind of action is effective.

It should be a matter of concern to everyone that women's position in theatre be improved. Women are 52% of the population. Audience research suggests that women account for around 58% of theatre audiences. Women accounted for 68% of holders of the City University's Diploma in Arts Administration by 1987. As a matter of simple justice, women and women's work ought to be better represented in the theatre. If theatre is acknowledged as important, then what the playwright has to tell us has an impact on our view of the world. It does not automatically follow that male playwrights will not write plays that are accessible and important to women. But if women writers are not being performed, then audiences of both women and men are missing the opportunity for a different perspective on the world. Women writers tend to write more and larger roles for women. An increase in the number of plays by women being performed could lead to greater opportunities for actresses. The new research should include some work on the particular problems facing actresses. The effect of having women in senior posts in theatre is to create greater opportunities for women in all areas of theatre. The appointment of more women general managers and artistic directors would be a major first step towards improving women's status in theatre.

In 1991 research should be seen only as the beginning this time. It is no longer enough to simply define the problem. This time we need to find out why the problem exists. And how we can begin to move towards a time when research on the status of women in theatre will no longer be needed.

(1) p 44, *'Theatre is For All'* Report of the Cork Enquiry into Professional Theatre, published by the Arts Council of Great Britain (1986)

The Plays

COCHON FLAMBÉ

Eva Lewin

beginnings.....

I wrote the first draft of *Cochon Flambé* one morning in bed before going to work. I thought of it then as a possible stand up comedy routine for a friend of mine's cabaret trio. A three minute summary of waitressing which they could muck about with as they saw fit. She and I had the same tedious box office job at the time, with no end in sight. I coped by semi diligent sulkiness and cynicism, she by brandishing a well honed anger at the hapless customers - mostly tourists vainly attempting to buy tickets for *Cats*. Her performing anger showed me the way and I tapped into my previous experience as a waitress in a City of London restaurant at the dawn of the Thatcher financial bubble. Not writing the piece as a formal play, but as conversational rant (hopefully entertaining) which could be changed, adjusted, experimented with, gave me the freedom to let loose. This was my piece of graffitti.

Although *Cochon* has gone through several drafts since then and has in fact become a short play, it is substantially what I drafted that morning. Having said that, it is thanks to the encouragement and advice of members of the Drill Hall Women Writers' Workshop, actresses and directors who have workshopped and performed the play that *Cochon* is a complete piece now.

Cochon Flambé was originally performed at the Drill Hall Arts Centre in 1988 as part of the Attic Work Season directed by Heather Goodman with Carol Ruggier and Laurence Gallio performing and in 1990 it was performed with a sequel *Diva Dream*, in the 'Out of The Attic' festival at the Soho Poly Theatre, directed by Ruth Ben-Tovim with Carol Ruggier and Tim Newton. The play was performed again in March 1991 at the Etcetera Theatre Club, directed by Bryan Bowen in London's First One Person Play Festival.

CHARACTERS:
WENDY..............................Young waitress, about 22 years old
MALE CUSTOMER...........A businessman, over 25 years

LOCATION:
A posh City of London restaurant.'Neo-Victorian', wood panelling etc.

ACT ONE.

Restaurant interior. Day.
WENDY is preparing for lunchtime rush

WENDY: Here I stand in my neat apron. Like a white fig leaf. My black blouse and my comfy slip-on shoes. I'm a slight figure only half visible in the dim light of the restaurant.
(Pause)
This place specialises in a Victorian feel. Tankards on the wall, sawdust on the floor, framed cartoons of long lost politicians. Tables lit by imitation ships' lanterns. A warm ambiance for businessmen and their lunchtime deals. The manager and his assistant creep around deferentially in three piece suits and expensive leather shoes.
(Pause)
I am a real waitress. This is my life. I didn't choose this job. The job centre got it for me. Peters and Co were kind enough to train me. Silver service and all that. A bright and shiny career in catering. It's a growth industry. I take home fifty-six quid a week, plus tips. It's not bad money except it's not enough. We get free lunches. I'm sick of them. And ten quid a day tips if you're lucky. "Excuse me, could you possibly leave the tip as cash? I don't get it if you add it on the American Express. The Restaurant keeps it." The customers don't like it if I ask for cash. It makes them feel embarrassed or angry. It's like begging they think. It is begging. I don't like it but it's my living isn't it? We're not meant to ask for cash tips either. The manager's giving the waitress with the most credit card tips an Easter egg. Just the thought of it makes me feel servile.
(Pause)
I told him to shove it up his arse.
(Pause)
I'm saving up to go to the Riviera.

Get a job with the Club Mediterranean.....

(MALE CUSTOMER enters)

An early bird at one of my tables. Just my luck. I'm not nearly ready. Good morning. I am here to serve you. I know the menu off by heart. Pâté. Salmon starter. Game pie, cold sliced lamb, ham, tongue, roast beef, side salad - lettuce, tomato, cucumber. Onions. Sliced French bread. Home made soup: French onion, yesterday, today, tomorrow and always. Our recommended wine is vintage red Burgundy St Aubin 1985, £11.95.

CUSTOMER: St Aubin. Thank you.

WENDY: I know him.
(Pause)
My first job was at a travel company, photocopying. My dad was really pleased, he said "you can use your O levels there". Excusez moi patron, l'appareil photocopy ne marche pas... I worked so hard there. I was really keen. I read all the brochures. I was a mine of information for customers whenever the boss'd let me get near one. I told him I wanted to be a courier. He told me to get lost. "We only recruit graduates for courier positions." Later he drew me aside. "Look Wendy" he said, "you're a bright girl. We'd like to help you but you've got to get some skills. Learn to type, use a wordprocessor. Then come back to us. "Wordprocessing: it's as bad as photocopying. You're just an appendage to a machine. If they could do it without you they would. Anyway, I had enough of studying, with A levels. All my friends had left school. When they were out having fun, I was stuck in doing homework. They stopped phoning. It was all too much. I had to go to one school for English,

another for Maths and another for Geography. Spent hours at bus stops. I was so lonely, and fed up with travelling, I packed it in.
(Pause)
I can remember bits: "come unto these yellow sands and then take hands", "The President of the Immortals had ended his sport with Tess". Your wine sir. Would you like to taste it?

CUSTOMER: No no. Pour it out. I'm sure its excellent.

WENDY: Okay sir. The customers here want you to flirt or be a bit servile. Clip your cigar sir? Excuse me while I reach over. You like that don't you? Means I tilt my tits in your direction. Too bad I wear my blouse done up to the top. So they can smile and wink and lick their lips and imagine my bare bum as I carry out the plates. And if they leave money on the table, I'll give them one of my special grateful smiles.
(She demonstrates smile)
I never used to be like this. I've got a ball of iron in my stomach. You might call it anger. In the morning it's cold. The bus ride here warms it up. By noon it's red hot. Nicking desserts cools it down. Cheesecake slices, chocolate mousses in little porcelain bowls, grapes, half finished bottles of wine. But it won't go away. Perhaps Mr Simmonds will come in today. He's a self-made man from the North somewhere. But he's alright. He's got a wide smile, lots of teeth. He makes Pauline giggle and always orders game pie - even if it really stinks. He sits askew from the table with one leg sticking out, so you trip over it if you don't watch out. Oh Mr Simmonds put your leg away please. "Sorry luv, my long leg's causing trouble again?" Pauline always says to him "jumping hurdles is extra". He's a kind man. Harmless. I'm sure if he

could think of a better joke he would. They're dying out though, men like him. They're just not nasty enough for a lean and thrusting competitive society.
(Pause)
The thing about customers is that unless you are actually doing something for them, they think you are skiving. It's food you see. Never come between a customer and their food. They can't bear it. It's torture to hold off from that crusty pie for two minutes more. I want my Branston pickle. Gimme gimme gimme. Come here. What the hell do you think you are doing over at that table? Having a good giggle eh? Passing the time of day? I don't exist do I? I'm just a walking grey pin-stripe. You can't see me, the real hungry me. Come here, come here. Waitress, Waitress... You're hiding from me, I know you are. Thinks I can't catch her eye behind that pile of plates and glasses she's carrying. You little whore, you bitch. I'll spill my mustard if you don't come. Spill spill spill. And the vinaigrette. You won't like that will you? Sticky slimy mess all over the place. That'll keep you busy. And so it goes. They just want their mums. Nubile mums, motherly mums, cuddly mums, bossy mums, fussy mums, doting mums and run around them mums. They make me sick. You get your own back though, by telling them confidentially (just as you serve their entrées) that the prawns they've just eaten were a weeny bit off, and then you offer them dessert on the house.
(to CUSTOMER) Here's some French bread to be getting on with.

CUSTOMER: Oh you're quite pretty really. Are you new here?

WENDY: No. We've met.

CUSTOMER: I don't remember I'm

46

afraid.

WENDY: Well, I'm not so lucky.

CUSTOMER: Could I have a lamp please?

WENDY: Oh my God. I don't believe it. "Are you new here?" The fucking cheek to come back. Oh no, no. He can't, the bastard. What's he want? Not me again. Oh no. He's not having me again. *(She flips back time when male customer raped her, and tries to defend herself)* You've come to the wrong toilet sir. "No I haven't miss." No use trying to laugh it off, to forget. It happened. Had against my will by male customer of Table 3. Silver service. Who cares? Who cares? Who'd believe me? A respectable man, frequent customer, versus young waitress. Don't make me laugh. The manager'd say I offered. He thinks I'd do anything for cash.
(She stares at the customer)
Look at him, so cool, so nonchalant. Popped in for roast beef, glass of vino, and a quick fuck. Goddamit, he's signalling. He wants a lamp. A lamp to lighten his darkness. Show up the blood in his beef. Give each little green pea its little round shadow. Glint softly on his gold watch strap, the thick hairs on his wrist. I'm going to make a nice bright light.
(Pause)
In the evenings at home I lie on the floor and look at my pot plants. I dream I'm in the jungle with roaring tigers, chattering monkeys and stampeding elephants. But I'm safe. I sleep in the lush grass and in the morning I swim like a naiad in the smooth brown river. Who can touch me there? No-one. No-one. No-one. That's freedom for you.

(WENDY gets out several large chunky lighters, empty wine bottles, *a wick and matches. She empties lighter fuel into bottle, adds wick etc. To make Molotov cocktail)*

I'll never come here again. No more polishing, slicing, carrying, slopping vinaigrette. I won't have to squirm and be servile and enunciate the menu like an act of religious devotion - ever again. Ever again. I'm going to tear up these black clothes and this pubic apron into thousands of shreds. No more slavery. Oh my skin stinks of this place - how long will it take to clear?

(The bomb is ready. She calls to CUSTOMER)

Sir, here's your lamp - catch!

(Big explosion)

Blackout.

CRUX

April de Angelis

CRUX was commissioned by Paines Plough Theatre Company in 1989. It had a first performance at The Towngate Centre, Basildon on March 8th, 1990 followed by a national tour ending at the Lyric Studio, Hammersmith.

Cast:
Joan:	Kathy Burke.
Madeleine:	Tina Jones.
Marguarite:	Anna Keaveney.
Bishop:	David Mallinson.
Agnes:	Adele Saleem.
Carl:	Steve Sweeney

Directed by Saffron Myers
Designed by Catherine Armstrong.

I had originally been commissioned to write a play about the crusades, as often happens after doing research I wrote a play only tangentially connected with them. I had come across a thirteenth century religious doctrine 'The Doctrine of the Free Spirit'- the followers of this doctrine believed in a sort of radical pantheism; that they were made from the same substance as God and therefore they could not sin, did not need to own property (how can you supplement God?) and had no room for a concept of guilt. These free spiriters lived in houses scattered across medieval Europe and one of these houses was a house of women. I was fascinated by the idea of women that lived with such an overwhelming commitment to a sense of self love.

The Doctrine of the Free Spirit, not surprisingly, ran into opposition from the established church. A church which was founded upon the idea of wretched human sinners and guilt. Free spiriters were persecuted. In 1309, a woman called Marguarite Porete was burnt at the stake for refusing to renounce her 'heresy' of the free spirit. These were the basic historical facts upon which I invented in writing *'Crux'*.

FIRST HALF

Against a red light MARGUARITE stands.

MARGUARITE: So many people, all pushed together like blades of grass, all shouting and crying out like they wanted something bigger than the sun, all pushed together and wanting to see, to see. Men on horses. Iron men. Heads of iron. People with sticks. Fire on the sticks. Children with small heads and faces turned up. Eyes. Someone crying in their throat. Strange sounds like surprise but longer. Someone crying...it's me! Fire on the sticks. It's me..

(Lights change. MARGUARITE exits)

JOAN enters with a bucket.
(She puts it down)

JOAN: Crossroads.

(Pause)

I could walk off in any direction now and no-one would try and stop me.
I could do anything.
Fart.
Anything.
This is my bucket.
(Pause)
It's hard to know if you've done bad or not.
Did I?
I don't know.
No-one can tell me.
Bucket can't tell me. No-one.
If you can think something in your head. It's as good as real. That's what they used to say.
I can think them now.
I can think them.
Back they come.
Back back.
Look.

(MARGUARITE enters. She has a stick and begins drawing with it on the ground).

JOAN: What are you doing?

MARGUARITE: Making something.

JOAN: What?

MARGUARITE: House.

JOAN: Making a house with a stick.

MARGUARITE: Making the pattern of our house.
In the earth.

JOAN: We lived in it.
Is it beautiful?

MARGUARITE: It does.

JOAN: House. Squat. A fat door.
Earth floor.
You built it.

MARGUARITE: From nothing.

JOAN: House from nothing.

(MARGUARITE continues to draw. Ignores JOAN. JOAN looks at her and whispers).

JOAN: Marguarite?

(MARGUARITE does not hear her. JOAN squats down and rubs her hands and arms in Marguarite's drawing. MARGUARITE takes no notice. JOAN rubs her face with her hands. MARGUARITE carries on drawing)

MARGUARITE: This is the house of voluntary poverty.

JOAN: A good house.

(A man runs across the stage with a cry, holding his head in his hands. Some coins are thrown across the stage after him.

49

MADELAINE enters)

MADELAINE: Dampballs! Fuckwit! Take your piss money!

JOAN: That's Madelaine. She's very nice.

MADELAINE: Needleprick! *(to JOAN)* If I was doing it for money that'd be a bloody insult. *(she exits)*

JOAN: I remember everything. Like it was. Everything. The beat of people's hearts. Their mouth shapes. Everything. *(the lights go ghostly)* The beat of their hearts.

(AGNES walks across the stage. Expressionless. Like a ghost)

JOAN: Agnes! *(whispers)* Agnes....? *(the lights go dark)* I do remember. Like I was new still.
Everything.

(Lights change.)

(The house is revealed. Windows open. Morning. JOAN stands awed and uncomfortable in the centre. She holds her bucket.)

MARGUARITE: In the beginning there was nothing. Then I said 'Let there be light'... *(lights up more fully)* And there was light!

(MADELAINE staggers out)

MADELAINE: Hark. Her Ladyship's up.

MARGUARITE: I saw the light was good. I separated it from the dark. I called it morning.

MADELAINE: Last night.
Don't remember going to sleep.
Don't remember nothing.

(AGNES enters briskly. On an errand.)

MARGUARITE: You drank our donation from the Sisters of Holy and Charitable Ways.

MADELAINE: I remember that...

MARGUARITE: All of it.

MADELAINE: Friggin nuns.

MARGUARITE: They've got a good brew.

JOAN: Hello.

(Pause, MADELAINE stares at JOAN. AGNES regards her from further off. MARGUARITE carries on)

MADELAINE: What's this?

MARGUARITE: She came last night.

(Pause)

JOAN: Joan.
That's my name.
Joan.

MADELAINE: Charming.
What's that?

JOAN: A bucket.
I forgot to let go of the handle when I left.
So it came with me.
(Pause)
It leaks.

MADELAINE: That's useful.

JOAN: It's a slow leak.

MARGUARITE: Where were you before?

JOAN: Before what?

MARGUARITE: Before last night.

JOAN: Oh.
Well...
I kept the fire.

It was dark inside.
There was a hole in the top of the roof to let the smoke out.
I used to look out of that hole at the sky or the stars.
I had four brothers and no yard.
I kept looking at the hole till I thought it was a dream and then a hole again and then a dream and then a hole.
(Pause)
And so on.

MARGUARITE: I see.

JOAN: Then one day I heard talking. About how earth was heaven and we were full of it. Heaven. And something came over me. And I looked at the hole one last time and ran away forever looking for here. Till I was here.

MADELAINE: Hallelujah.

(MARGUARITE walks over to JOAN. She has another bucket or she fills JOAN'S bucket with water).

MARGUARITE: See this.

(She scoops up a handful of water)

JOAN: Yes. I see it.

MARGUARITE: That's you.

(MARGUARITE tips the water back into the bucket)

JOAN: Ooh. I'm drowned.
I never felt a thing.

MARGUARITE: All that in there is god.

JOAN: I'm in there too.

MARGUARITE: You and god. The same. Inseparable. Made of the same.

JOAN: The same! *(Pause)* I...

MARGUARITE: Go on.

JOAN: *(whispers)* I can't hardly believe every bit of me is god.

MARGUARITE: Every bit.

JOAN: Even...

MADELAINE: Even your shit hole's holy.

JOAN: Oh.

AGNES: We're good.
People leave us things. Because we're good. This is silk.

MADELAINE: Fart. It's not.

AGNES: Crusader silk.

MADELAINE: Let's try it?

AGNES: No.

(MADELAINE snatches it. Tries it on)

MADELAINE: *(mocking)* Our house is the house of Voluntary Poverty. People leave us things because we're good. Pies or scarves. This is silk.

AGNES: Give it back.

MADELAINE: Account nothing your own.

AGNES: You've kept something.

MADELAINE: I haven't.

AGNES: Have.

MADELAINE: What?

AGNES: A shilling.

MADELAINE: What shilling?

AGNES: Man threw it. You kept it.

MADELAINE: He threw it. I threw it back. He thought that's what I'd fucked him for.

AGNES: You kept it.

MADELAINE: No.

MARGUARITE: Have you kept it? A shilling?

MADELAINE: No!

MARGUARITE: Madelaine?

MADELAINE: No.

MARGUARITE: No?

(Pause)

MADELAINE: I'm saving it.

MARGUARITE: What for? Old age? Throw it away.

JOAN: You could throw it in a ditch. *(Pause)* Or a puddle...

MARGUARITE: Keeping it's like selling.

MADELAINE: It's different.

MARGUARITE: It's like turning god to nothing.

MADELAINE: It's different.

MARGUARITE: A fuck should always be beautiful.

MADELAINE: Oh Ecstatic.

MARGUARITE: I'm right.

MADELAINE: You'd piss bliss you would.

MARGUARITE: Think of the house. We gave up everything. We got more back.

MADELAINE: It's not much. A shilling. *(Pause)* It's nothing.

(Pause) You might be glad of a shilling. *(Pause)* Fuck.

(MADELAINE throws away the shilling. MARGUARITE places the bucket of water centrally. The women begin to wash their faces and arms)

JOAN: Even my arm.
Oh great arm...

(MADELAINE takes off the scarf. Dips it in the bucket and hands it back to AGNES. AGNES flicks water at MADELAINE. MADELAINE retaliates. AGNES gives a cry. MADELAINE upturns the bucket. Mayhem. It turns into a sort of wild game)

AGNES: Water everywhere!

MARGUARITE: Like the flood.

MADELAINE: God's piss.

MARGUARITE: Like the flood.

JOAN: Wet fur animals. People in wet beds drowned!

MADELAINE: Ha!

MARGUARITE: Just water in the world. No one could stop it.

JOAN: I'm wet now.

AGNES: People drowned and spluttered dead.

(Lights change. The women's scene fades into the background.)

(Focus on the MANSERVANT and the BISHOP. They are in the traditional pose of the confessor and client.)

BISHOP: Have you anything to say?

MAN: I don't believe so, no.

BISHOP: There must be something.

MAN: Something...?

BISHOP: Some thing. Some little thing. Something.

MAN: Oh. Something *(Pause)* There is. Now you come to mention it.

BISHOP: Well?

MAN: I met someone.

BISHOP: And?

MAN: And...it was a girl.
Well, a woman. *(Pause)*
And that's all. And that's it.

BISHOP: Did you lie with her?

MAN: What?

BISHOP: Did you lie with her?

MAN: Did I lie with her?

BISHOP: Did you lie with her?

MAN: No. Yes.

BISHOP: You serve a man of the church. Well?

MAN: Well?

BISHOP: Was there skin?

MAN: What?

BISHOP: Was there skin?

MAN: Skin?

BISHOP: Involved. Skin, was it involved. Was it?

MAN: It was involved.

BISHOP: And spittle?

MAN: No!

BISHOPS: No....

(Pause)

MAN: I'll never do it again it was all my fault. *(Pause)* And hers. *(Pause)* And that's all. I can't think of any more.

BISHOP: Ah.

MAN: Dampballs.

BISHOP: Pardon?

MAN: That's what she called me. *(Pause)* I wish I was more like you. Gooder.

BISHOP: I'm guided by a stronger light. That's why I'm a Bishop.

MAN: I'll never do it again. I promise.

(Lights focus on the women. They finish washing.)

AGNES: They all drowned. Maybe they were bad.

MARGUARITE: They were busy. Not bad.

MADELAINE: *(to AGNES)* You ought to be careful. What you get up to.

AGNES: What?

MADELAINE: What you get up to. Mooning about like a moon.

AGNES: Don't.

MADELAINE: Lovesick. Meet your boyfriend in a forest sick.

AGNES: Liar.

MADELAINE: Who wants a cuddle in the forest?

AGNES: I'm not listening.
I've got the name of a saint.

MARGUARITE: Saints are not better than anybody.

JOAN: I don't mind a cuddle.

AGNES: Agnes.

JOAN: Sometimes I cuddle my bucket.

MADELAINE: Saint Agnes!

AGNES: Saint Agnes.

MARGUARITE: The back wall. This morning, I noticed. It's crumbling. We need mud. To mend it. That's all. Mud.

JOAN: I'll help.

MADELAINE: Mud.

MARGUARITE: There'd be no wall without mud. And no house without a wall. Our house.

MADELAINE: Your house.

MARGUARITE: Our house.

AGNES: One day a solider came to her house.

JOAN: Whose house?

MADELAINE: Miss holy boots.

AGNES: He had a sword. He was all sweaty. She wouldn't do what he wanted.

JOAN: What?

MADELAINE: Milk her goat. What else?

JOAN: Oh...

AGNES: So she ran down under her house which was in ancient Rome where they kept fires in those times to heat up the house. She hid there and never made a sound even though it was hot as hot and it hurt worse than a pinch all over. In fact it was so hot that she blew up like a giant bump and died.

JOAN: What a horrible bump.

AGNES: She stayed the same for hundreds of years. Never changing. You can still see her. In a church somewhere...

MARGUARITE: (wryly) How wonderful. Still, she did what she wanted. Like we do, here.

MADELAINE: No, she didn't do like us.

MARGUARITE: Maybe she did.

JOAN: I don't think I'd want to be a bump. Even an old bump.

MARGUARITE: Mud anyone?

MADELAINE: God says she don't feel like doing anything today.

JOAN: Even if it was old as a chimney.

MARGUARITE: Well, if that's what she says.

(MARGUARITE exits)

JOAN: Old as peas
Old as sausage
Old as hedge
Old as armpit...

MADELAINE: Old as your friggin armpit.

JOAN: I was just contemplating...

MADELAINE: Did she tell you?

JOAN: What?

MADELAINE: She must have. Marguarite.

JOAN: What?

MADELAINE: When you come here. At first. What you have to do.

JOAN: What?

MADELAINE: *(to AGNES)* Don't we?

AGNES: Yes...

MADELAINE: A dance.

JOAN: A dance?

MADELAINE: Oh yes!

JOAN: I see.

AGNES: One with lots of spinning in it.

(Does a spin)

JOAN: Spinning.

MADELAINE: And you have to do things with your arms and legs.

(She demonstrates)

JOAN: Do things with your arms and legs...

(She has a go. They watch her. Copy her)

JOAN: *(to herself)* Foot like this. Arm like this.

MADELAINE: Arm like this!

JOAN: Spin like this which makes the world tip.

MADELAINE: What a divine inspired dance!

JOAN: Thank you.

AGNES: Makes my heart fast. Makes everything fast. Don't like it.

(MARGUARITE re-enters)

MARGUARITE: What's this?

MADELAINE: Joan wanted to dance.

JOAN: This and this... I made up a dance.

AGNES: Don't like it.

MARGUARITE: It's a fine dance.

JOAN: Thank you.

MADELAINE: Fucking inspired.

MARGUARITE: A fine dance.

JOAN: I made it.

(They continue to dance.)

JOAN: I feel sick now. All that spinning!

(She collapses. Dance fades. They rest. MARGUARITE looks at the house)

MARGUARITE: How shall we speak of you and not speak of ourselves? Worship you and not ourselves? Praise you and not ourselves? Our very flesh and taste, our spit, the blood of our wombs, us, us, us. We the divine on earth how shall we deny our being in you and you in ourselves? And who shall stop us, who? We who are in heaven now in the glory of our creation. Who? Who shall stop us? Who?

Lights change

MADELAINE and the MAN in the forest. A meeting.

MAN: You're bloody late.

MADELAINE: Better late than never.

MAN: Thought you weren't coming... after last time.

55

MADELAINE: Changed my mind. That's not a crime.

MAN: No.

MADELAINE: Let's not hang about then.

(They kiss).

Lights change

AGNES alone in the forest

AGNES: Are you here?

(Pause)

Close my eyes. Imagine you're here.
I imagine your curly beard.
I imagine it's all...curly.
Can feel it rough.
Feel it on my neck, rubbing that soft bit behind my ear.
Or on the hollow that leads to my shoulder like a river leads to a sea.
I can feel it there.
You could get inside my dress with me and we could pray.
I love you.
You're all I think of,
As if we'd swapped bones.
I'll wait for you.
Wait.
Come.
No-one would know.
No-one.

(JOAN enters. She is collecting mud.)

JOAN: It's me.

AGNES: Go away.

(Pause)

JOAN: I'm looking for mud.
For the wall.
It's an errand.
Are you looking for mud?

AGNES: I might be.
Can't you look for it somewhere else?

JOAN: I could. Or we could look for it together.

(Pause)

AGNES: No. I think I'll watch you. Anyway. I'm waiting for somebody.

JOAN: Who?

AGNES: No-one you know.

JOAN: Will they come?

AGNES: You've got mud on your cheek.

(JOAN wipes it with her sleeve)

I hate mud. It's dirty.

JOAN: Worms like it.

AGNES: Worms are stupid.

JOAN: They haven't got heads. That's why. *(Pause)* Have you been here long? At the house I mean... not here on this spot. Have you been there long?

AGNES: Longer than you.

JOAN: Oh. I ran away.

AGNES: I left home. I had a longing. That's why.

JOAN: A longing!

AGNES: You only know what it's like if you've had one.
I had one.
Like running inside.
That made me want to leave.
Don't go they said.
That inside you making you go is a devil.
You'll end up like a stone turned up by a plough wishing someone would put you in their pocket and bring you back.

(Pause)

How would you like it if someone pushed up to you?
Pushed up to you hard so your back hurt against the thing you were being pushed?

JOAN: I wouldn't like it.

AGNES: No.

JOAN: No.

AGNES: He pushed me up by a wall and said you like that. And he pushed against me. I could feel blood in my mouth because I'd bitten my mouth.
How would you like that?

JOAN: I wouldn't.

AGNES: That's the thing in you that's the devil he said.
The thing you want.
Put your hand between your legs and find out.
I said the thing in me was not the devil and he said that was a trick.
I'd find out my father said.
Ask a priest, and he laughed.
I went though.
I still went.

(Pause)

I came here.
And the longing went away.

JOAN: Where did it go?

AGNES: I don't know. (Pause) But it came back. Like something with it's claw in me.
In my flesh.

JOAN: A claw?

AGNES: Haven't you found any mud yet?

JOAN: How does a longing feel?

AGNES: Like you want to swallow all the time and you can't.

(JOAN practises some swallowing.)

(Lights up on MADELAINE and the man. Post-coital.)

MAN: There's a twig sticking in my back. *(Pause)* Why can't we do it at your house?

MADELAINE: Because.

MAN: Aren't men allowed?

MADELAINE: Not inside. We could fuck in the yard if you like. Only I was thinking of others before myself.

MAN: I think I'll stick to the woods. *(Pause)* How was it?

MADELAINE: How was what?

MAN: You know.

MADELAINE: Oh that. Middling to middling.

MAN: You enjoyed it.

MADELAINE: You should know.

MAN: Do you love me?

(MADELAINE begins to get up)

Where are you going?

MADELAINE: Going.

MAN: Stay here. We can count twigs.

MADELAINE: I got things to do.

MAN: Like what? What do you ever do?

MADELAINE: What I like.

MAN: You want the best of everything. You do.

MADELAINE: So do you.

MAN: You're not right.

MADELAINE: Sod off.

MAN: Me and you.

MADELAINE: Sod off.
Where would that get me.
Back where I started.
No thanks.

(MADELAINE brushes herself down)

MAN: I love you.

MADELAINE: Mind out.

MAN: People want things for themselves. Stay here. With me.

MADELAINE: This is the last time.

MAN: What?

MADELAINE: Last time I see you.

MAN: Why?

MADELAINE: I feel like it.

MAN: You bitch. You think you can do that? You got a thing coming.

MADELAINE: What are you? God almighty?

MAN: Bitch.

MADELAINE: Stink-bastard.

MAN: What about us?

MADELAINE: What about us?
(Pause)

MAN: You should take money for what you do.

MADELAINE: I gave that up. Years ago. Goodbye.

MAN: You think you can do that.

(MAN grabs her arm)

MADELAINE: Let go!

(She gets free.)

MAN: You think you can do that?

MADELAINE: Yes.

(She exits)

MAN: No. *(Pause)*
You'll make me do something.
I could have been a bishop, me.
Bishop of France. Big, bloody bishop!

Lights change.

JOAN alone

JOAN: *(sings)* Lavender's blue dilly dilly,
Lavender's green.
When I am king dilly dilly
You shall be queen.
How do you know dilly dilly
That this is true
Because my heart dilly dilly.
It told me so.

(Pause)

(calls) Ready!

(Pause)

Agnes!
I'm coming to find you now.

(Pause)

I bet you're behind a big tree.

(Pause)

I'm not scared of trees.
Not even if they're in a clump.
Agnes?

(Pause)

(shouts) Bucket and me are coming!

(JOAN exits. AGNES emerges from hiding)

AGNES: Shall I tell you something?
I wait for you every night.
To keep awake I pinch myself.
Look.

(She shows her arm. JOAN re-enters)

JOAN: Agnes?

AGNES: What?

JOAN: I don't understand this game.

AGNES: You are supposed to be looking for me.

JOAN: But you weren't hiding properly.

AGNES: You hide. I'll look for you.

JOAN: Me hide?

AGNES: Yes.

JOAN: Alright. I will. Then you can come and find me.

AGNES: Yes.

JOAN: Right.

(JOAN exits)

AGNES: When I think about you.
Those holes in you,
I could cry.
My tongue could lick your hands clean,
Lick the blood away
Even if it came back and back to eternity.
Use up all my spit licking you
All till I dried up like a husk and blew away in the wind.

That there was just you,
Your body between the devil and us.
Like a thin biscuit
Holding back a tide
A tide longing to flood
Longing.

(JOAN enters.)

JOAN: Agnes?

AGNES: I'm still counting!

(JOAN exits)

AGNES: And they nailed you. Nailed you.
Bang bang bang.
They probably laughed as they did it.
Their breath smelt.
Banging, banging.
Greasy leather.
Pushing against you.
And it hurt it hurt
All the banging
As you held back the longing
Held it.
Blood spurting everywhere
Your fingers twitched
Twitching.

(Pause)

Later all your flesh dropped off.
You left it for rotten.
And stepped out, light.

(Pause)

If I had a knife I'd carve your name on my chest.
Deep.
To hold back the longing.
I'd cut off my hair for you
Stick something in my leg.
I love you.
Look.

(She bites her arm. MARGUARITE enters.)

MARGUARITE: I found you.

AGNES: I wasn't hiding...oh, it's you. Are you looking for mud too?

MARGUARITE: No. Looking for you. What's this?

AGNES: What?

MARGUARITE: A dog bite you?

AGNES: Oh that.

MARGUARITE: Yes. That. Here. *(She takes AGNES' arm)* I want to tell you something.

AGNES: Let go.

MARGUARITE: No. You think where you'd be if it wasn't for me.

AGNES: You followed me.

MARGUARITE: Wasn't for our house.

AGNES: Don't know.

MARGUARITE: Think.

AGNES: Don't care.

MARGUARITE: Don't you?
Thirteen. You'd be married, in the fields or dead.

AGNES: I wouldn't be in the fields.

MARGUARITE: You can say what you like.

AGNES: I will.

MARGUARITE: Here, you can.
Say, do what you like.
No one tells God what to do.
And we're God.

AGNES: You're telling me.

MARGUARITE: I'm telling you
Before this house
It was a cold world
Where I was wrong

I did the bidding of others.
I was as small as a beetle.
I weaved other peoples' pictures.
Now it's different.
Say after me 'This is my flesh'.

(Pause)

Say it.
This is my flesh. I like my flesh.

AGNES: Let go.

MARGUARITE: I like it because it keeps my bones warm. Go on.

AGNES: My bones warm.

MARGUARITE: I like my skin...

AGNES: My skin because it's all over me.

MARGUARITE: I like the inside of my mouth because it's wet and soft and hard as fish.
I like the feeling that when I touch myself a part of me could turn to water. Go on.

AGNES: Could turn to water...

MARGUARITE: That feeling goes right out of my fingers. To my hair even.

AGNES: My hair even.

MARGUARITE: I could shout. I love that.

AGNES: Love that.

MARGUARITE: That's how God feels all the time. That's how it feels to be God. *(She lets go of AGNES)* Remember.

AGNES: You want me to go.

MARGUARITE: No.

(Lights change. Exit AGNES, enter MADELAINE.)

60

MADELAINE: You should chuck her out.

MARGUARITE: No.

MADELAINE: Why's she here?

MARGUARITE: Is that philosophical or ordinary?

MADELAINE: I mean it.

MARGUARITE: Where else should she be?

MADELAINE: Somewhere.
Some nun's house.
Down a well. I don't care.
Tell her.

MARGUARITE: What? Goodbye, the well's first to your right.

MADELAINE: You should tell her.

MARGUARITE: Why should I tell her?

MADELAINE: It's your house.

MARGUARITE: You live here.

MADELAINE: She doesn't think what we think.

MARGUARITE: She will.

MADELAINE: Why will she?
She'll think her own sweet way.
People don't change.

MARGUARITE: You did.

MADELAINE: You didn't.

MARGUARITE: Thank you.

MADELAINE: You're the same.
Same as I saw you in the market, the first time.
Talking to people on and on.
Your hair. Wild.

MARGUARITE: It was bloody freezing.

MADELAINE: It was dark. I listened to you till it was dark. Making promises. Turning things on their heads. Easy as picking flowers.

MARGUARITE: You came with me.

MADELAINE: You can't keep living your talk.

MARGUARITE: Why not?

MADELAINE: You'll let her stay.

MARGUARITE: She's no harm.

MADELAINE: Here. No-one asking things of me. I like it. Don't want it to stop.

MARGUARITE: It won't.

MADELAINE: Promises

MARGUARITE: The wall's nearly finished.

(Lights change. MARGUARITE and MADELAINE exit. AGNES enters)

AGNES: I said things. I said them.
She would never have said them.
Agnes.
She was beautiful. She wore a silver dress.
She died on a stake.
It went straight through her and came out the other end.

(Pause)

You'll never come now.

(JOAN sidles on.)

JOAN: Agnes.
I've been hiding for ages.
All crouched down near a stream.
Then it got boring.

(Pause)

61

Just now I never heard nothing.
I heard a big gap.

(Pause)

Come back to the house.

(Pause)

You may have a hold of the bucket
if you like.

They exit

There is a cry in the darkness.

BISHOP: Ah!

(The MAN hurries on.)

MAN: What?

BISHOP: Dream! In my mouth. See
anything.

MAN: No

BISHOP: Nothing?

MAN: Nothing.

BISHOP: The lord was very tiny.
Like a raison.
He was sitting in my mouth. On
my tongue.
He was tiny and smiling.
I wanted to swallow.
My whole mouth began to ache.
I could feel my spittle beginning to
drench our lord.
Beginning to turn into a great river
and wash him down my throat.
I wanted to say 'Get out quickly
lord'. But I knew if I did he'd be
crushed like a fly on the roof of
my mouth. The waters were rising
like the waters of a great vat. I
prayed hard. I prayed hard 'Hold
on to a tooth'.

MAN: What happened?

BISHOP: His hands were too tiny.
He said 'There's work to be done'.

Then he slipped.

MAN: He'll be alright. He's the lord.

BISHOP: I'm not a murderer.

MAN: Perhaps he could swim?

BISHOP: What does He mean
'There's work to be done?'

MAN: Dunno...

BISHOP: My hems feel heavy.
I could sleep for a year.

MAN: You sleep. You look nice
asleep.

Lights down. Lights up on the house.
MARGUARITE stirs mud in
preparation. JOAN watches.

JOAN: I got that mud.
Me.
I found it.
On the ground.
What have you put in it?

MARGUARITE: Straw.

JOAN: Straw? Have you always
made walls.

MARGUARITE: No. I was a weaver.
I used to sit in a small room.
Up and down. Up and down.
On the loom all day.
Up and down.

JOAN: Up and down.

MARGUARITE: I worked for a
weaver. He used to watch me and
talk. 'There's lots of talk' he said,
'People coming here and preaching
with words. Preaching ideas and
begging.'

JOAN: Preaching ideas and begging.

MARGUARITE: I'd spit on them.

JOAN: Ptt!

MARGUARITE: He was a git.

(Pause)

JOAN: He was a git.

MARGUARITE: 'Margery.' That was his name for me. 'I know you've been listening to them, Margery. I've seen you. I have.' 'No' he goes on. 'Don't listen. Don't. Shut them out. You must live by the sweat of your brow. Don't forget.' Then I felt something in me. For the first time. Like a fire starting. 'What about you' I said. 'You!, must you live by the sweat of my brow an all?'

JOAN: Must you live by the sweat of my brow an all!

MARGUARITE: 'Margery!' he said.

JOAN: Margery!

MARGUARITE: But I was all fired up.
Like I'd seen something.
Like I wanted more than his face and that room.
I left.
That's how I left.
Before I came here I was nothing.
Now I make myself like an Eve with her own clay.
I could be anything.

JOAN: I could be anything.

MARGUARITE: Anything.

Lights down

Lights up on the BISHOP and his MAN. They sit posed.

BISHOP: Karl?

MAN: Yes?

BISHOP: I get restless. Sitting in this chair all day. I don't feel like praying all the time. Sometimes I put a hood on and go out. I like going out. In my hood. I walk the streets. Sometimes I bless the people. Sometimes I shout at them. Depends.

MAN: You've been active in your time. Active. That's why you're restless. Now.

(Pause)

You've told me things. Stories. Remember? Knees?

BISHOP: Knees?

MAN: Knees.

BISHOP: Knees....
The blood came up to my knees!

MAN: Did it?

BISHOP: Yes! To here.
(He pulls up his clothes to reveal his knees)

MAN: Goodness. That was a lot of blood.

BISHOP: Yes. And I was on a horse. I kept thinking 'Why doesn't somebody open the gates and let the blood out'?

(Pause)

That's the way to lame a horse. Can't see where it puts its feet. Ha ha.

MAN: Ha ha.

BISHOP: Look! *(the BISHOP climbs up on his chair)* The city. I can see it.

MAN: Oh yes.

BISHOP: Yes. There's a good view

from this mountain. The sun is shining and its spires glisten like they're made of frozen rain.

MAN: How very beautiful.

(Pause)

How lucky we were to get to the top of this mountain. Thanks to you. You are brave and a good climber. Thank goodness you came. Thank goodness you are our leader.

BISHOP: I'm making a plan now.

MAN: Are you thinking we might have a seige?

BISHOP: Yes. A long one.

MAN: Oh rejoice.

(They arrange themselves as for a long seige.)

BISHOP: Thirst.

MAN: An important part of a seige.

BISHOP: Mouths shrink.

MAN: You dream you've eaten a hill of salt.

BISHOP: You dream of lakes.

MAN: Of being a duck.

BISHOP: Peaches.

MAN: You drink your own piss till even that dries up.

(BISHOP shoots the MAN a look, the MAN settles down to sleep)

BISHOP: Torment.
Wild thoughts.
That's when they come.
Seep up from hell.
Push them away. Fight.
Want want mixed up with thirst all mixed up this is a test.

Cool flesh.
Be strong.
I want someone to pee into my mouth.
Then I want to kiss the bit that pees.
I want someone to shit into my canonical hat.
Then I want to wear it.
Nothing else.

(Pause)

Jesus.

(Pause)

The devil has a prick the size of a sow.

(Pause)

It's being so close to the city.
Their thoughts have drifted over the wall and into my head. Into my head! They're such filthy bastards!

(Pause)

Christ says this is a city of desecrators!

MAN: I'd just got to sleep.

BISHOP: The city of a nation waiting to swamp Christ's lands.

(He approaches the MAN in a threatening manner)

If they come across you, a christian, they'd behead you or disembowel you, no questions asked. First though, they'd cut off your feet and wave them in your face and sneer 'Where's your god now'!
That's what they'd sneer.
Then they'd drink your blood.
Then fuck you both before and after you'd passed over.

(Pause)

(He addresses a 'crowd')

Brothers!
If you're asking what you get out
of this.
Remember.
Anyone fighting under the sign of
the cross today is guaranteed
eternal life.
I can give you that in writing.
Also,
Mohammed's people are wicked
But their city is full of rich things.
(Pause)
Let us lift the cross high.
Let us give the cry for holy war.
Let it ring out.
Holy war!

(They both give a loud cry)

MAN: What happened then?

BISHOP: Then?

MAN: Then.

BISHOP: We stormed the walls and
slaughtered the lot.

(Pause)

They lived luxurious lives.
Lives of luxury.
Sweetmeats and mathematics.
They took baths and rubbed each
other in scented oils.
They did that to each other.

MAN: I've got a report.

BISHOP: Like a scout?

MAN: Like a scout.

BISHOP: What did you see?

MAN: A house.

BISHOP: What sort of house?

MAN: I don't know if I should say.
In your company.

BISHOP: Say, say!

MAN: I'll speak very low...

*(He comes close to the BISHOP.
Whispers . The women come to life
around the men. They cannot see
the men but continue their daily
ritual.)*

MAN: *(audibly)*....right in the middle
of your bishopric. Like a piece of
the city. Floated down...

BISHOP: I can see them. Should I
speak to them?

MAN: You could try.

BISHOP: They're ignoring me.

MAN: What did you say?

BISHOP: Embrace Jesus.

MAN: What did they say?

BISHOP: Which one's Jesus.

MAN: They think they can do what
they like. They think they can do
things with a person and then leave
him in a wood.

(Pause)

He said there was work to be done.

BISHOP: Who?

MAN: The little raison Jesus.

BISHOP: He was right.

MAN: What are they doing now?

BISHOP: They're taking off my
clothes.

*(BISHOP is taking off his own
clothes)*

MAN: No!

BISHOP: One of them's laughing.
They've got my shoes.

MAN: What are they doing now?

BISHOP: Things.

MAN: Tell me.

BISHOP: They're waving my shoes in my face and they're shouting.

MAN: What?

BISHOP: Where's your god now?
Where's your god now?
Where's your god now?

Lights change.

BISHOP looks skew-whiff.

BISHOP: Man is a corrupt and dirty animal.

MAN: What happened?

BISHOP: We must lay on the floor, face in the dust. Then we'll have a chance. Chance small as a crack of light in a cupboard.

MAN: Don't lay down there.
You'll get fluff on your hat.

BISHOP: Here's a piece.

MAN: That's amazing.

BISHOP: What?

MAN: What does that remind you of?

BISHOP: Fluff.

MAN: That's how big that house looks to the almighty.

(MAN gets down on his knees and begins to blow the fluff about. They begin a game of blowing the fluff. It goes under the chair.)

BISHOP: It's gone under the chair.

MAN: Leave it.

BISHOP: Then the house won't get any light.

MAN: Won't get anything.

BISHOP: Like a seige.

MAN: A seige. Just say the word.

BISHOP: Like holy war.

MAN: That's it.

BISHOP: There's work to be done.

MAN: Holy war.

(Pause)

I'll get some mates.
We'll go into town.
We'll put the word about.
Bishop's orders. Holy church's orders. Lots of orders.
Don't give this fluff house nothing.

BISHOP: Nothing!

MAN: Then we find someone.
And we do something.
For instance kill their cow.
That's an example to the rest of them.
Like a seal on a bargain.
So they know what an order is.
So the house gets nothing.

BISHOP: Nothing. Bishop's orders! That's me.

(BISHOP puts his arm round MAN'S shoulder. They exit.)

We stormed the walls and slaughtered the lot...

JOAN alone at the house. She waits. She looks into the distance.

JOAN: *(shouts)* Hello!

(She picks up her bucket. She bangs on it with her shoe)

66

Hello! Hello!

(*She waves and jumps about, waits.*)

I made a mistake.
Thought I saw someone.
Someone coming.

(*MADELAINE has come out. She watches JOAN without JOAN knowing.*)

Shut my eyes.
Shake my head to get rid of the old look.
Walk to the place.

(*She walks with her eyes shut to stage front*)

Don't look yet.
Imagine. Imagine a pot of soup.
Don't knock it over, doddle-head.
Steaming, smelling. Cabbage floating.

(*She squats down*)

One eye at a time.
Look.

(*She opens her eyes*)

Bugger it.

(*Pause*)

Where are you soup?
Soup-soup. Soup soup ....

MADELAINE: Over here.

JOAN: Who's that?

MADELAINE: Soup.

JOAN: Soup don't speak.

MADELAINE: Don't be bloody rude. Anyway, I'm the spirit of the soup. Hot and cruel.

JOAN: Oh.

MADELAINE: I was asleep in my big pot in the sky. Heard someone calling me.

JOAN: Me.

MADELAINE: Nice sleeping. Then a voice. A squawk. Horrible like mouldy peelings.

JOAN: That was....me.

MADELAINE: You! What do you want? It better be good or else I'll boil over onto your foot.

JOAN: I'm hungry.
No-one's bringing us food like they used to. Yesterday I saw a man. I shouted at him. But he ran away.

MADELAINE: That was clever.

JOAN: He shouted something back but I never heard it. Thought if I closed my eyes the people might come back, up the way to our house. People with things that are drippy with fat or juice, or an egg, or apple slice with a clove or a pig's foot or a pie with a crust and hot steam coming out of it ....

MADELAINE: Shut-up.

JOAN: Or a toasted fish. Toasted in the fire. Can feel it now buttery scaly, feel it in my mouth with it's juice dripping down the side of my mouth.

MADELAINE: Shut piss up.

JOAN: You're not the soup spirit.

MADELAINE: Never.

JOAN: You're not polite.

MADELAINE: Turnip head.

JOAN: You shouldn't say things about heads. God made my head.

MADELAINE: A glorious elevation.

JOAN: Thank you. *(Pause)* Christ have mercy.

MADELAINE: What?

JOAN: That's what he shouted. That man. I remember now.

(AGNES enters slowly. She is collecting stones. Using her skirt to collect them. They watch her.)

JOAN: Here's a stone. It's like a face.

(AGNES takes it silently)

MADELAINE: Here's one like a bum.

(She tosses it to AGNES)

Thank you. Don't mention it.

(Pause)

What do you want them for?

(Pause)

What for?

(JOAN puts one in her mouth. Spits it out)

JOAN: You can't eat them.

MADELAINE: What for?

(She takes a handful of stones from AGNES' skirt and throws them on the ground)

What? *(AGNES ignores her)*

JOAN: Try again, Shut my eyes...

MADELAINE: Don't start that. You'll make me go raving. I can feel it.

(MARGUARITE enters.)

MARGUARITE: The wall's finished.

MADELAINE: I'm so glad. Have you had breakfast?

(Pause)

We haven't. There's been nothing of that sort for a while.

MARGUARITE: I found another patch. Another patch that needed seeing to.

MADELAINE: Haven't you noticed anything?

MARGUARITE: I nearly missed it.

MADELAINE: It's quiet.

MARGUARITE: In a corner.

MADELAINE: There's usually people. Talking. Questions. Who's lost teeth? Who's dead? Who's doing it with who? What's the meaning of life?

MARGUARITE: Nearly left it for the rot to set in.

MADELAINE: Well?

MARGUARITE: I want to write a book.

MADELAINE: I'm going to scream.

JOAN: Can I scream?

MARGUARITE: A book translating the divine fabric of my own existence into a text resplendant with an enlightening sense of the perfection of living here and now in the egalitarian glory of creation.

MADELAINE: You can't write.

JOAN: What's a book?

MARGUARITE: I could learn.

MADELAINE: We're deserted.

MARGUARITE: They'll be back.

MADELAINE: Will they? Maybe if there's a miracle.

JOAN: Will you make a miracle?

MARGUARITE: A miracle. Why not?

MADELAINE: Why not? You're cut from God's cloth.

JOAN: Will it bring a sack of food?

MARGUARITE: *(to MADELAINE)* You say it's a miracle we've been here this long.

MADELAINE: I can't talk to you anymore. Your head's gone soft. Soft with being Marguarite this and Marguarite that. Miracles are for people with nothing.

MARGUARITE: We've always had nothing. We don't start needing things now. We don't need anything.

MADELAINE: I do. I need food. I need a drink. I need three drinks.

JOAN: I'm going to wait for the miracle. All night. I'll sing so it knows where to come.

MARGUARITE: You sing.

JOAN: I will. Something a miracle might be partial to.

MADELAINE: You can wait as long as you like. I'm going.

JOAN: Where?

MADELAINE: If the sky had a mouth.

JOAN: What?

MADELAINE: We'd all know everything.

MARGUARITE: Madelaine.

MADELAINE: What?

MARGUARITE: You'll be back.

(A Pause. MADELAINE leaves)

JOAN: If I was the sky and I had a mouth I'd look down and eat myself.

(She flinches. AGNES continues to pick up stones.)

Lights down.

The BISHOP and his MANSERVANT are spotlighted. The BISHOP sits on his chair. He holds his crozier with a string tied to it. On the bottom are attached a bunch of grapes. The game the BISHOP plays is to pull the grapes away each time the MAN reaches for them. The BISHOP laughs. The MAN looks disgruntled. Lights down slowly. Laugh fades.

Lights up. Shadowy, night.
AGNES is sorting out bits of stone on the ground around her.

AGNES: Here's some stones. Small.
Bitter.
Bits of stones.
Sharp like teeth.
They can bite even though they've no mouth.

(She puts the stones into her shoes. She walks about.)

Are you here?
I'm getting better.

(JOAN enters.)

JOAN: Is it you?
I've been waiting.
You're small for a miracle.
I thought you be bigger, with more hair.

AGNES: It's me.

JOAN: Oh.

(Pause)

It's me.
Your friend. Joan.

AGNES: You're always following me.

JOAN: I'm not. I just want to ask you something.

(Pause)

You see. I knew you weren't the miracle.
Because I think it's me.
I'm the miracle.

AGNES: How could you be?

JOAN: I've got something.

AGNES: What?

JOAN: Something we could eat.
I hide her in the woods. When I go there she follows me about. She's clever.

AGNES: What is it.

JOAN: It's my chicken. I'm very close to her and so I'd rather not eat her. I couldn't eat her. But everyone's hungry...I'm hungry.

(Pause)

AGNES: What do you think?

JOAN: What do you think?

AGNES: No. I mean about you being heaven?

JOAN: I think that's what I am.

AGNES: Oh.

(Pause)

That's there's no hell?

JOAN: Only what's made by a person in their own heart for their own selves.

AGNES: Where's god.

JOAN: Everywhere. Everything's god.

AGNES: Me and you?

JOAN: Me and you.

AGNES: Do you love god?

JOAN: I do.

AGNES: You don't.

JOAN: I do.

AGNES: I feel sorry for you.

JOAN: Me?

AGNES: Can't you feel the dark? Feel it like it's resting on your skin. Ready. Can't you feel it like another skin that could tighten and tighten and slowly choke you? Can't you feel its warm fingers on the soft bit of your leg. Moving up your leg? It wants to touch you. Wants you to cry out. Can't you smell the dead? That wet in the air is the sog of their grave beds. It wants to get in your ears. Death looks for holes. That's why they put the dead in them. That's evil. It waits out there. Waits.

JOAN: Why? Why does it wait?

AGNES: I feel sorry for you. God's listening now. He's heard what you said. He knows you only love yourself. He's upset. He's nearby. Very close.

JOAN: Close?

AGNES: Near the trees.

70

JOAN: The trees!

AGNES: He's sitting in one and listening.

JOAN: Why is he up a tree?

AGNES: Listening and crying and shaking his head and saying to himself he thought you were a nice girl.

JOAN: A nice girl....

AGNES: Thought you were a nice girl and he's sorry he'll have to put you on his burn list. What a shame he says.

JOAN: What's he say that about me for?

AGNES: A shame.

JOAN: Why's he put me on his list?

AGNES: A crying shame.

JOAN: What list's that?

AGNES: When he thinks about all your nice hair flaming up and going to black ash and falling off so you look like inside a bad egg and all your hands and feet crisping up like bacon he shakes his head harder.

JOAN: I do love him.

AGNES: And all that going on and on forever in a huge pot in eternity with people trampling all over each other to get to the rim for ever and ever and the pot is hot metal hot metal and everyone screams and their flesh is burnt and comes back and is burnt and comes back and there's no water.

JOAN: I do love him.

AGNES: Only fires.

JOAN: I do.

AGNES: Hurting that never stops.

JOAN: Love him.

AGNES: He hates to do it. Has it got a name?

JOAN: What.

AGNES: The chicken.

JOAN: Just chicken.

AGNES: Chicken.

Lights down.

MARGUARITE alone outside the house

MARGUARITE: I left the weaver's.
As I was leaving his wife stood in the doorway.
Like a shadow in the doorway.
Cutting out the day.
She looked at me.
And she spoke.
You better know.
You better know my girl
You better know
There's no-where else to go
You leave here and everything's the same forever
The land getting stonier and stonier
The bread flatter and flatter
Cows thinner.
Dinners wetter.
It's more of the same.
It's more of the same.
So don't go thinking anything's different.
Do go thinking that.
You'll crash down if you do
You'll crash down
Think of me one day saying this.
Don't hope for anything.
If you want to know truth
Stick your head in a bag
It's that dark.
No wild hopes.
Everything's made that's going to

be.
So keep your hands at your side and think of me one day saying this.

(Pause)

Think of me.

(She exits)

BISHOP and man sit picnicking.

BISHOP: Saint Augustine was a venerable man.

MAN: He had a venerable beard.

BISHOP: And everywhere Augustine went...

MAN: Boredom was horribly feared!

(Pause)

BISHOP: What about... he always took a spare beard?

MAN: Then you've used 'beard' twice.

BISHOP: Does that matter?

MAN: It's a bit repetitive. Beard and beard.

BISHOP: I like it.

(Pause. They continue eating)

BISHOP: That reminds me. Did I ever tell you about the city?

MAN: Once or twice.

BISHOP: I was just about to leave the city. Evening. The light caught the stones, made them look like precious stones. Things were beginning to stink. Then in the distance there was someone walking. Walking. Picking their way among the dead. And they were bending over and taking things from the dead. It was a girl. I was on a horse. She was wearing a dress, it clung to her knees with the blood. You remember?

MAN: I wasn't there.

BISHOP: You be the girl.

MAN: I wasn't there.

BISHOP: Hello.

MAN: Hello.

BISHOP: What've you got there?

MAN: Where?

BISHOP: There. On your wrist.

MAN: A bracelet.

BISHOP: That's pretty.

MAN: A bracelet with blue stones.

BISHOP: Very pretty.

MAN: I took it off a dead person.

BISHOP: That's naughty.

MAN: Is that your horse?

BISHOP: Yes.

MAN: What's its name?

BISHOP: Richard.

MAN: Oh.

BISHOP: How did you get into the city?

MAN: I don't know.

BISHOP: You do.

MAN: Through the gates.

BISHOP: That's a lie. The gates are

72

locked. She found another way in.

MAN: I'm going to wear this bracelet when I comb my hair. I pulled it off her hand.

(Pause)

BISHOP: Do you see?

MAN: Her mouth was open and there were flies in her mouth.

BISHOP: Karl?

MAN: What?

BISHOP: She got in another way. The girl. A secret way.

(Pause)

Imagine a city.
You burn it. That's good.
Then imagine it with its fountains,
Its streets, its birds.
That's better for you.
It responds to your touch, like a woman or a horse.
That's better.
If it's against you, burn it.
If you can make it yours from the inside
That's better.

MAN: What do you mean?

BISHOP: I'm thinking of somewhere nearer to home. Finding a way in. Inside. Making it yours.

MAN: What way?

BISHOP: Up to you.

MAN: Me?

BISHOP: You.

(Pause)

MAN: That girl, what happened? Did she die?

BISHOP: Don't remember.

Lights down.

Lights up on JOAN. She sits on the ground. Dazed. AGNES is digging.

JOAN: Scratches. I've got scratches.

AGNES: She made a fuss.

JOAN: She knew.

AGNES: They're not deep.

JOAN: She always knew everything.

AGNES: They'll disappear. In a few days.

JOAN: She gave me such a look...

AGNES: Then it will be like it never happened.

JOAN: She was my friend.

AGNES: She was a chicken.

JOAN: Sometimes in the evenings, the sun caught her feathers. They went redder than flowers. She was soft, like she was made of feathers all the way through.

AGNES: It's dead now. We killed it.

JOAN: Don't. She made such terrible cries. Each one scratched my heart. I never knew she had sounds like that in her.

AGNES: They hate water.

(Pause)

How do you feel now?

JOAN: Horrible.

AGNES: How?

JOAN: Like there's something inside

me.

AGNES: What?

JOAN: I don't know. Like a heavy thing.

AGNES: Hot or cold.

JOAN: What?

AGNES: The thing. Is it hot or cold?

JOAN: Cold, I think. Cold.

AGNES: How does it make you feel?

JOAN: Like a tree with no leaves.

AGNES: Good.

JOAN: It's not?

AGNES That's how it feels to know your sins and love god.

JOAN: I liked it better the way I was before.

AGNES: That's the way to burn.

JOAN: Are we going to, you know... *(she whispers)* eat her?

AGNES: No.

JOAN: No?

AGNES: No.

JOAN: But...

AGNES: No we are going to bury her. With a stick on top.

JOAN: I don't understand.

AGNES: Trust me.

JOAN: I wish I had something. A feather.

Lights down.

Lights up on MARGUARITE. She sits alone. A silence. MADELAINE enters. She has a wine skin. She sits down heavily.

MARGUARITE: Three days.

MADELAINE: What?

MARGUARITE: You've been away.

(Pause)

Is that wine?

(MADELAINE takes a drink then throws the skin aside.)

MADELAINE: Empty.

(Pause)

So wine isn't leaking from our tits yet?
No divine wine.
No miracle.
Fancy that?

(Pause)

I'm not staying.

(Pause. She looks at MARGUARITE)

Your face...

MARGUARITE: Dirt.

MADELAINE: Beautiful dirt.

MARGUARITE: I left the house. I walked into town. Then I was on the ground.
Someone rubbed my face in the street.
Spat on me.
Left.

MADELAINE: There was no thunder and lightning then. When you was on the street. No salvation?

MARGUARITE: No. I'm thirsty.

MADELAINE: Thirsty's the last of your worries. People won't give you anything now.

MARGUARITE: They like us. They like us because we've got an idea. An idea of everyone as better, more.

MADELAINE: Did you see the mud when your face was pushed in it?
Did you?
I don't think you did. Did you?
People look after themselves. In the end.
Oh they're all full and fine when the going's good
but when the wind changes they go small and hard
They're not stupid.
Things have changed.
Can't you smell it?
It's even in the wind.
Like ash in the wind.

MARGUARITE: It's not the end. No.

MADELAINE: At night I don't sleep.
I watch the dark.
It's different.
Something's in it.
Roosting in it.
Skin wings, heavy, claws.
I can hear its breath
nearly.
I listen for it.
It listens back.
Worse is coming.

MARGUARITE: Come here. What you've had's like a dream.

(*MADELAINE moves away*)

MADELAINE: Feels real. I'm not staying. I came back to tell you.

MARGUARITE: Building this house wasn't labour. It was like it built itself, easy. As if it wanted to be built.

MADELAINE: To tell you.

MARGUARITE: How did you get the wine?

MADELAINE: Can you hear what I'm saying?

MARGUARITE: How?

MADELAINE: Bought it.

MARGUARITE: How?

MADELAINE: I borrowed the money.

MARGUARITE: Did you?

MADELAINE: What do you think?

(*Pause*)

MARGUARITE: It's the taking the money. That's like selling. That's hell.

MADELAINE: Christ. Listen.
The church don't like us.
The priests.
The church has got the church.
What have we got?
Hot piss is all we've got.

MARGUARITE: We don't need things.

MADELAINE: They don't need us.
They've got books.
They've got fires.
They don't like what we say.
This house.
I'm telling you.

MARGUARITE: God's will is our will and our will is God's.

MADELAINE: That's what they hate.

(*Pause*)

They'll come. Here.
I know they will.
They'll take us.
Burn the house.
They don't want it

They don't want it in our heads anymore.

MARGUARITE: They won't burn it.

MADELAINE: I came to say. That's all. Then go.

(JOAN enters shouting.)

JOAN: Go away go away go away...

(She sees MARGUARITE and MADELAINE)

I keep seeing bits of food dangling before me, a whole load of tormenting vegetables including a horrible and violent cabbage, laughing at me.

(Pause)

The miracle never came.
Something else came.
Things feel different. Like I've bitten into a bad nut.

(MARGUARITE empties out a sack. Out comes a loaf, apples etc.)

JOAN: The miracle! It came. Even a miracle loaf.

(She begins to eat something)

MADELAINE: Miracle food?

MARGUARITE: I stole it. In town. I stole it. I was nearly caught. But I was clever.

(AGNES has hobbled on.)

AGNES: Taking something. That's wrong... A sin.

MARGUARITE: We can't sin.

AGNES: It's wrong.

MARGUARITE: People take what they need.

AGNES: If I took something of yours?

MARGUARITE: I haven't got anything.

AGNES: If we're hungry. That's a punishment.

MARGUARITE: That's stupid.

(Pause)

AGNES: I'm going. Leaving.

(Pause)

Joan?

(JOAN makes a move towards AGNES)

MARGUARITE: They're coming. To burn the house.

JOAN: Burn it?

MARGUARITE: Burn it. Even the bit where you sleep.

MADELAINE: Marguarite!

JOAN: Burn it?

MARGUARITE: Burn it down.

JOAN: No?

MARGUARITE: Turn it to ash. I'm staying.

AGNES: Joan?

JOAN: I don't know.

MARGUARITE: I'll throw things at them.

MADELAINE: What?

AGNES: Joan?

JOAN: I don't know. Burn it.

MARGUARITE: Stones.

MADELAINE: Stones?

MARGUARITE: Lots of stones.

AGNES: Joan?

JOAN: I'll hit them with my bucket.

MARGUARITE: And mud.

JOAN: I'll get some more.

MARGUARITE: We'll curse them. Shout.

JOAN: I'll call them things. I'll call them... dampballs.

(JOAN runs into house)

MADELAINE: It won't work.

MARGUARITE: How do you know?

MADELAINE: It can't.

MARGUARITE: Can't it?

(Pause)

It's better.
Better than going back to before.

(MARGUARITE walks to the house)

(Pause)

MADELAINE: Fuck!

(She goes into the house. AGNES is left alone)

AGNES: My feet hurt.
Like there's a hot coal between each toe.
I've got a saint's name. Agnes.
She died burning on a giant wheel.
She lit up a whole port doing that.

(The MAN enters. They see each other.)

Lights down.
End of first half.

SECOND HALF.

Lights up on the BISHOP who has been promoted to POPE.
He sits on his chair. His MAN stands at a respectful distance.

POPE: There's been a lot of us popes.
That's historical.
A lot of us.
We all look the same.
Serious, similar. With hats.

(Pause)

Sometimes I forget which one I am.
I always know I am one though
I've got the costume
And on occasion I'm addressed formally.

MAN: Your Popeship?

POPE: Look.

MAN: What?

POPE: On the floor.

MAN: There's nothing. I swept that floor.

POPE: Now there's nothing. But before I found something.
A thing with legs.
It walked right past my chair.
Six silly legs all walking. Scuttling happy.
Then just when it thought there was nothing in its universe that could ever touch it again...I squashed it with my foot.
Now nothing will ever happen to it again.
Do you want to see it?

MAN: No thank you.

POPE: Go on.

MAN: Alright.

(The POPE takes it out of his hat and holds it out on the palm of his hand.)

MAN: There's nothing there.

POPE: Ha ha.

MAN: Honestly.

POPE: Playing dead! It's escaped. Never mind. You'll find it.

MAN: You're different since you got your promotion.

POPE: Course I'm different. I'm a pope.

(The MAN begins looking for the bug.)

That house. We never burnt it.

MAN: No.

POPE: No. We changed it.
Now there's just a few records lying about.

MAN: They'll turn to dust.

POPE: Crumble. Then you can sweep them away.

(Pause)

I remember the first one. I remember her. Do/her for me.

MAN: I can't.

POPE: Go on.

MAN: Ooh. Ooh. Hobble hobble.

(He hobbles about)

Ooh. Feet hurt.
I'm burning up.

Oh. Ah.

POPE: Haha. That's her. That's good!

(AGNES appears)

POPE: What do you want?

MAN: She followed me. I found her.

POPE: I see.

AGNES: I want a holy man to put his hand on my head.

POPE: You do?

MAN: I'll do that. If you like.

AGNES: Are you holy?

MAN: I live here, don't I?

AGNES: My feet could be flames. I've got something in the woods.

POPE: Have you?

(AGNES begins 'digging')

AGNES: I buried it.

POPE: A body?

AGNES: *(laughs)* Not a body! Something dead and out of torment.

(Continues digging)

Look. Nearly there.

(She pulls something out)

POPE: Ah.

AGNES: Smells.

MAN: What is it?

AGNES: I killed it. It's got worms now, all over its wings and head. All climbing over each other. Small and white. *(She hugs it to her. She begins to eat the bird)* Come on

bird. *(She eats)*
There's something in me.
Burning me.
Put your hand on me.
Save me.
Drive it out of me.

POPE: Come here.

(AGNES comes)

I will drive it out of you.
I can do that.
I will do it.

AGNES: Thank you.

POPE: Come here.

AGNES: To you?

POPE: To me. *(AGNES goes to him. The POPE stands with AGNES in front of him)* Townspeople.
Here's a poor daughter for you.
A poor daughter.
Full of something.

AGNES: It's in me.

POPE: She's been opened up like a door. An ill wind's blown in.

AGNES: Inside me.

POPE: A wind full of imps, devils and small evil things.

AGNES: Burning me.

POPE: Put there by a foul ungodly house.

AGNES: Taking me.

POPE: This poor daughter.

AGNES: I'm burning up.
There's something in me.
Taking me.
And shaking me,
Shaking me.

BISHOP: A house where God won't

go.

AGNES: Won't go.

BISHOP: And it's here, near. Near here!

AGNES: Banging. banging. Drive it out of me. Out.

POPE: Her flesh tormented.

AGNES: I can smell the bird!

POPE: She could be your daughter. Do you want this to happen to your daughter?

AGNES: Drive it out!

(Lights change. AGNES exits)

POPE: She turned out alright. In the end.

MAN: She did.

POPE: Look! There it is. I've found it.

MAN: What?

POPE: Six legs!

MAN: Where?

POPE: There. Tread on it.

MAN: Me?

POPE: Squash it. Quickly. *(Pause)* Go on. *(MAN hesitates. Treads on it)* Good! Hiding and playing dead! The dead never come back do they?

MAN: Never.

POPE: They're mostly forgotten.

MAN: Mostly.

POPE: That's good.

Lights down.

Lights up. Back to the house.
JOAN runs on. Stops.

JOAN: There's no-one.
  No-one. Just me and my bucket.
  I could do anything now.
  If I could think of anything...

(Pause)

Close my eyes...
  I can hear noises...I can.
  See someone's hair in a plait, see
  their knee,
  Their mouth.
  They go to speak. They speak air,
  they go, their plait goes. No-one.
  Come back. I want to smell
  someone, their neck or hair please.

(Pause)

There's not even echo.
  Nothing. Big bored space. Frozen
  yawn space.
  Ghost space.

(Pause. She hears something)

Marguarite?

*(AGNES enters. She wears a veil
similar to a nun's veil.)*

AGNES: Joan.

JOAN: Didn't see you...

AGNES: It's cold. You're standing
  with bare feet and the ground is
  damp. Wet.

(Pause)

You should be inside. It's morning.

JOAN: Agnes...?

AGNES: Yes?

JOAN: Do you ever think things?

AGNES: Yes

JOAN: I mean...about before?

AGNES: There's plenty of work to
  be done. Useful work. Scrubbing,
  sweeping, bread-making, pot
  scouring...

JOAN: Sometimes I think of it. I
  can't help it. We're in the same
  place with all the past sucked out
  of it. Till it's an empty din.

AGNES: It's different now. We're
  bathed in god's love.

JOAN: Like a holy bath. *(Pause)* Do
  you ever think of her?

AGNES: No.

JOAN: Sometimes I think she lives
  in the woods and watches us!

AGNES: That's the devil putting
  thoughts into your head.

JOAN: Watches us.

AGNES: You should be inside.

JOAN: I was just...cleaning my
  bucket.

*(JOAN begins wiping it with her
skirt. Spitting on it. Wiping it)*

JOAN: Look, there's a stone...

AGNES: Throw it away.

(She does so)

It's different now.
  She's not in the woods.
  Not anywhere.

(Exit AGNES)

JOAN: That man.
  He never liked me.
  That's because I hit him with my
  bucket.

(Pause)

I hit him quite hard.
For a first go.
(Pause)

They all came. From town.
Lots of people. All shouting.
All talking about their daughter.
There was too many heads and not
enough bucket.
They took us.
On the way to the town one of
them pulled my hair till it came out
in a bunch.

(Pause)

I knew they'd ask me things.
I felt their asking things like pokes.
Pokes all over. Poke poke.
I thought I'll stand there.
Heart wobbling
Eyes bobbling
Head wagging
Knees sagging
Boobs swingling
Armpits tingling.
Then I'll say something and it'll be
the wrong thing to say and I'll fall
over on the spot and just wished
I'd stayed looking at the hole.

(Pause)

Back here things are the same but
different.
Like a tree with no leaves.

(Pause)

Sometimes I think she's in the
forest.
Watching.
I know that's a bad thing to think.
A bad thing like being friends with
a ghost.
But I can't help myself.

(Pause)

I can't hardly look at a fire now.
Even if I am cold.

*(She cleans her bucket vigorously.
Lights dim. Then lights up on*
MARGUARITE. *She stands ghost
like. The lights flicker red. We hear
the sound of flames.)*

JOAN: Marguarite?

Lights fade to blackout.

We hear the noise of a farmyard.
MADELAINE *stands. Shouting.*

MADELAINE: Get off that fucking
fence! Do you think I put it up so
you could climb all over it? Do
you want the pissin' pig to make a
break for freedom? Moron. *(Pause)*
You do? Come hear and say that.
Don't let your sister eat mud
either. She'll get worms and then
she'll be eating your dinner and all
and then you'll be sorry. I swear
that by god's cock.

*(AGNES and JOAN have entered.
She notices them.)*

AGNES: Good morning.

JOAN: Good morning.

MADELAINE: What do you want?

AGNES: We're on a visit...

JOAN: To the needy of this parish.

AGNES: Joan.

MADELAINE: And?

JOAN: We brought you something.

MADELAINE: What?

(JOAN pulls out a large rafia mat.)

JOAN: I made it.

AGNES: Joan's been very busy.

MADELAINE: What is it?

JOAN: A large rafia mat.

MADELAINE: Oh.

AGNES: For the floor.

MADELAINE: We haven't got a floor. Mud, but no floor.

AGNES: May I see the baby?

MADELAINE: Round the side.

(AGNES goes)

JOAN: Well...

MADELAINE: Well.

(Pause)

JOAN: Is God looking after you?

MADELAINE: He's too busy visiting the land with scarcity.

JOAN: *(whispers)* He might hear you.

MADELAINE: He never usually does why should he start now?

(Pause)

JOAN: You've got a nice pig.

MADELAINE: That's all I've got.

(Pause)

JOAN: Madelaine?

MADELAINE: Don't start. Don't you start.
I've got enough on my plate.
I get up at dawn.
I don't stop.
The babies don't stop.
They're like bags of crying.
I haven't got time to think.
Haven't got time to make stupid mats.

(Pause)

JOAN: I knew you wouldn't like it. It was my favourite.

(Pause)

MADELAINE: I do like it.

JOAN: Do you?

MADELAINE: I'm trying not to get too attached to it. It'll probably end up in the pig like everything else round here.

JOAN: Do you ever think about before?

MADELAINE: Sometimes. Forget it.

JOAN: I can't. It comes back.

MADELAINE: I know.

(Lights change. Flashback. The yard sounds disappear. MADELAINE and JOAN stand alone. The BISHOP sits in his chair although he is not yet lit.)

JOAN: No.

MADELAINE: Yes.

JOAN: No

MADELAINE: Yes.

JOAN: It's wrong.

MADELAINE: Piss off.

JOAN: Isn't it wrong?

MADELAINE: Do it.

JOAN: I can't

MADELAINE: You can.

JOAN: I don't know.

MADELAINE: You do. Do it.

(The BISHOP in his chair, with the MAN at his side, becomes illuminated, enter the scene)

MAN: Madelaine de Planisolles and Joan.

BISHOP: Joan?

JOAN: I've just got the one... the... Joan.

BISHOP: You lived in the house?

TOGETHER: Yes.

BISHOP: You lived according to the doctrine of the free spirit?

TOGETHER: Yes.

BISHOP: You did no useful work and lived a life parasitical upon the godfearing community around you?

TOGETHER: Yes.

BISHOP: You are sometimes called 'turlupins' due to the obscene and unnatural acts you perform singly and together?

(Pause)

TOGETHER: Yes.

BISHOP: You lived in the belief that your will and the will of God is one and inseparable?

TOGETHER: Yes.

BISHOP: That ownership of private property is an act of wilful dismissal of the true nature of God and being in God?

TOGETHER: Yes.

BISHOP: That sin is a fallacy, your actions being of a divine nature?

TOGETHER: Yes.

BISHOP: You do now renounce the doctrine of the free spirit and all its practices and do embrace God and the true faith? You understand and accept the true sinful nature of your selves, of the flesh and accept the fathership of God, his guidance and his house on earth, the holy church?

(They speak simultaneously)

MADELAINE: Yes.

JOAN: No.

(Pause)

MADELAINE: Yes.

JOAN: No.

MADELAINE: She means yes.

JOAN: I don't know.

BISHOP: Do you renounce the doctrine of the free spirit and all its practices?

MADELAINE: Yes. We do.

JOAN: Lying's a sin.

MADELAINE: She believes in sin. She's saying yes. Say yes.

JOAN: Yes.

(Lights change. AGNES re-enters. We hear the yard noises)

AGNES: It bit me. That baby.

MADELAINE: I should have told you it bites. Only I didn't want to encourage you.

AGNES: We better go.

JOAN: We have several more mats to distribute. Goodbye.

MADELAINE: Goodbye. Joan?

JOAN: What?

MADELAINE: I'll see you.

(Pause)

JOAN: Goodbye.

(Lights change. MADELAINE alone. Lights dim.)

MADELAINE: Marguarite?

(Lights come up to reveal MARGUARITE. She stands/sits impassively, looking out. Lighting suggests a cell.)

MADELAINE: There's just you left. We're going. Speak to them Marguarite. Say yes.

MARGUARITE: What can they do?

MADELAINE: You could go away. Start a new house.

MARGUARITE: Would you come?

MADELAINE: You've been alone before.

MARGUARITE: I could start again.

MADELAINE: You could. If anyone could.

MARGUARITE: Would you come?

MADELAINE: I'm too old.

MARGUARITE: How old?

MADELAINE: Dunno. I feel old.

MARGUARITE: Who asked you to come here?

MADELAINE: No-one. I asked. *(Pause)* Say yes.

MARGUARITE: I could.

MADELAINE: Yes.

MARGUARITE: But I don't feel like it.

MADELAINE: Don't you see

anything?

MARGUARITE: What?

MADELAINE: You can't choose anymore.

MARGUARITE: Can't I?

MADELAINE: No.

MARGUARITE: What can they do?

MADELAINE: Put you in a fire.

MARGUARITE: They won't.

MADELAINE: Won't they?

MARGUARITE: No, they won't. Why should they?

MADELAINE: This is real. This isn't ideas in your head. This is this. Here, now. That's the real. No miracles here. You have to face that. What are we? Mouths that have to be fed. That's what.
We're born, we grow, we shrivel, we die.
You have to take what you can.
For us that's fuck all.
You'd throw it away with both hands
Forget being God.
Take what you can.
Forget ideas, ideas.
The house was nice, now it's over and the real bit begins.

MARGUARITE: The real bit?

MADELAINE: Speak to them.
(Pause) What else?
The house is different now.
It's darker with doors.
I'm not going back. *(Pause)*
I told them I was going to marry a good man of this parish. That or sell ribbons. I'll probably sell ribbons. *(Pause)* You always used to talk. Bloody talk talk. It's easy to say yes. Think of them as someone you fucked once, then

84

discarded. They're nothing. It's bloody easy to say yes. I hate you for not saying it. *(Pause)* You want to make me feel I've done wrong. Like you wanted me to feel the house was more yours by rights because you were more god than I was. Well, God turned out to be nothing. *(Pause)* Speak to them. *(Pause)* To me. *(Pause)* Marguarite?

MADELAINE is left alone.

Lights go to blackout

BISHOP, MAN, MARGUARITE.
They all sit still. A strange light.

MAN: *(to MARGUARITE)* We can wait all day. All year. *(to BISHOP)* Can't we? She's the last. She's not saying anything.

MARGUARITE: What do you want me to say? *(Pause)* Just tell me. I'll say it.

MAN: You could say anything.

MARGUARITE: I could. If you could tell me what.

MAN: We can't do that. That misses the point.

MARGUARITE: Why?

MAN: It just does.

BISHOP: What is the true nature of God?
See it my way.
Can't you?
You people say you're God,
So you ought to be able to see it my way.
It isn't easy being a bishop.
I had to study for years.
It can be very boring
But I did it.
Now, I'm a man of God.
I look after his will on earth,
The way things should be.
I'm appointed.

MARGUARITE: Who by?

BISHOP: By the Church.

MARGUARITE: Who appointed the Church?

BISHOP: God.

MARGUARITE: How do you know that?

BISHOP: I can speak to God.

MARGUARITE: How?

BISHOP: In my prayers.

MARGUARITE: How do you know it's God answering?

BISHOP: Who else would it be?

MARGUARITE: How do you know your god's the right one?

BISHOP: God is god.

MARGUARITE: You can't be sure. You're telling me to say I'm not god but you can't tell me a reason I'm not. You read a lot of books for nothing.

MAN: He can tell you.

MARGUARITE: Can he?

MAN: Yes. He can. Can't you?

BISHOP: Yes.

MARGUARITE: Go on then.

(Pause)

BISHOP: Poor sinner.
God looks down on us.
God likes a pattern
He likes order.
He doesn't like to think of himself

scattered in tiny mouthfuls inside every Tom, Dick and Harry. Each bit doing what they wanted.
Each bit speaking from their own mouth.
Each clamouring for their own way
Each thinking they had the right to expect the world to turn for them.
That would be chaos.
One god wanting bread
The other sausage
Others wanting other things
Others others.
A world of mini gods.
Hellish.

MARGUARITE: What if god was in all of us? Every part of us? We wouldn't be turning against each other scrabbling for a bit of this or a bit of that. Bread, sausage or whatever, because somewhere in us we'd all know we were god. All know that somewhere we wanted the same things. That that feeling you had when you had a laugh was the same feeling we all had. We'd know that. We'd know we needed nothing except ourselves. A world of gods. Heaven.

(Pause)

BISHOP: I've been patient. I've explained. I'm not unreasonable. It's simple enough. One God in one place. The rest of us - we're like shit on God's boot. We have to know that. Then when we're dead it'll be alright. Some of us like me, are closer to God because we pray and read a lot of books. We help people like you. Who don't pray and read a lot of books.
You're lucky.
You've been found in time.
You've been given a choice.
Do you embrace God's house?

MARGUARITE: *(to herself)* Just say yes.

(Lights up on the group.)

MARGUARITE: You want me to say yes.

MAN: Yes.
(Pause)

MARGUARITE: Yes.

(Pause)

MAN: Yes?

MARGUARITE: Yes.

(Pause)

MAN: That's it then.

BISHOP: Is it over?

MARGUARITE: Yes.

(Pause)

BISHOP: Let's have a drink. To celebrate.

(MAN gets some wine)

MAN: Shall I give her some?

BISHOP: Give her some.

(They pass it round. They all drink. MARGUARITE drinks deeply. It runs down the side of her mouth. The BISHOP and MAN sit in their usual pose)

BISHOP: We've some things to discuss.

MARGUARITE: My house.

BISHOP: The house.

MARGUARITE: It's not much. When you look at it.

MAN: No. It's not.

(MARGUARITE begins to laugh. They watch her. She laughs more. They look sterner)

MAN: What's so funny?

MARGUARITE: When I was a girl I lived in a dream. I'd wander down to a stream and stare at the water. Imagining things.
Imagine it took me somewhere
Twisting in its silver water.
A new land.
The day would go.
I'd get back. I'd get a cuff.
Stupid! You could have fell in and died.
I'd think 'But the stream is so magic'
More real than them.
More real...

(Pause)

We are born. We are. Our flesh is beautiful. More beautiful than cake or the stars. Just like we breathe air and it is everywhere.
That's how we are to god.
You can't put air in boxes and call it this air and that.
It's all air.
That's how we are to god.
All one.
Divine and intoxicating,
Or just plain divine.

(Pause)

MAN: That's like saying no.

MARGUARITE: I don't want to die. I don't want to live in your house.

BISHOP: Do you deny the true nature of God?

MARGUARITE: I don't need God anymore. I am God.

(Lights change)

MAN: She was mad. It was like she lit that fire herself.

BISHOP: Who lit the flames?

MADELAINE: Marguarite?

MAN: A soldier lit them.

MADELAINE: Speak to them.

MAN: There were a lot of people.

BISHOP: She was quite popular or else people hated her. It wasn't clear.

MADELAINE: Marguarite!

MAN: Fire eats the legs first.

(Lights focus on MARGUARITE)

MARGUARITE: On why I let myself be burnt.
That's a stupid beginning.
After all, I didn't pile up the sticks, logs, sticks.
Didn't arrange them so as to allow the optimum amount of air to be pocketed within its criss-crossing.
So as to help the flames be big and strong.
And hot.
I did not pass sentence on myself.
Didn't tie myself to the stake.
I didn't bring the flaming oil dipped rag tied to a stick to light the sticks, logs, sticks.
I burnt though.
All I felt when I saw the fire creep close was a terrible fear
Of pain,
Of dark nothing forever.
The thing is though
It was the going back
I'd been god for too long
Too long to say 'I am not god'
To be plain after being radiant
To be stupid after being inspired
To be single after being the world
There was no going back. No.
So I burnt.

Lights down. A cry. The sound of flames

The MAN walks in from one direction, MADELAINE from the other. They knock into each other.

MADELAINE'S basket falls to the floor. They look at each other. MADELAINE picks up her basket and leaves. The MAN watches her go.

MAN: People ask for things. They ask for them. And if they ask for them then that's their look out. They can't turn round and blame another person for giving them what they asked for in the first place. So I don't feel bad about it. No! It's funny. You can feel close to someone, so close that your skin touches but you can forget them. Forget everything.

(Pause)

Sometimes people ask me why I do my job. That's easy. It's a good job!

He exits

JOAN and AGNES in the woods. JOAN is laden down with mats, bucket etc.

JOAN: Agnes? Can we stop for a bit. My legs feel sleepy.

AGNES: We're on a tight schedule.

JOAN: *(looks about her)* Are we?

AGNES: Just for a minute.

(They sit down. JOAN on her upturned bucket)

JOAN: I don't mind it in the woods. Not anymore.

AGNES: It's a shortcut.

JOAN: There's blood on your hands.

AGNES: A thorn. Scratched me.

JOAN: Oh. *(Pause)* Do you think mats could be popular?

AGNES: Pride, Joan.

JOAN: I was thinking of trying some round ones.

AGNES: Round?

JOAN: It was just a thought. *(Pause)* Do you believe in spirits?

AGNES: No.

JOAN: Sometimes I think I see them. In the woods. In a tangle with the trees. Their skirts in a tangle. One of them looks like her.

AGNES: Say a prayer.

JOAN: She laughs and calls out to me.

AGNES: A long one.

JOAN: When I gave that last mat away they said would I mind if they cut a hole in the middle and used it as a skirt I said no but how would you get in and out of doors with it - it would be like wearing a small haystack and...

AGNES: That's our minute.

(She gets ready to leave)

JOAN: Agnes...

AGNES: It's nearer two.

JOAN: Agnes... I've had a thought.

AGNES: A thought?

JOAN: Of...going.

AGNES: Going?

JOAN: Yes.

AGNES: Where?

JOAN: Don't know. A town. Somewhere new. Exciting.

I've had ideas. Like flashes.
Like they've been called into my
head.

AGNES: How far do you think you'll
get?

JOAN: Don't know. *(Pause)* I've got
some mats.
I made them in my spare time.
I thought I might make mats.
Live that way.
Have a room in a town.
These are going to start me off.
I'll live on what I make from them
and I'll make some more. I worked
it out.

AGNES: By rights they're not yours.

JOAN: What?

AGNES: Those mats.

JOAN: Not mine?

AGNES: Not while you were fed our
food. Working on our premises.
No.

JOAN: These were going to start me
off.

AGNES: By rights.

JOAN: Oh. *(She puts down the mats)*
Some of them have got different
patterns.
I made them up.
There's even one like feathers.
I'd never seen them before. Except
in my head.

(Pause)

I'm still going.
I'll remember the patterns or make
up new ones.

(She exits)

AGNES: Go on then.

(Pause)

No-one's here.

(Pause)

House of correction.
My house.
This morning there was frost on the
flags
Frozen prayer breath.
That house could be made of ice.
All sounds flint.
Even whispers turn to cuts.
Faces in it. Meet you sharp.
Carved from a cold wood.
Thin arms. Prayers.
All good words over and over.
Floating from the body.
That's a husk.

(Pause)

The world would have been perfect
No death or cancers
No babies dead
No age or stink
No bloody festering wounds
But for me.
Me.
I'll get better.
Let me show you.

*(She takes off her top. Her body is
painted with many small red
crosses)*

Lord. Why will the longing never
leave me?

(Whispers, like a prayer.)

I'm glad to be here.
Glad to be here
Glad to be here
Glad.
Glad.
Glad.

Lights down.

*POPE sits sleeping in his chair.
He gives a cry. Wakes. MAN runs on.*

MAN: What?

POPE: Dream. In my ear. Can you see anything?

MAN: It's dark.

POPE: Anything else?

MAN: Just dark.

POPE: There was a creature living in my ear.
A half breed angel. Half devil half angel.
It wore black silk and drank red wine.
It had black furry wings and tickling fingers.
It kept slithering up and down my ear passages,
playing slides.
It kept laughing. And slithering.
Take off your hat take off your hat it said
and it slithered all over again.
Sliding.
What does it mean?

MAN: I don't know.

POPE: Will it stay long?

MAN: I don't know.

POPE: Why doesn't it just die?

MAN: It sounds tricky.

POPE: Why doesn't it wear white silk like other angels?

MAN: It's perverse.

POPE: Why doesn't it just die?

MAN: Sometimes things don't.

POPE: I'd go to sleep now, except it will be slipping around my head.
It's not right.
It should be dead.
It shouldn't be able to talk and drink.
Things like that shouldn't happen.
It should be forgotten and dead like a little charred fish.
Why isn't it?

MAN: Sometimes it's hard to keep things dead.

Lights change.

JOAN enters.

JOAN: Crossroads. I could walk off in any direction now and no-one would try and stop me.
No-one..

(She looks about her sees, a stick. Picks it up)

It'll be night-time soon. There'll be a moon.

(She draws a moon)

Moon. So-on.

(She looks pleased with herself. She begins to draw in the earth)

This is the house.
I'm making it in the earth.
The pattern of it.
House. Squat. A fat door. Earth floor.
And a mat.

(Pause)

Think something. It's as good as real. That's what they said.

(The women come alive round JOAN and watch)

Here's a fire.

(She draws it)

It's bright.
We sit round it.
It lights our faces.
I can see us.
I can't stop seeing us.
Even if I close my eyes.

It's as if we shone.
As if we shone.
As if we shone.
As if we shone.

Lights down.

CUT IT OUT

Jan Ruppe

I first came across self-laceration in December 1988 in a rather sensationalised article in a women's magazine. I was shocked. Not just because of the topic, but because I had been within an inch of harming myself six months previously and had thought I was going mad. I was unaware that others cut themselves and that the problem was so widespread. I had already begun to write my first play but until I read that article I didn't know the subject matter.

I started writing, firstly, because, as an actress, I wanted there to be parts for women that were challenging. There are nearly twice as many actresses as actors and a great deal less work. When the work comes it is often unsatisfying. Having spent years learning how to play a variety of roles it is soul destroying to find yourself up against thousands of other people for parts which do not move, interest or excite you. There are some good parts for women but not enough. Secondly, I had always chosen to write at moments of tension. Poems, stories, letters. Just as my desire to do something about improving parts for women reached its peak I had a miscarriage and suffered severe depression for the first time. I had never had any patience for other people's depression and when it happened to me I did not acknowledge it. I pretended it wasn't happening. I tried to 'snap out of it' and I nearly cut myself. I didn't know what was wrong with me but I knew it was my fault and that it was never appropriate to cry. Fortunately I chose to start writing a play instead of harming myself to get whatever it was out of my system.

I had the character of Laura before I learnt about cutting. She was someone who did not allow herself to get angry or cry. To express need was a weakness to her. Exactly as it had been for me. Once I read the article I found case history after case history of men and women who cut themselves described in those terms.

I have noticed both before and since researching the lives of self-harmers that many of us, if not all of us, have the seeds of self-doubt and self-hate which can lead to such extraordinary action. One person commenting on the second draft of this play said I ought to show something about Laura which tells the audience why she is 'not like the rest of us'. What it is about her which makes her cut herself where we would cry or scream. The problem is there is nothing. She is like the rest of us. All of us have known moments when it was inappropriate to vent our feelings. We have all 'bitten our lips' on occasion. We are all capable of choosing a dangerous form of release in private for fear of the repercussions of expressing ourselves in public. Many of us do. Drink, drugs, food disorders, banging walls. I think there is a fine line between the acceptable and non-acceptable means of self-abuse.

All the characters in this play display some self-doubt or self-hatred, yet they are all normal and identifiable people. I fear the eighties did much to make things worse for everyone's self-respect. Not just because of the much repeated observation that physical image was so important and so thrust on us by the media during that period, setting role models for many, especially young women, which we could never live up to, but something far crueller took place and continues. An 'emotional image' was set up for us. The image of the tough no-nonsense woman. The power-dressing, incredibly intelligent, incredibly tough (and of course still incredibly beautiful) superwoman was the ideal woman to be. Women who cried were soft. Sure to go to the wall. Many women aspired to this ideal and still do. Running a home and family and never letting it get you down was a picture of women coming across at me again and again from the women's magazines I spent the decade addicted to. It was in the adverts on television. It was everywhere. And it has contributed to the feelings of inadequacy of many thousands of women. Men too have been and continue to be victims of 'new images'. Ironically, the image of the caring considerate 'Renaissance man' has grown at the same time as that of the tough, dependable woman. The character of Jason is just such a victim. He is apparently confident but promotes an image of himself as a 'new man' which in reality he cannot live up to. I believe that until and unless we recognise and respect each other as individuals and stop labelling each other and creating unrealistic models for ourselves, self-laceration will continue and grow along with all the other forms of abuse which proliferate in our society.

'Second String' are to produce *'Cut it Out'* at the Duke's Head in Richmond from July 1st 1991.

CHARACTERS:

Laura
Ruth
Mark
Jason
Female Doctor

ACT ONE

SCENE ONE:

The living room of a one bedroom flat in London. Stage right is an exit to the bedroom. Stage left an exit to the kitchen and bathroom. Upstage centre, the entrance to the flat. There is a sofa centre stage and occasional furniture in the matt black/chrome look, including a dining table upstage. Athena type pictures on the wall. LAURA is looking in the mirror which is on the 'fourth' wall. She studies her reflection for a few moments before pulling faces which get increasingly grotesque. Lights come up on the rest of the room as RUTH enters carrying shopping bags which she dumps on the floor and returns to shut the door. LAURA jumps and moves away from the mirror.

RUTH: Oh God! It's murder out there. What's the time? Oh Jesus!

LAURA: I've just got in myself.

RUTH: Look at this *(she pulls a bright orange outfit from one of the bags)* What do you think?

LAURA: It's um.... orange.

RUTH: It's my colour. Mind you it didn't look as bright as this in the mag. Where is it? *(she looks around and then picks up a copy of 'Options')* I can't wait to try it on. *(exits into bedroom)*.

LAURA: What time are you going out?

RUTH: *(off)* I'm not. They're coming here.

LAURA: They? Coming here? Who?

RUTH: *(off)* Two men.

LAURA: It's bad enough trying to sleep in here when you're having sex with one man but two?

RUTH: *(off)* They're brothers.

LAURA: *(Pause)* Oh, well, that's alright then.

RUTH: *(entering)* One of them's for you.

LAURA: I don't want one. I wish you wouldn't do this Ruth.

RUTH: *(looks in the mirror)* Oh why does it never look like it does in the mags? *(Pause)* I'd give my right arm to have longer legs.

LAURA: I'm not up to another blind date. Not tonight.

RUTH: *(sits on sofa and gets make-up bag out)* He's gorgeous. You'll like him.

LAURA: That's what you said about the last one.

RUTH: You did like him didn't you?

LAURA: No.

RUTH: You slept with him.

LAURA: So.

RUTH: Laura!

LAURA: Don't tell me you've never slept with someone you didn't like.

RUTH: No. I may hate them afterwards but I love them at the time.

LAURA: *(Pause)* He was heavily into tying up.

RUTH: *(drops make-up)* Was he? Lucky cow. I've been walking around with rope in my bag for ages waiting for a man who's still got the guts to ask that.

LAURA: Not tying me up, tying himself up.

RUTH: Oh.

LAURA: *(lying on the sofa)* Tell him I'm ill.

RUTH: *(packing up make-up)* When you moved in here you said you wanted to get out more. Meet people. Maybe even find a boyfriend.

LAURA: I never said....

RUTH: I try to arrange that and look at the thanks I get. You've got through just about all the men I think of introducing you to. Not one's been good enough.

LAURA: They all fell into two categories. The one night stand or 'You're just like one of the lads Laura.' I don't know which is more humiliating.

RUTH: You don't give them a chance. You frighten them off. You're too hard.

LAURA: *(Pause)* Has it ever occurred to you that there are other things in life apart from men?

RUTH: Of course not.

(RUTH exits into kitchen)

LAURA: I saw the perfect man today. He was dark and handsome. Not too tall. A manageable sort of size. Slightly Italian looking or maybe Irish. You know the type. He had a smile in his eyes which said sincerity and sensitivity. And you could see he was strong. What a wonderful combination.

RUTH: Probably thick as too short ones. Or a charmer.

LAURA: Great! I can't even dream now. I bet he was the caring type. Someone with respect for women. A man who could converse with you intelligently for hours on feminist issues.

RUTH: Do you know what my perfect man is like? He's the kind of man who could converse with you intelligently for hours on feminist issues.... and then take you home and fuck your brains out! *(Pause)* I know what you're afraid of. Another Richard. They're not all like that, you know.

LAURA: I wish they were. He loved me how I was.

RUTH: He used to beat you up for Christ sake. *(Pause. She begins to lay the table)* It's not a big deal anyway. I just thought it would be nice to have them around for a quiet meal.

LAURA: *(looking at the outfit)* Quiet?

RUTH: Peter's mine, by the way. Yours is Jason. Peter's taller. Do you know I think I've finally found a man who will let me do what I like with anyone else? I know you and Jason will be perfect for one another. He's recovering from the break up of a long standing relationship so he's lonely too. And he's got money. Big in advertising. Oh God it's nearly eight! You'd better get changed. And put some make-up on for once. Laura? Laura? *(LAURA is staring in the mirror)*

LAURA: Um?

RUTH: Stop it. I hate it when you do that.

LAURA: You haven't asked me how it went.

RUTH: *(Pause)* Oh, God, sorry.

96

(Pause) How did it go?

LAURA: Bad. I had all the right answers in my head I just couldn't get them out of my mouth. Before I went in I was a calm, intelligent woman who knew how to do the job I was being interviewed for standing on my head. Once I got in there I felt about five years old. I was shaking like a leaf. I kept saying to myself. Why did you wear these clothes? You look all wrong. And they know you're too young to be in charge of the marketing of a firm this size. How can you possibly? What on earth possessed you to apply? They're only seeing you at the end of the day as a joke. You're a joke.

RUTH: *(Pause)* You probably got the job. I'll put the dinner on.

(LAURA stares in the mirror.)

LAURA: What a waste of time. No. Not that. You are not going to do that.

RUTH: *(re-enters)* What?

LAURA: What are you going to give them to eat?

RUTH: Macaroni Cheese.

LAURA: Oh not again! There's still some four days old out there. Can't you cook anything else?

RUTH: No. *(Pause)* I'm very sorry, Laura, that I went to so much trouble for you. *(Goes into bedroom. Slams about)*

LAURA: Ruth! I'm sorry. I didn't mean to upset you. I'm just no good at this boy-girl thing. I always feel I'm in a game where everyone else knows the rules except me. I'll get changed. I'll make an effort. Just don't expect too much of me.

RUTH: *(re-enters)* Alright. What are you staring at?

LAURA: You've got my coat on.

RUTH: I'm only going to get some fags.

LAURA: You can have mine.

RUTH: O.k. Are they...*(puts her hands in Laura's coat pockets)* What's that? *(pulls out a packet of razor blades. She freezes)*

LAURA: *(taking them from her)* They're in the bedroom.

(RUTH remains still in the living room. LAURA goes into the bedroom and returns with cigarettes. Gives them to RUTH)

LAURA: *(Pause)* Do you want me to move out? I'd understand if you did. I know I'm not much fun.

RUTH: *(taking off coat)* I've told you before. You can stay as long as you like. Oh yes, I almost forgot. Your Mum called.

LAURA: Oh. Thanks.

RUTH: *(Pause)* Aren't you going to ring her?

LAURA: No. She'll only want what she wanted last week and the week before. For me to come home and just 'be there' while she tells my father she's leaving him again. I've been my mother's mother for far too long. It's about time she learned to stand on her own two feet. *(takes coat and exits into bedroom)* I'll get changed.

(A banging noise is heard below. LAURA re-enters)

RUTH: What on earth? He's at it again.

LAURA: What does he do down there?

RUTH: *(puts her ear to the floor. A quieter couple of bangs are heard)* I think he's having kinky sex with someone. *(another loud bang)* Perhaps not.

LAURA: You don't think he's experimenting on his animals, do you? *(another bang)*.

RUTH: How? By dropping heavy objects on them to test their backbones? He's a vet not a scientist. Maybe he's having kinky sex with one of his animals? Mark! Leave the poor thing alone! *(the banging stops)*.

LAURA: He had another woman down there last night. Did you hear him?

RUTH: No, but I heard her. Oh where is Peter? He should have been here ages ago. *(Exits into kitchen. Pause)*

LAURA: Oh no! I've just remembered who Peter is. He's the one who always says. 'Is anything happening?' every time I answer the phone. I think he thinks that because he's out of work too at the moment that we're all in the same boat. I've never even met the guy and he's obsessed with my job prospects. It's like he's checking to make sure I don't get out of the boat before him. I say I'm still not working. Then that's the end of the conversation. What time's he due?

RUTH: Seven-thirty. Eight at the latest. We'll go in the other room until his brother comes - Jason's coming later. Well, he said he might not be able to make it but I told him about you and then he seemed keen.

LAURA: What? What did you tell him?

RUTH: Just that you were nice.

LAURA: Yuk. Certain personal details about my past didn't happen to worm their way into the conversation I suppose?

RUTH: He was interested in you.

LAURA: Ruth. I wish you would please not talk about me. It makes me feel... dirty somehow. And you expect me to dress up for someone who may not even be coming? *(Pause)* If Peter says 'Is anything happening?' I will chuck that Macaroni Cheese that's suffering in the kitchen in his face.

RUTH: You wouldn't dare.

LAURA: *(Pause)* No I suppose not.

(The doorbell goes)

RUTH: Oh God he's here! *(she rushes past LAURA into the bedroom)*

LAURA: Well, I suppose I'm getting the door then. *(she goes to the door and sees MARK)* Oh Mark? Hi.

MARK: Hi. What is it?

LAURA: What's what?

MARK: What do you want?

LAURA: What do I want? What do you want?

MARK: I want you to tell me what you want.

LAURA: What are you? My fairy Godmother? *(Pause)* Look, hang on. I'm in the flat, you rang the bell, so you're the one who's supposed to tell me what you want. Aren't you?

MARK: I came up because you called me.

LAURA: I didn't.

MARK: Well someone did. Shouted through the ceiling.

LAURA: Oh. That was Ruth.

MARK: Well?

LAURA: Well what?

MARK: What does she want? Look maybe I should go out and come back in again.

LAURA: No. No. She was just shouting because we heard you.... you were banging downstairs. I mean you were making a noise and Ruth was rather disturbed so she was shouting for you to stop. And you did. So that's alright then, isn't it?

MARK: Right. Sorry about that. *(goes to the door)* I don't suppose you've changed your mind about the job?

LAURA: No. Thanks Mark but I don't think being a receptionist is my sort of thing. I'm no good with people. *(MARK is about to leave)* Um. Mark?.. What um... What were you doing downstairs?

MARK: I was punching the wall.

LAURA: Oh right. Fine.

MARK: *(going)* See you.

LAURA: Yeah bye.

(He exits. She contemplates punching the wall and then does so. It makes a dull thud and hurts her hand. The bell goes again. LAURA goes back to open the door)

Why?

JASON: *(from behind a large bunch of flowers)* Why not?

LAURA: Oh. Ruth! Bunch of flowers to see you.

(She sits. He is still in the doorway)

JASON: Well. You don't stand on ceremony here, do you? Do you mind if I come in?

LAURA: *(not looking up)* No. Please.

JASON: *(Walks into room. Glances at mirror.)* You must be Laura. Is that right?

LAURA: Yes, that's right. *(She looks up. He strongly resembles her 'perfect man')*

JASON: Nice to meet you Laura. *(Pause. He sits on the sofa and rests the flowers beside him)* I'd better intro..

LAURA: Can I get you something? *(together)*

JASON: No thanks. *(Pause)* When I last spoke to Ruth, she said you were unemployed.

LAURA: That's right. We're all in the same boat.

JASON: Oh yeah....in a sense, I suppose. We're all God's children after all.

LAURA: What? I mean we're both unemployed.

JASON: Oh no. I've got a job.

LAURA: You got out before me then. Well done.

JASON: You're obviously very bitter about it Laura. I can understand

99

that. *(Pause)* Is anything happening on the work front with you?

(LAURA stares at him for a moment then walks into the kitchen, returning with the four day old macaroni cheese. RUTH enters from the bedroom.)

RUTH: Oh No!

LAURA: I can't do this.

JASON: What?

LAURA: I can do this. *(She squashes it in his face. Laughs)*

RUTH: Laura. That's not Peter.

LAURA: It isn't, oh God! I'm so sorry. I thought...Ruth said...If you'd heard the conversation we were having... I'm sorry. I'll get something to clean you up. *(She exits to kitchen)*

RUTH: I tried to stop her. *(gives him tissues)* Is Peter on his way?

JASON: No. He's got a job interview in the morning. He thought me coming to take you both out would be better than a phone call.

RUTH: Oh. *(Pause)* I said she was fun didn't I?

JASON: You said she was shy!

(LAURA enters)

RUTH: I didn't think you'd do it.

LAURA: I know. That's sort of why I did it. *(wiping his face)* God I'm sorry. Are you alright?

(JASON takes the towel from her and does it himself)

JASON: You thought I was Peter. I've heard he has this effect on women. I should have introduced myself. I'm Jason. Peter's brother. *(He shakes her hand.)* Would you like to go for a drink?

RUTH: Peter's not coming. *(exits with flowers)*

LAURA: That's very nice of you. Especially after...Oh God I feel so awful about that. *(she takes her hand away. There is macaroni on it. She wipes both their hands. They laugh.)*

JASON: It's alright. It's funny. I've never had such a welcome. You've got....character.

LAURA: Thanks. I think. You make me sound like a quaint old building.

JASON: Can I use your bathroom?

RUTH: *(entering)* Straight through, left hand door.

(JASON exits)

RUTH: Go for it.

LAURA: I wish I'd had time to change. *(looks in the mirror)* I look dreadful.

RUTH: Don't worry. He fancies you. I can tell.

LAURA: What? Oh God, that's what I'm worried about.

(JASON returns but RUTH takes him straight back out again. LAURA tidies herself in the mirror. RUTH practically hurls JASON back into the room.)

RUTH: *(loud whisper)* Go for it! *(exit)*

JASON: She's not very subtle is she?

LAURA: She keeps trying to pair me off with people. Take no notice.

JASON: It's nice of her. I'm grateful to her anyway. (LAURA brushes a piece of macaroni cheese from his shoulder) Ruth told me you were pretty.

LAURA: She didn't.

JASON: She did. She's been going on about you so much I had to see you.

LAURA: You didn't.

JASON: I did. I got the feeling we'd known each other for years when I walked in.

LAURA: You didn't.

JASON: I did!

(They both laugh. RUTH enters.)

RUTH: I'm going round to Tony's place. You can tell Peter I'll call him sometime OK? (goes to door) Have fun!

LAURA: Can I get changed? Do you mind? Only I've just got in.

JASON: Of course I don't mind. We don't have to go out, you know. In fact, why don't I get us something to drink while you change? What were you making for dinner?

LAURA: Macaroni cheese.

JASON: I've suddenly lost my appetite.

LAURA: So have I.

Lights down

SCENE TWO:

Two hours later. JASON is pouring drinks. Wine for LAURA, orange juice for himself. He empties the wine into LAURA'S glass. Soft music is playing in the background.

JASON: I've poured you another.

LAURA: (off) Thanks. I won't be a minute.

JASON: You said that a minute ago. (Pause) How long has it been since you worked?

LAURA: (off) About a year.

JASON: That's a long time. (Pause) Have you had many interviews since?

LAURA: (off) A few. I felt like I was just going through the motions, though. If I'd been offered any of the jobs I would have turned them down. I wasn't ready to go back.

JASON: And now?

LAURA: (off) Ah! Got it! (she enters with a poster). Here it is. I designed that myself. I thought for a while I might go in that direction. Stop marketing other people's products and services and concentrate on the creative side. What do you think?

JASON: What's it selling?

LAURA: Nothing. That's the logo of the company. It's just promoting their name. Recognition is the first rule of advertising. Oh. But you know that of course.

JASON: Sure. (Pause) You know, I may be able to get you a job in an art department. It'd only be secretarial to start with but you'd get opportunities later.

LAURA: That would be great! (Pause) What I said before about not working. I am ready to go back now. More than ready.

JASON: I've been throwing myself at

work lately. I'm in danger of making fifty grand this year if I'm not careful. It gets so meaningless after a while, though. I wonder what I'm doing that's of any value for all that money when there are people so much worse off than me. *(Pause)* What made you stop work?

LAURA: *(Pause)* Oh. Well. I was depressed and.... you know. It was silly. Nothing really.

JASON: A year off work? It can't have been that silly.

LAURA: Let's not talk about work any more. Cheers.

JASON: Cheers.

LAURA: Don't you ever drink?

JASON: No. I've got the constitution of a potential addict. If I started drinking I'd never stop. If I smoked I'd be an eighty-a-day man.

LAURA: What about sex? *(instant regret)* Sorry. *(They laugh)* Ruth said you'd split up with someone recently.

JASON: Did she? Yes. Three years seem to have gone as though they never happened. I've been walking around for weeks feeling nothing but guilt.

LAURA: It can't be all your fault.

JASON: It is. We never should have been together in the first place. *(Pause)* I'd been going out with a girl for about a year before that. Never an argument. One day she just waltzed past me with another man. As if I wasn't there. I went out with Claire on the rebound. No. It was revenge. Not that I didn't like her.

LAURA: But you didn't love her?

JASON: I don't know. I don't think so, no. *(Pause)* No, I didn't.

LAURA: I don't think you should be so hard on yourself. We all make mistakes.

JASON: Yes but I made one and spent three years trying to justify it.

LAURA: At least you were brave enough to stop the rot.

JASON: I hadn't thought of it as brave.

LAURA: I know it's hard. I had to leave someone I cared very much for last year.

JASON: Ruth told me.

LAURA: *(Pause)* What did she tell you?

JASON: That you left someone. That he used to hit you. That you lost a baby.

LAURA: Paints a lovely picture doesn't she?

JASON: She said you moved in with her because you had nowhere else to turn.

LAURA: Did she say anything else?

JASON: Does it get worse that that?

LAURA: No. No. So you know why I've been off work. Good old Ruth.

JASON: She's concerned about you.

LAURA: Ruth sentimentalizes and sensationalizes everything. There are a hell of a lot of women who are worse off than me. *(Pause)* You think I'm hard now.

JASON: Hard?

LAURA: Cold. Hard-hearted.

JASON: I don't think you're as tough as you make yourself out to be. *(Pause)* I think it's admirable what you've come through.

LAURA: I'm lucky.

JASON: Hitting women is despicable.

LAURA: Hitting anyone is despicable. So you don't think there must be something about me that asks for it?

JASON: No! You can't have it both ways Laura. You can't not give yourself credit for things you've achieved but blame yourself when they go wrong. Give yourself a pat on the back every now and then. I mean you must have been bright to have been a marketing manager at twenty.

LAURA: That was just luck.

JASON: You see. You're doing it again. Don't be grateful. Be proud. I recognise myself in you. That's why it makes me so cross to see you so apologetic. *(Pause)* You nearly apologised then, didn't you?

LAURA: I can't imagine you being like me. You're so confident.

JASON: I'm not grateful anymore. You don't have to be nasty. Just respect your own opinion. Don't give in to other people.

LAURA: I don't give in. I just give. That's been my trouble. My trust has been abused in the past but maybe those that abused it are the losers. I coped.

JASON: It doesn't work like that Laura. If you give. People take. Because they can. It's irresistible.

LAURA: So you're saying I'm irresistible?

JASON: *(Pause)* I'm glad I came over tonight.

LAURA: So am I.

JASON: I haven't been able to talk to anyone like this for a long time.

LAURA: Me neither.

JASON: It's been fun.

LAURA: Fun? I've been staying with Ruth for six months and she thinks I'm the most miserable person out.

JASON: People need two things to discover a quality in themselves. The opportunity and the support. Dance with me. *(He gets up)* Here's your opportunity. *(She gets up. He puts his arm around her.)* And here's your support. *(They dance slowly)*.

Lights down

SCENE THREE:

Two weeks later.

MARK: Just for once say yes. Go on. Be really wacky and leave the flat, walk two hundred yards down the road and have a couple of drinks with me. I know it's dangerous. I know it's frightening but just for the hell of it, eh?

LAURA: I'm sorry.

MARK: Why not?

LAURA: Because in the first place we wouldn't be going out as mates would we? You think of me as a potential girlfriend and I just don't think of you that way.

MARK: Look, if you've got something to say don't beat about the bush. Just come right out and say it won't you?

LAURA: Sorry.

MARK: No problem. I'd hate to be thought of as someone's potential girlfriend. What about the second place?

LAURA: In the second place. I think.... I might.... have met someone.

MARK: You think you might? Who was he, the Invisible Man?

LAURA: He's Ruth's boyfriend's brother.

MARK: Very cosy.

LAURA: He's coming over tonight.

MARK: I see. *(Pause)* What's he like? This Ruth's boyfriend's cousin's....

LAURA: He's great.

MARK: Don't you mean sweet? Isn't that what women say about their boyfriends? 'He's so sweet.' Someone said that about me once. I was nearly sick.

LAURA: He's not sweet and he's not my boyfriend. I only met him a couple of weeks ago and we get on very well. He's just split up with someone and things are a bit difficult for him at the moment.

MARK: Doesn't sound very good so far.

LAURA: He's really very nice. He's very caring. Very intelligent. Fun to be with and a real gentleman. You don't mind me saying this do you?

MARK: No. I think I'm falling in love with him myself. Hey, what have you done to your hand?

LAURA: Oh. Slammed it in a drawer. Nothing serious. Oh yes, I've got a job. Jason got it for me.

MARK: Oh! He's got a name too!

LAURA: Stop making fun of me. He's got me a job in an advertising agency. Just asked a friend of his apparently and they said yes without even meeting me.

MARK: You could have had that job at my place. Mary, the receptionist I've got now is useless. She keeps getting the animals confused with their owners. Last week she sent out a letter to Mr and Mrs Spot. *(Pause)* Well at least you're not staying in to be miserable. I'm going to the pub. On my own.

LAURA: Why don't you ask one of your other women?

MARK: What other women?

LAURA: We've heard you.

MARK: Oh no.

LAURA: Oh yes.

MARK: Is that why you don't want to go out with me?

LAURA: No. I'm just saying you're not exactly stuck for company when you want it, are you?

MARK: I suppose not. Oh well. Have fun. I might just be able to get ten in before closing if I hurry.

LAURA: That's another thing about Jason. He doesn't drink.

MARK: *(Pause)* Drop him.

LAURA laughs. MARK exits. Lights down.

SCENE FOUR:

Later the same evening. JASON and LAURA are sitting on the floor playing Monopoly.

LAURA: Two hundred pounds.

JASON: What? Have you got all the stations?

LAURA: Yes.

JASON: You haven't got Fenchurch Street.

LAURA: I have. I landed on it last time you went to jail.

JASON: Oh yeah. There. Two hundred. You'll be laughing on the other side of your face when you land on Mayfair.

LAURA: We'll see. *(she throws the dice)* Buy it!

JASON: Where's all this money coming from? How come you've still got a five hundred left and I'm down to fives and ones?

LAURA: It's a tough game, the property business. Your go.

JASON: *(takes her hand as she passes the dice)* What have you done?

LAURA: Oh. Got carried away chopping vegetables.

JASON: I've been wanting to say something.

LAURA: Yes.

JASON: The last few weeks. Talking to you about Claire and everything. Well, I wanted to say thank you. That's all.

LAURA: *(Pause. LAURA smiles then pulls her hand away.)* Your go.

JASON: Now. Will I pay a fine or take a chance? *(takes a chance)* Go to jail. Move directly to jail....

LAURA: One two three...Oh. Here I am in Mayfair. Now. Who do I pay my rent to? What? Gone to jail?

Oh well, I'll stay here for a bit anyway *(She dances her piece over him)* La la la la la....

JASON: I take back everything I ever said about you being a dignified and lovely person.

LAURA: *(during the above)* La la la la la......

(They wrestle for the piece she has in her hand. End up lying on the floor. He kisses her.)

I was wondering when you were going to do that.

JASON: *(sitting up)* Maybe I shouldn't have.

LAURA: Why not?

JASON: *(Pause)* I've lost a lot of friends in the past. Female friends. Because I slept with them.

LAURA: I've lost a few male friends that way too. *(Pause)* Well. One or two.

JASON: I've had one night stands and affairs before but not any more. I value people more than I did then.

LAURA: Yes. You can have so much respect for someone and it attracts you to them and you sleep with them and the respect goes and the attraction goes.

JASON: Respect is more important.

LAURA: *(Pause)* Just one night between passion and indifference.

JASON: It's frightening.

LAURA: It frightens me.

JASON: Sex spoils everything.

LAURA: You don't want to sleep

with me, do you?

JASON: It's not that I don't want to. I just don't want you to end up thinking badly of me after all the fun we've had. I can't have a relationship with you, Laura. I'd end up leaning on you just like I did Claire. I don't want to make the same mistake again. You don't deserve that. *(He has been moving closer to her during the above and is now right next to her).*

LAURA: *(has been staring fixedly at one spot throughout his speech)* I love it. Sex. That's the trouble.

JASON: Oh God.

LAURA: What's the matter?

JASON: I've thought about nothing but you in weeks.

LAURA: I've thought about nothing but me in twenty five years.

JASON: *(Pause)* I'm going to Manchester on business on Thursday. I'm not sure how long for. Could we write to each other? You've got to care to write.

LAURA: O.k.

JASON: Have I wronged you?

LAURA: No. You've been a friend to me and I do want to preserve that but I can't let you go and not... Trust me. I will always think well of you no matter what. I will never lose respect for you. But I want you to stay tonight. *(she kisses him)*

JASON: You're special. You're very special. *(They kiss again then get up and go towards the bedroom. He stops her.)* I'll tell you something else.

LAURA: What?

JASON: Next time. I'm banker.

Lights down.

SCENE FIVE:

Six weeks later. RUTH is on the phone.

RUTH: How dare you! How dare you talk to me nicely! I saw you with her. *(Pause)* Who? How many are there? *(Pause)* Yes that one. *(Pause)* Oh, well that's different then. I mean if you've known her for years. Let me tell you something. I've known my sixty-two-year-old boss for years but I don't stick my hands down his blouse! *(Pause)* Yes I can talk! I may have seen other men but not under your nose and I didn't, have never, would never talk about you the way I heard you talking about me. I am not easy. I am very, very difficult! Friends? You don't know the meaning of the word. Take care? I hope you die horribly and soon! *(Pause)* And if your dick was as big as your mouth we might have had a better sex life! *(She slams the phone down)*

LAURA: *(entering)* Da da! This is the first time I've walked in here feeling like a human being. I have just received my first wage packet. Mind you it feels like I've been there six months instead of one. *(puts her bags down).* I've got drink. I've got fags. Any calls?

RUTH: No.

LAURA: Any letters?

RUTH: No.

LAURA: Alright, what's wrong?

RUTH: *(looking in mirror)* I've split up with Peter. *(screws her face up and cries)*

106

LAURA: For goodness sake... I mean... it's not as if you spent any time together really *(RUTH cries)*....Well....he slept with other women didn't he? *(more cries)* I'm sorry but he... he wasn't good enough. You need someone who really cares about you. Jason's made me realize that.

RUTH: Oh! Jason! Jason! Jason! That's all I hear from you these days. What makes him such an expert? They treat you like a goddess until they're bored with you. Then they find someone else to treat like a goddess. And they play the nice guy to the bitter end. Because they don't want to hurt you. That's what they say, but really it's their image they don't want to hurt. 'Take care' he says. He doesn't care about me. Give me a so-called bastard any day who tells you he's only interested in one thing before he sleeps with you. That's honest. Then you know where you are. You can make a choice. You're not left feeling like a fool.*(Pause)* Oh why did he have to do this to me now? Just when I'm going away. I was looking forward to 'Total Quality Management - The First Step' but not feeling like this.

LAURA: You didn't say you were going away.

RUTH: Only about five times. I asked you yesterday what I should wear. Don't you remember?

LAURA: No.

RUTH: There's no point talking to you these days. Your head's in the clouds. *(Pause)* I feel rotten.

LAURA: Have a drink. There's still some whisky in the kitchen. We're both celebrating. Me getting paid and you getting shot of someone who isn't fit to wipe your boots.

(exits into kitchen) But don't tell Jason I said that. *(laughs)*

RUTH: *(to herself)* Fucking Jason. *(LAURA returns)* I think you think too much of Jason.

LAURA: How can you think too much of a person? You can't love a person too much. The trouble with this world is there's not enough love in it.

RUTH: *(Pause)* Have you listened to yourself lately? These days your mouth opens and I hear Jason talking.

LAURA: I'm not going out with him you know. I did sleep with him. Once. But we decided we'd be better off as friends.

RUTH: You decided or he decided?

LAURA: We decided.

RUTH: And have you seen or heard from him since?

LAURA: You know I haven't. He knew he was going to be busy up in Manchester. Look don't sit there looking so sceptical. We are just friends. It's what I want too.

RUTH: Rubbish. You're in love with him.

LAURA: I am not. Why do you say this?

RUTH: It's obvious! Not a day has gone by since you met him when you haven't mentioned something he's said or done or wants to do. If he'd wanted a relationship with you, you would have said yes, wouldn't you?

LAURA: Yes, but..

RUTH: But he didn't, did he?

LAURA: No but if he had we would just have leant on each other.

RUTH: What else are relationships for?! Why is it such a crime for you to need someone? You need someone and just because it's not convenient for you to be in love with him doesn't mean you can make yourself not be. Admit it.

LAURA: *(Pause)* Alright. I admit.... I admit I haven't slept properly since he left. I've lost my appetite. And this job is a constant reminder of him. Do you know they had the nerve to ask me to make more of an effort to be sociable? They're the ones who are comfortable in their jobs. Know everybody but no-one speaks to me. I'm supposed to make an effort! I escape into dreams about him. I see us in years to come maybe running our own company and me taking time off to have babies. But I'll get over what I'm feeling now. It may be what you call being in love but it will pass. It gets in the way. By the time I see him again I'll be able to look at him and say 'that's my good friend Jase, who I love, but like he was a brother.' Besides, it may still happen. He won't be on the rebound forever. Come on you're not drinking.

RUTH: I've had enough. That's another thing they both do. Peter and your precious Jason. Every time things don't go quite their way they hit the bottle.

LAURA: Jason doesn't drink.

RUTH: If he told you that he's a liar.

LAURA: He is not.

RUTH: Alright then he's very creative with the truth. For Christ's sake Laura he drinks! They both do! Like fish! I've seen the state they both get into. You think the sun shines out of his arse. It doesn't. Forget him. He doesn't give a damn about himself or anyone else.

LAURA: He does! He cares about a lot of things. Himself. People. The Environment. He gives money to charity. Peter I don't know but you don't know Jase.

RUTH: He cares? He cares so much about himself you'd've found him downing a bottle of this stuff on his own if you'd gone over to Peter's two months ago. He cares so much about the Environment his company advertises enough products to destroy the world five times over. But that's business. That's what gives him the luxury to sit back and decide which charity to be seen to support this week. Everything they do is for show. I can see them getting pissed together in a few weeks and having a good laugh about you and me. Peter will say I told him he was brilliant in bed - which is far from the truth - and that he 'let me go' because he's an old-fashioned guy who couldn't take the pressure of being unemployed and unable to wine and dine women in the manner to which he's become accustomed. He's got thirty grand in the bank of course but that's his idea of poverty. Jason will say how sad it is that we can't all be rich and good looking and terribly caring as well and he'll use you as an example of the sort of unfortunate woman who's been attracted to him in the past because of his generosity and friendship to show how wonderful he is to his new girlfriend. *(She realises she has let the cat out of the bag but LAURA doesn't twig).*

LAURA: You're jealous! You're jealous because Peter's dumped you. Perhaps if you hadn't had so many other men. Perhaps if you didn't just want sex and nothing else, Peter would have had more respect and you wouldn't be saying the things you are now!

RUTH: And Jason cares so much about you he's been seeing another woman ever since he got to Manchester! *(Pause)* That's why he went there. He's known her for years. Peter let it slip just now. Huh! Using his brother's behaviour as an example to justify his own. *(Pause)* I'm sorry Laura. I wasn't going to say anything but you asked for it.

LAURA: You're lying.

RUTH: And you thought you weren't in love.

LAURA: What's her name?

RUTH: Hermione.

LAURA: Oh well. That makes me feel a bit better.

RUTH: I'm sorry Laura.

LAURA: I don't believe it. Jason would have told me. Maybe that's why he hasn't been in touch? He met her again after he got there and doesn't know how to tell me.

RUTH: You're not listening. That's why he...

LAURA: Poor Jason. He's afraid I'll think badly of him. *(She stares at the floor).*

RUTH: Laura? *(Pause)* Laura? I'm going out.

LAURA: Um? Tony's?

RUTH: No. There's no Tony. He was just an invention to make Peter think he had competition. The truth is I haven't seen anyone else since I met him. I wanted someone who wouldn't mind me seeing another man so I wouldn't want to anymore. And I found him. And now he doesn't want me. *(She laughs resignedly and goes to the bedroom. LAURA remains staring. RUTH re-enters wearing a coat.)* Laura? Laura just don't... hurt yourself will you?

LAURA: What do you mean?

RUTH: I... just don't want you to be hurt that's all.

LAURA: I'm alright. I don't care what you say. I don't believe it. You don't know him. *(LAURA takes the bottle and exits into the bedroom. RUTH goes straight to the sofa and fishes around until she finds a first-aid box. She hurriedly puts it in her bag and exits. LAURA hears the door and returns to the sitting-room. She puts down her bottle. Walks up and down. Obviously tense. Deep in thought. From time to time she shakes her head. Eventually she goes to the sofa. Looks for the box. Can't find it. Realizes RUTH must have it.)* Ruth!

Lights down

SCENE SIX:

LAURA'S place of work. No set. LAURA enters carrying a bag/case. She stops in her tracks as if someone has spoken to her.

LAURA: Laura. No. I've only been here a few weeks. Yes. Assistant secretary to the Art Director. [Yes I'm the one who sits around all day with bugger all to do.] Oh, you earn that much Fiona? That's nice. [Yes I probably do earn less than half that.] No. No. I didn't see that. [Quite frankly I couldn't care less if Ken Barlow fucks goats.] God I hate women! *(Pause)* Me?

Yes thank you. I went to Paris actually with my boyfriend. It was great. Came as a complete surprise to me. Got home Friday night. Got whisked away. Yes he is. Wonderful. He's in advertising as well. He got me this job. He said it was just a start. I used to be in Marketing. That's half the trouble with this job. I'm over qualified to be doing odd-jobs. [No. I don't care if you do think I'm arrogant.] *(She picks up her bag. Starts.)* Yes. That's his name. Do you know him? Oh. It's you I've got to thank for the job then. Thank you. Well. He wouldn't have mentioned me. He's just split up with someone. It's all a bit difficult at the moment. *(Pause)* Hermione? Yes I know...of Hermione. I don't think I'd better talk about it anymore. You know. [HELP!] God! I've got to go. It was nice talking to you Fiona. I'll probably see you tomorrow. *(She walks, slowly clutching her bag. Spotlight closes in on her. She faces front.)* Dear Jason. I'm the most despicable person in the world. I've done the most despicable thing. I know you'll find out. I wanted to tell you myself. I told them at work you were my boyfriend. I know it was wrong. I know what we agreed. I know you have someone else and I hope you're happy. I want you to be happy more than anything else. I should have told you before. I love you. Not as a friend. I'm in love with you. I've never said that to anyone. Even now I can write it but I couldn't say it if you were here. I wish you were here. I don't expect you to love me. I don't expect anything. I won't ask you for anything. I just have to know that you forgive me. I know you'll understand. I know you are my friend. I hope you don't think too badly of me. That's all. Lots and lots of love. Laura.

Lights down.

SCENE SEVEN:

The flat. The same day. LAURA has arrived home from work. RUTH has the phone receiver in her hand. There are a couple of suit cases by her side. She is wearing a 'Smart girls carry condoms' T-Shirt.

RUTH: How much did you hear?

LAURA: It doesn't matter.

RUTH: I had to tell her. I had to tell someone.

LAURA: How long have you known?

RUTH: A while.

LAURA: What have you done with my box?

RUTH: It's under the bed. Only please don't...

LAURA: Who were you talking to about me?

RUTH: Rachael. She's a friend. You've never met her. She's concerned about you.

LAURA: How can she be concerned about someone she's never met?

RUTH: *(Pause)* Why don't you just get angry with me?

LAURA: I'm not angry with you.

RUTH: Well you bloody well should be! You're just doing this on purpose to make me feel guilty. Well I don't care. I'm going out. *(She moves to the door.)* Laura? *(Pause)* Laura?

LAURA: Ruth. Don't tell anyone else.

(RUTH exits. LAURA remains seated for a moment. She gets up, still deep in thought. Walks up and

*down, stops and suddenly bashes
the sides of her head with the
palms of her hands. Then exits to
the bedroom. She returns with the
box and lays out: razors, scissors,
bandages, gauze, pins on the floor
and sits, cross-legged before them.
She is very tense. She rocks slightly
back and forward as she picks up
a razor and cuts her arm. She
continues to rock as she watches it
bleed, letting out a sigh of relief.
She covers the cut with a piece of
gauze and repeats the process
twice more. Finally she rests her
hand on her forearm and presses
down letting out a bigger sigh and
leaning forward with the top half
of her body. She bandages her
forearm. Pins it. Packs up the box
and stands. She catches herself in
the mirror. Her face creases up at
the realisation of what she's done.
She cries out angrily at her
reflection.)*

Lights down.

End of Act One.

ACT TWO

SCENE ONE:

*LAURA is seated in front of the sofa.
Looking out front. It is a few hours
later.*

LAURA: There's a disease where
you feel too well. You feel so
extremely healthy. So excessively
happy. Your mind is so clear, your
emotions so stirred, you feel you
might explode. And all around you
is wonderful. The air seems clearer
than ever imaginable. The sun
brighter. It's too wonderful.
Everything is just too perfect.
Suffering from this disease people
have killed themselves jumping
from cliff-tops believing they could
fly. Elation doesn't cover it. Even
ecstacy has a limit but this feeling
is of a boundless energy...and

impending doom. *(pause)* I've felt
this way ever since I met him. He
made me feel wonderful. And yet...
he was somehow frightening. And
that made it all the more exciting
being with him. Almost unbearable
so I had to get away from him to
enjoy him. *(She is laughing. Pause)*
Even now I can't stop it. If I bleed
the pain without relieves the pain
within. It is painful - always
ecstatically dancing on a cliff-top -
maybe today I could fly? But it's
only a temporary measure. It
doesn't help now any more than it
ever has. These wounds will heal
and I will build up more and more
inside until I need to re-open them.
I want it to stop. Please God make
it stop. Take away his voice in my
head. His name. The memory of his
words. His movement. His laugh.
All of it wonderful. So extremely,
excessively wonderful. Here it is
again. Meditate on him for a
moment and I feel I can do
anything. Anything at all. There it
is again. It's a brick. No, an anvil.
And it's going to drop on my
head.... soon?

(Enter RUTH and MARK)

RUTH: *(switching on the light)* She's
probably asleep. Oh God! Laura?
Are you O.K.?

LAURA: Um?

RUTH: I'll put her to bed. *(She gets
LAURA to her feet and takes her
into the bedroom. Re-enters).* When
I left she was just sitting there. She
often goes into these trances. I
wish I hadn't given her box
back. The last month or so it's got
worse. She keeps saying she'll
sleep on the sofa and I know that
sofa's hard as rock. She'll take a
razor to herself before she goes to
sleep. Like someone taking sleeping
tablets, I suppose. She never seems
to do herself any real harm. I've
turned a blind eye up until now
because I didn't know what to do.

MARK: How long has she been doing this?

RUTH: I don't know. I noticed it when she first moved in.

MARK: Why didn't you do something?

RUTH: I thought it was just a passing thing. She was depressed then. I thought she'd stopped until recently. What would you have done?

MARK: Something. Anything. I would have told me for a start. (Pause) I would have asked her about it. Got her to see a doctor.

RUTH: I've tried but every time I get close she changes the subject. Bites my head off if I mention doctors then I can't get the words out. That's why I had to find you. She'll listen to you.

MARK: I hope so. (Pause) Well I suppose you'd better run.

RUTH: Look it's bad enough that I feel guilty because I haven't been able to help her; then she makes me feel guilty because I try to help her and now you're making me feel guilty because I'm not helping enough. What am I supposed to do? Besides I have got to go. I can't miss the last train. I'm supposed to be in Birmingham now but I was terrified of what she might do. (Pause) Alright I can't cope with it anymore. Alright?

MARK: Don't worry. I'll talk to her.

RUTH: Thanks Mark. Here's the spare keys and my phone number. Let me know how she is. Oh. My friend Rachael gave me this magazine. There's an article in there all about people who do what she does. I've got to go.

MARK: Ruth?

RUTH: What?

MARK: Do you?

RUTH: Do I what?

MARK: Carry condoms?

RUTH: Oh, well.....not exactly. I thought it might help to bring up the subject. Bye. (exits)

MARK: Bye. (picks up magazine and lies uncomfortably on the sofa. LAURA enters wearing a dressing gown.)

LAURA: Mark? What's going on? What are you doing here?

MARK: Ruth asked me over.

LAURA: Oh you mean you and Ruth...

MARK: It's not like that. Ruth starts her course in the morning. She's just left.

LAURA: Oh God. I forgot. I've been a bit preoccupied lately.

MARK: So Ruth was saying.

LAURA: What? What was she saying?

MARK: She said you haven't been yourself.

LAURA: I haven't been myself. Yes, for once Ruth has hit the nail on the head and come up with a precise analysis. I have not been myself Mark. No. I have not.

MARK: That's why I came over.

LAURA: Do you want some coffee?

MARK: I thought we could go for a drink. Catch last orders.

LAURA: I'd rather not. I've got

things to get on with. I've left my job so I've got to start thinking where I might go for another one. Who put me to bed?

MARK: *(Pause)* Ruth.

LAURA: Oh. Do you mind if I make myself a cup?

MARK: Sit down.

LAURA: What?

MARK: Sit down. Please. *(Pause. She sits)*. Ruth said... She said that you've been hurting yourself. On a regular basis. For a long time. On purpose.

LAURA: And you believed her?

MARK: I saw the state you were in just now. Ruth doesn't know what to do about it. She thought I might.

LAURA: And do you? Do you know what to do?

MARK: I think you should see a doctor.

LAURA: There's nothing wrong with me.

MARK: Do you want to talk to me about it?

LAURA: Look. If you're going to be Ruth for a week, you have to do certain things: Talk rather than listen; throw things around the flat and then wonder why you can't find anything; spend money you can't afford on outrageously garish outfits and then say you've got no clothes and cry. Cry at every available opportunity.

MARK: Do you cry?

LAURA: Don't ask questions. Ruth never asks questions. It never occurs to her that anyone else has got anything to say and if their silence makes her uncomfortable she talks round in circles. Makes allusions. It's very amusing to watch.

MARK: I'm not Ruth.

LAURA: No. You don't have her sense of adventure in the clothing department.

MARK: *(MARK looks at his clothes. Pause)* Do you cry?

LAURA: I have a roof over my head. I could have a job if I hadn't jacked it in. I have my health. I'm quite intelligent. Not bad looking. Why should I cry? Ruth cries because she can't cope with anything unexpected. I like unexpected things. I thrive on them. Coping with disaster strengthens a person's character. Falling apart never does any good. Just makes you feel awful.

MARK: Cutting yourself makes you feel good? *(Pause)* Tell me about it.

LAURA: Why you?

MARK: I think I can help.

LAURA: Oh I get it. It's this new animal psychology thing. You want to practice on me before you risk one of your poodles and Ruth thought. 'Laura looks as if she's a pork pie short of the full picnic, I'll let Mark use her'. Well, have you got a pen and pad? Wait a minute, you're on the sofa. I'm supposed to be on the sofa.

MARK: Stop it.

LAURA: Now then. How can I arrange this? Yes. We'll put this chair here for you. Close enough so you can hear my innermost relevations but far enough away so you don't have to get personally involved.

MARK: Laura stop it!

LAURA: Would you like me to bark? Would that make you feel more at home?

MARK: Laura. Half an hour ago I was sitting, quite happily, in the pub having a quiet drink when I was yanked out by Ruth and brought over here. I didn't come to sit and listen to your sarcasm.

LAURA: Well fuck off then! By the way. What's Ruth doing to pay you for this kind gesture, as if I couldn't guess.

MARK: *(goes to leave)* I came here to help you but you obviously can't appreciate that. Read that. It's about women like you. Women who cut themselves.

LAURA: Mark. You and Ruth are exaggerating this out of all proportion. All it is....Oh I can't go into the reasons why I got so upset earlier. It was silly. It will sort itself out. It won't happen again. I got upset over nothing. Childish. If Ruth hadn't found out about me... what I do, I could have gone on doing it without badly hurting myself or anyone else. There's nothing to talk about.

MARK: Nothing? You think it's perfectly normal to do that to yourself again and again?

LAURA: It's normal to me. It doesn't hurt anyone else. Unlike the drug users and alcoholics of the world I don't degenerate after I 'cut up' and I'm a lot nicer to be around afterwards. It doesn't affect my brain and I never do it badly enough to do myself any real harm.

MARK: What if you slip one day?

Go to do a bit of blood letting and cut a vein or worse? What about the scald marks on your legs and the nicks on your face? Why do you do it? Tell me.

LAURA: I can't.

MARK: Would it help if you wrote it down? Write it to me in a letter.

LAURA: No. I hate writing letters. All your personal thoughts come out. Things you wouldn't say.

MARK: Exactly. It would make it easier.

LAURA: It's stupid. You only live downstairs.

MARK: Nevertheless. *(Pause)* Does he know?

LAURA: Who?

MARK: Jason.

LAURA: No. He's in Manchester. I'm not seeing him.

MARK: Ruth said you've been cutting yourself more recently. Is it because of him?

LAURA: God no! He wasn't my type in the end. A bit flash really. All talk.

MARK: So you admit you've been worse lately?

LAURA: Would you go now please? I've got things to do. I do appreciate you coming round and I'm sorry Ruth asked you to come over here for nothing.

MARK: She had good reason to. Will you at least go and see a doctor? That's what they're there for.

LAURA: I'll think about it. Mark. You won't tell anyone, will you?

MARK: No.

LAURA: Thank you.

(He exits. Lights focus on LAURA who faces front.)

LAURA: Dear Jason. I can't believe the letter I wrote you yesterday. I don't mean the part about loving you. That's true. But today I feel so good. I feel I could fly. *(Pause)* I'm not sad. I would be fine if I never saw you again. Not that I wouldn't like to. Just knowing you are somewhere in the world and a great and wonderful person who has made me feel alive again is more than enough. I hope you and your girl are happy. I hope you'll get in touch soon. I just couldn't leave you with that distressed letter I wrote yesterday. I don't want you to worry about me. Lots and lots of love. Laura.

SCENE TWO:

The door bell goes and the lights come up on the whole room. LAURA answers it. The doctor enters the flat.

DOCTOR: Hello Laura. I'm sorry I don't have much time. I'm on route to four other patients, I'm afraid I shouldn't make house calls unless you are bedridden, you know.

LAURA: I know. I'm sorry. I just couldn't....I didn't want to go out. I can't go out.

DOCTOR: *(sits and looks at records)* Right. Now what can I do for you?

LAURA: Well. Do you remember when I came to see you last?

DOCTOR: Yes. The miscarriage. Did you have any problems?

LAURA: Yes.

DOCTOR: Irregular bleeding. Stomach cramps. That sort of thing?

LAURA: No. Nothing... physical.

DOCTOR: What? You felt a bit upset afterwards, did you?

LAURA: Yes. Yes I felt...a bit upset. I think.

DOCTOR: *(Pause)* Well. It's only to be expected. It's natural to experience....

LAURA: A sense of loss. That's what I felt. I felt I'd lost something. A part of me. A valuable and important part of me.

DOCTOR: Yes, well, you see the body gets ready to do something which it's not then able to do so a sense of loss....

LAURA: Not just physical. I felt empty. Emotionally empty. I didn't care about anyone. Especially me. I was dirty. Something ugly and worthless was stuck on me replacing something good and whole. *(She stops suddenly. Pause)*

DOCTOR: Is that what you wanted to see me about?

LAURA: Yes you see I've never had much sympathy for depression. I don't like it when people get depressed or angry or emotional. I get impatient. It's such a waste of energy. *(Pause)* I was depressed. I felt angry, emotional and I had no patience. I hated myself. I still.... *(she stops)*

DOCTOR: I'm not in favour of tablets for the treatment of depression. They may relieve you in the short term but they can become addictive. What I will do is refer you to a psychotherapist who will counsel you. There is a very long waiting list, however. And hopefully by the time your turn comes round you won't be feeling so bad. You really ought not to stay indoors. Get out. Have some fun. It shouldn't be hard for a young girl like you. Do you know what I do when I'm depressed?

LAURA: What?

DOCTOR: I get an old movie out on video; have a bath; sing in the bath and paint my toe nails then curl up and watch the movie. Have a bar of chocolate if I'm feeling really wicked. It's very easy to let the devil depression get the better of you. I know it's old fashioned but thinking positive and looking on the bright side is the best and most natural cure in the world. Do you have a boyfriend?

LAURA: No.

DOCTOR: Good. Go out with your girlfriends. And if you do find a boyfriend. Come back and see me. We don't want you getting pregnant again do we?

LAURA: No.

DOCTOR: Well. At least not until the time is right. *(Pause)* Was there anything else?

LAURA: *(Pause)* No. No. Thank you.

DOCTOR: I'll refer you to a psychotherapist at St. Georges. You should get a letter in a week or two. If you're still feeling off in a couple of months come back and see me again. And I think you should come and see me next time.

LAURA: Yes. Thank you. Bye.

DOCTOR: Goodbye. *(she exits).*

(Lights focus in on LAURA).

LAURA: Dear Jason. Where are you? What are you doing? What are you thinking? Have you forgiven me? You said I might write and I have. But every word is torn out of me and it hurts. You said yourself. 'You've got to care to write'. Well I have. I care. Is this your cold cruel way of telling me you don't? No. That's not fair. I understand. It must be difficult for you to reply. But please. I would rather you said you hated me than ignored me. Do I have to say again? I know you don't love me. I know you have someone else. I'm sure she's what's best for you. God knows I'm no good to anyone. I'm sure she's lovely. Take care. Lots and lots of love. Laura.

Lights down.

SCENE THREE:

LAURA is lying on the sofa, reading. RUTH enters noisily with cases. Shuts the door. Drops the cases.

RUTH: I'm home!

LAURA: Oh yeah, so you are.

RUTH: *(coming round beside her)* How are you?

LAURA: I'm fine, you?

RUTH: Oh yes. Listen, Laura, I've been thinking while I was away.

LAURA: *(sitting)* Oh, do you want to sit down?

RUTH: Listen to me. I've known for a long time about what you've been doing and I didn't mention it. I just want you to know it's not because I didn't care. I didn't know how I could help. But now I do.

LAURA: Ruth I...

RUTH: No, please, let me say this. I should have done something sooner.

I know that now. I rang a crisis line for people who do what you do and I spoke to Rachael as well, she's got a cousin whose friend used to cut herself. Anyway, they told me on the phone that people who do this often come from broken homes, perhaps lost a parent or a child. They feel a sense of rejection and then later they fear rejection in their relationships and I thought of course, I mean that's you, isn't it? That's exactly your problems.

LAURA: I know you mean well, Ruth...

RUTH: Let me tell you what they said. I asked them what we should do and they said that self-lacerators need to express themselves instead of hurting themselves. Talk to someone, get angry, cry. The very last thing you need is to be on your own which is what I've been leaving you to do. All I'm saying is from now on I'm here. If you want to shout or scream or cry or thump someone - not too hard. If you want to talk about anything. I don't mind. O.k.?

LAURA: Ruth, next time I feel like having a row with someone you'll be the first to know.

RUTH: Great. *(She picks up her cases and takes them into the bedroom. LAURA closes her book and puts her head in her hands.)*

Lights down

SCENE FOUR:

LAURA: Jason. I've fallen into a bottomless pit and there's nothing to hang on to. All you have to do is tell me you forgive me. Please. Laura. *(Lights grow. LAURA is cutting herself. RUTH enters from the bedroom, stops, and watches. LAURA senses her there. Looks up*

and sees her.)

LAURA: Go away! *(RUTH exits. LAURA throws her razors etc to the floor.)*

Lights down.

SCENE FIVE:

JASON is shutting the door of the flat. RUTH enters from the bedroom.

JASON: I feel as though I've been kidnapped.

RUTH: You have. Would you like a drink while you're waiting? I don't see why we shouldn't be civilised about this.

JASON: No, thank you.

RUTH: Oh, no, of course, you don't, do you? Seeing you and Peter out of your brains so many times was a figment of my imagination.

JASON: I did drink. I don't anymore. People change.

RUTH: Yes. Some more often than others. An orange juice, perhaps?

JASON: No, thank you. Look, Ruth, I can't stay here for long. I've got to get back up north.

RUTH: You'll stay until she gets here. She's been falling apart since you left.

JASON: She seemed fine last time I saw her. She was happy.

RUTH: Because she thought you'd come back and see her. Because she thought you were going to be such a good friend. And she was hoping for more. Because you didn't tell her the real reason you were going was another woman and not business at all.

117

JASON: You shouldn't have told her. That's what's upset her. Not me.

RUTH: And let her hope for all eternity? She would have found out eventually anyway.

JASON: This cutting you say she does. There was nothing about it in her letters.

RUTH: What letters?

JASON: When I left I said we should write to each other. I thought she understood. I meant us to be mates. She's written to me dozens of times. Three times a week sometimes.

RUTH: Did you write back?

JASON: No.

RUTH: Why not?

JASON: I didn't know what to say.

RUTH: Why didn't you tell her about Hermione?

JASON: I didn't know what to say.

RUTH: It's amazing how a man can be so eloquent when he wants to get a woman into bed and suddenly become speechless when he doesn't care to repeat the experience.

JASON: I know you think I've behaved badly.

RUTH: Is it that obvious?

JASON: I didn't want to hurt her. I didn't lie to her, though. I told her I couldn't have a relationship with her. There was no point in rubbing it in with the reasons why. That would have been cruel.

RUTH: You still slept with her first.

JASON: Afterwards.

RUTH: Oh great! 'I don't want you for a girlfriend, but since you're here...'

JASON: Look, she's obviously not coming.

RUTH: She could walk in that door any minute. *(Pause)*

JASON: What do you want me to do?

RUTH: Talk to her. Two months ago you convinced Laura you were the most wonderful human being she'd met. How God only knows, but she's convinced. You are going to be as good as your word. For once you are going to have to prove that you care, not just say it.

JASON: And what do I tell her about Hermione?

RUTH: The truth, of course.

JASON: You want me to tell her that I'm in love with someone else? That I slept with her knowing that? The thing is, Ruth, I'm just lazy about keeping in touch with people. I thought she'd forget about me. Then she told someone she was my girlfriend and it got back to Hermione. She went up the wall. Then, on top of all that, Laura starts writing letters saying she's in love with me. I know I took the coward's way out, but I only did what most people would in that situation. I let it go. I thought she'd give up eventually. Is that what you want me to tell her? If she's falling apart now, how much worse will it be if I tell her that? *(There is a key in the door. They both look. Neither moves. The door opens.)*

MARK: Oh, Ruth, I'm sorry. I thought no-one was here.

RUTH: That's alright. Come in,

Mark. This is Jason. Jason - Mark.

JASON: Hello.

MARK: Hi.

RUTH: Mark's our neighbour.

JASON: Laura mentioned you.

MARK: Likewise. *(Pause)*

RUTH: We're waiting for her.

MARK: Oh, I just saw her go out. *(slight pause)* I wasn't going to rob the place. I wanted that magazine. There was a phone number.

RUTH: I know, I rang them. It's no good though. She won't stop. Did you speak to her while I was away.

MARK: Yes. I managed to get her to see a doctor.

JASON: How is she?

MARK: Apart from mutilating herself every now and then she's fine.

JASON: I can't believe she could do that.

RUTH: She didn't tell me she'd been to a doctor.

MARK: Well, apparently she's been referred for psychotherapy at St. Georges but she said there's a huge waiting list and it might take six months or more before she's seen. I thought she might have heard something.

RUTH: Six months?! She can't wait that long. What are we supposed to do in the meantime? That's ridiculous!

MARK: I know. And I've been thinking about it. If she went private she could see someone tomorrow. I've got some money but

I think it's going to be difficult to get her to take it. Perhaps if you suggest it first, between us we could persuade her. I'd talk to her myself but you know what she's like, she...

RUTH: No. Jason's got a better idea, haven't you Jason?

JASON: What? *(Pause)* Look, I've got to go. I don't know what I'm going to say to Hermione about why I'm so late.

RUTH: You'll think of something. But just before you go Jason, I'd like to give you the opportunity to show what a truly kind person you are. Laura was telling me how you care about things. The environment, people. How you give money to charity. Well Laura's a person Jason and she's in need of some charity at the moment. Perhaps you could donate something. Nothing much. Just a thousand pounds.

JASON: Well I...

RUTH: That is right what Laura was saying about your having so much money but it not meaning anything to you?

JASON: Well that's true but I can't just...

RUTH: Or was that all bullshit too?

(Pause. JASON sits down. Takes out a pen and cheque book and starts writing. He pauses)

RUTH: What's the matter? Run out of ink?

JASON: No. I've forgotten her surname.

RUTH: Waterford.

JASON: *(He hands her the cheque and goes to the door.)* Will you tell

119

her....tell her I'm sorry. Tell her I'll write to her.

RUTH: No.

JASON: Why not?

RUTH: Because you're not and you won't.

JASON: *(Pause)* Goodbye Ruth. *(He goes)*

MARK: So. That was Superman.

RUTH: Yeah, well, he's done his bit I suppose. Maybe he is sorry. Somewhere deep down.

MARK: Or maybe he doesn't have a deep down. Just a mouth and a cheque book. How could she fall for that?

RUTH: Do you know where she went?

MARK: No idea. How was the course?

RUTH: Good. I couldn't concentrate though. I kept feeling I should be here. I left three days early. I don't think they believed my sick relative story. It's not entirely untrue is it? I mean, I've got a sick friend. She is sick, isn't she?

MARK: Why did you ask him here?

RUTH: I thought it would help. I thought if she could see him for what he is...

MARK: But she won't will she? Not now. We'll hand over the cheque and she'll think her knight in shining armour has saved the day.

RUTH: What does it matter? So long as she... *(LAURA enters)*

LAURA: Hi Mark. Not working today?

MARK: I'm on holiday.

LAURA: Oh, what's the weather like?

MARK: What?

LAURA: Never mind. You both look so serious.

MARK: We were just talking about you.

LAURA: Oh, great! That's why you look so miserable. What have I done?

RUTH: It's what you haven't done. We know you haven't stopped.

LAURA: Stopped what? Oh, not that again.

RUTH: It's not certain how long you'll have to wait to see... the person... your doctor's referred you to, so we've got you the money. So you can see someone straight away.

LAURA: Money? For me? Where from?

RUTH: *(Pause)* Jason.

LAURA: What? When did you see him?

RUTH: Today.

LAURA: Where? Where is he?

RUTH: He was at Peter's. I went over there to get some things and there he was. He said he was sorry. He asked me to give you this.

LAURA: A thousand pounds. No letter? No message?

RUTH: No.

LAURA: Did he say?...Has he forgiven me?

RUTH: What for?

LAURA: Never mind. When am I going to see him?

RUTH: I don't know. Look, why can't you just forget about him?

LAURA: How could you tell him? He'll never want to see me now. He'll think I'm mad.

RUTH: He doesn't want to see you anyway.

MARK: Ruth, why don't you put the kettle on and I'll make us some tea.

LAURA: Did he say that?

MARK: The important thing is you've got the money. As long as you agree to see someone. Will you?

LAURA: I'm already going to see someone, I just don't know when.

MARK: Well, now you don't have to wait.

LAURA: He didn't say anything else? Are you sure? I'd like to write to him. Thank him.

RUTH: Thank him? Laura, he doesn't give a shit about you.

MARK: Ruth!

LAURA: God, you just can't stand to see me happy, can you? I bet he's been writing to me and you've hidden the letters. He's my friend. You're the one who doesn't give a shit about anyone but yourself. He's my friend. He's my friend.

RUTH: Your friend! (LAURA tears up the cheque.) What are you doing?

LAURA: I said I wouldn't ask him for anything and I won't.

RUTH: Do you realise what I've been through to get that?

LAURA: You said he gave it to you.

RUTH: I had to ask him for it. It wasn't easy. He didn't want to see you. He couldn't wait to get back to his girlfriend. That's what he's like. This was all I could get from him and you tear it up.

MARK: This isn't helping matters, Ruth.

RUTH: How could you? After all the trouble I've been to?

LAURA: I didn't ask you to. Well, I didn't, did I? All I've ever asked you to do is leave me alone. But no, you had to stick your nose in. Telling him what I do so now he'll never speak to me again. I don't want his money. Why couldn't you just mind your own busines. (RUTH rises)

MARK: Where are you going?

RUTH: Out. I'm sick and tired of worrying about you. Walking on eggshells in case I say the wrong thing. Lying awake wondering what you're doing to yourself in here. Everything I've done today just to have you throw it back in my face. Well, at least I don't feel guilty anymore.

MARK: Look Ruth...

RUTH: I've tried to help her, Mark, you know that. She doesn't want help. She wants to be a martyr. Cold and silent. Greta Garbo wanting to be alone, all sad and mysterious and dramatic and slicing herself to pieces. Well, I don't think it's mysterious, it's very common actually. There are hundreds of thousands of people who lacerate themselves on a daily basis all over the country. So you're not special. You're just pathetic. Pathetic and stupid. (*exits*)

LAURA: She's right.

MARK: No she isn't and you know it. Don't start sulking.

LAURA: I'm not sulking.

MARK: This has to stop, Laura. And don't start telling me about seeing a therapist at the hospital. That could be six months from now.

LAURA: I've been fine for the last six months. Why not the next?

MARK: You have not been fine. Have you? You can't tell me it makes you happy taking a razor to yourself of an evening.

LAURA: Not happy, no. But I need it. It relaxes me. I can't imagine ever not needing it.

MARK: There must have been a time when you didn't. When do you feel the need and when don't you?

LAURA: I don't know.

MARK: Yes you do. Tell me the first time it happened.

LAURA: Oh, please.

MARK: Tell me. I know you'll feel better. I know it'll help.

LAURA: Help! Everybody wants to help. You make me feel so inadequate and useless. I can help myself.

MARK: Then do it. Here's your opportunity.

LAURA: By myself!

MARK: You need support.

LAURA: Opportunity. Support.

(*Pause*) Alright, I'll tell you the first time. But it won't make any difference. I was twelve. I walked into the kitchen from the bathroom one day and heard my Mum and Dad having an argument. I couldn't get anywhere else in the house without going through the living-room but I didn't want them to see me. I couldn't stay where I was because if they came in they'd think I'd been listening on purpose. They said hateful things to each other. I couldn't cry because they'd hear that. I wanted to go in and shout at them to stop but that would only make them angrier with each other and me as well. Then I had the brilliant idea of making a cup of tea. I'd make lots of noise so I couldn't hear them but they'd hear me and come in. I'd act all innocent. End of problem. But they didn't hear anything. The kettle boiling was drowned by their bellowing. I was so angry. Suddenly I had the urge to pour the boiling water on my foot. It was agony at first but then I felt the most incredible sense of relief. Tension gone. Anger gone. They came in when I screamed. I got the usual lecture about what a clumsy, stupid girl I was, but they stopped arguing and, anyway, I didn't care anymore. Later I found less conspicuous ways of wounding. Then it started again when I broke up with Richard. Again when I...wasn't well when I moved in here. And then a couple of months ago.

MARK: When Jason let you down.

LAURA: He didn't let me down.

MARK: Alright. (*Pause*) Do you feel any better now?

LAURA: Yes. Yes, I do. (*Pause*) I'm shattered, Mark.

MARK: Ruth didn't mean what she

said.

LAURA: I know. She's a good friend. So are you.

MARK: Will you do something for me before I go?

LAURA: What?

MARK: Will you promise to talk to me next time? I won't stop you. But maybe we can find another way of getting out that anger. You could punch the walls with me or something.

LAURA: Now that is stupid.

MARK: Maybe. Is it a deal?

LAURA: It's a deal. Thanks, Mark.

MARK: Sleep well tonight.

LAURA: I will. *(He goes. She goes to the mirror.)* So, it's a deal, is it?....Liar! *(She scratches her face with her fingernails. MARK re-enters)*

MARK: Oh, by the way, I forgot to tell you, Mary walked out on me today. Would you believe it she's allergic to cats? So if you want the job it's yours.

LAURA: *(Pause. LAURA turns slowly)* Fine. When do I start?

MARK: *(Pause)* Oh, God. Laura. What have you done?

LAURA: Well, *(She goes to the door and shuts it)* I wouldn't go to you if my cat had a thorn in its foot. The diagnosis would appear to be that I have multiple abrasions on my left cheek. An examination of my fingernails would lead any half-competent medical practitioner to the inevitable conclusion that I have scratched my face. Quite badly. *(She sits)*

MARK: I thought we were in this together.

LAURA: Well, I lied. That's what I'm like you see. You never know where you are. I say one thing and do another. You're wasting your time talking to me.

MARK: Look. You are sick. We've got to do something.

LAURA: We haven't got to do anything. I'm supposed to wait. I got a letter. They'll see me August. Next year.

MARK: *(He is pacing)* You can't wait that long!

LAURA: I can. You can go now.

MARK: *(Pause. He sits down and picks up the magazine).* No. I'm staying.

LAURA: I'm asking you to leave.

MARK: I'm not going. *(Pause)* Where's the article on self-laceration?

LAURA: I think Ruth's making a poster out of it. *(Pause)* Do you want some information? I can tell you how to do it if you like?

MARK: Go on, then.

LAURA: *(Pause)* Well, it's really very simple. What you do is you get a razor or a fingernail. Best start with a fingernail, razors are for the more experienced. And you take a piece of virgin flesh and you tear into it. It helps if you're feeling angry or are in the presence of someone who's really pissing you off.

MARK: Do it then. Again. Show me.

LAURA: Shut up.

MARK: No. Go on. Do it. You're the expert. Show me. Here. We'll do it together. *(Pause)* Is this part of it? A two minute silence before the act itself. I want to get the whole process right.

LAURA: Stop it. I don't need this. It isn't fair. I want to be on my own.

MARK: No you don't.

LAURA: Don't tell me what I want.

MARK: You need me here.

LAURA: I don't need anyone.

MARK: So, you're an expert. When does one get to graduate from fingernails to razors?

LAURA: Stop trying to be clever, Mark. It doesn't suit you.

MARK: *(Pause)* I can remember a time when we were friends. You don't talk to me like a friend anymore.

LAURA: You're not being a friend to me.

MARK: I am.

LAURA: You're hounding me.

MARK: What do you call being a friend? Someone who ignores you? Someone who isn't there when you need them? Someone who beats you up?

LAURA: You really have been having a good old chat with Ruth, haven't you? How dare she? How dare you! It's none of your business. It's my life and it's my body.

MARK: It's your problem.

LAURA: Yes. Exactly.

MARK: So you admit it's a problem?

LAURA: It's a figure of speech.

MARK: It's a problem.

LAURA: Well, it's mine. Maybe I don't want to solve it. Maybe I think I'm alright as I am.

MARK: If you thought you were alright as you were you wouldn't cut yourself. You can't hide it. We both know you do it, and we both want you to stop.

LAURA: No we don't. You just want to boost your image. Demonstrate what a kind, compassionate man you are.

MARK: *(rises, crosses to the wall)* I do not! *(He punches the wall with his fist. Long pause)*

LAURA: I wish he was here now. He wouldn't shout at me.

MARK: No because he doesn't give a damn. Look what he's done to you. You were a quiet, thoughtful girl with a bit of a sharp tongue, and ever since you met Mr. Advertising you're a nervous wreck. And where is he now? With someone else. He used you. Laura.

LAURA: He didn't. You don't understand.

MARK: There's nothing to understand. I can see what he's done.

LAURA: He's done nothing. It was my fault.

MARK: What? What was your fault?

LAURA: Everything! You think you care about me? You don't know anything about me: what I'm like; what I do. I seduced him. Not the other way around. I wanted him even though I knew he didn't want me. I used to make Richard hit me. I'd goad and goad him until he did it, then watch him suffer in his guilt. I chose them and I took the consequences. Not their fault, mine! That's what kind of person I am. You think I'm quiet and thoughtful? You don't know me. I'm a lying, ugly, selfish bitch. Do you know I love to have sex with complete strangers? Men I don't even like! I love it! I use them! Poor Laura, who Ruth has to look after and Mark has to befriend has had two abortions and a miscarriage. All I'm good at is destroying things. I made Richard hate me. Ruth hate me. Jason run a mile from me. Even the baby I wanted didn't want me. No-one wants to look after me for long. Well, that's fine, because I don't need anyone, OK? OK? *(MARK goes to her and hugs her)* Go away. Go away.

MARK: Why can't you care for someone who cares for you?

LAURA: Why can't you? *(Pause)* You see? You see what I'm like?

MARK: I love you.

LAURA: No. I don't want to be loved. I don't want to.

MARK: You're worth a hundred Ruths and a thousand Richards and a million Jasons and I know it and they know it and I wish to God you knew it too.

LAURA: I'm horrible. Horrible.

MARK: Alright, you're horrible. And you're lovely. You're lovely.

Lights down

SCENE SIX:

MARK and LAURA are sitting at opposite ends of the sofa. LAURA is staring at a painting. MARK looks from the picture to LAURA

MARK: I thought you were supposed to lie down on a couch and talk about your childhood.

LAURA: *(concentrating)* Shows what you know.

MARK: I think you've been done. They've discovered your level of intelligence and they're trying to send you bonkers to provide long term work for themselves.

LAURA: Sssssh.

MARK: *(Pause. Quietly.)* What exactly are you supposed to be achieving?

LAURA: I'm meant to be focusing on my picture.

MARK: Did you paint that?

LAURA: Yes.

MARK: Really? It's beautiful. *(he walks up to it)*

LAURA: Yeah, yeah.

MARK: No it is. *(Pause)* It's you, isn't it?

LAURA: Do you think it looks like me? Do I look like that?

MARK: Well not exactly. Your nose is a shade brighter yellow in real life. But it's pretty.

LAURA: I must get on. *(She rises. Takes down the picture. Puts it by the sofa facing inwards.)*

MARK: Sorry. *(Pause. They both stand still not looking at each*

other. Then MARK looks up)
You're not going to change your
mind about me, are you?

LAURA: *(She shakes her head)* I
find it hard....to do what they ask
me to. The exercises. The soul
searching. Talking hurts. I don't
feel safe unless I'm on my own
and I need to feel safe. For a
while. I need to cut if I want to.
And I need to do it in private.
(Pause) I'd lie to you and go back
to square one. I don't have the
strength to be honest very often.
Maybe in a few years? But that'll
be too late for you. *(Pause)* It can't
get worse anyway. It's getting
better already. *(She lets out a small
laugh).* Still, I know where you are.

MARK: *(Pause)* I'll be going away
for a while.

LAURA: Oh. *(Pause)* Ok. *(He goes
to the door.)*

MARK: Goodbye Laura.

LAURA: Goodbye. *(He exits. She has
tears in her eyes. She cries softly
and then starts to giggle. She gives
out a little cry which is a mixture
of sadness, fear and joy. She
breathes deeply and sighs with
relief which echoes that which she
experienced after cutting herself.
She sees herself in the mirror and
pulls funny faces. Laughing to
herself.)*

Lights down.

ITHAKA

Nina Rapi

"ITHAKA" had a staged reading at Riverside Studios in June 1989.

The cast were:

SULA:	SHARRON MCKEVITT
SHADOW:	DONNA DOUBTFIRE
LENNA:	CORINNE GABLE
MOTHER/DEBORAH:	MICHELLE READ
FATHER/OFFICIAL:	TED DAWSON
BROTHER:	LAURENCE GALLIO
LOUISE:	JACKIE SKARVELLIS
DIRECTED BY:	RUTH BEN-TOVIM

"...theatrically inventive, often surreal, witty and funny in its sensitive charting of Sula's quest for love and freedom." (David Hunter, Literary Manager, BUSH THEATRE)

" I was impressed ...an intelligent approach to a series of complex and interrelated issues." (Fiona Branson, Artistic Co-ordinator, RESISTERS theatre company.)

" We enjoyed the piece ...strong moments...claustrophobic intensity..." (Mel Kenyon, Literary Manager, ROYAL COURT)

I am not clear as to when exactly *'ITHAKA'* started. I had written a short story called *'Convict'* and on joining the Workshop in Spring 1988, I submitted it, together with two outlines for plays and a number of poems, to Attic Work, the workshop's annual show of new work. The story very much dealt with submission, domination and entrapment. I had been playing in a band for a few years and was rather cut off from women's politics in general and theatre in particular. My image of feminism at the time was one of 'Big Sister is Watching you'. I was dreading that I would be admonished for submitting such a story and was rather hoping it would pass unnoticed, even though, having written in isolation for some time, I badly needed responses and feedback.

To my surprise, *'Convict'* was the one piece that was picked out. Cheryl

Robson and Janet Beck who were selecting the material, both liked it and suggested I developed it into a script. I thought it was a very introverted piece, as it was mostly concerned with inner realities, and worried that it might not work well on stage. But I overcame these anxieties with the excitement of writing a script, something I very much wanted to do. I used to love the theatre as a child when I lived in Thessaloniki, missed it as an adolescent while I lived in Kastoria, a small town with only the worst of touring companies visiting it and that very rarely, and I reclaimed it again when I first came to this country. I later abandoned it completely and hardly ever went near one, becoming absorbed as I was in politics and later music. Coming back to it, this time as a writer, was exhilarating.

So I wrote out some rough scenes and an even rougher 'plot'. Catherine Carnie who was Artistic Director of the PARK Theatre at the time, had been enthusiastic about it and so we met at the PARK, to discuss it. I had never been to an empty theatre before and the feeling was amazing. Being given that space just to explore the theatrical possibilities of my script felt such a privilege. Things were going extremely well and the script developed to a twenty minute length but due to a number of complications, including actresses dropping out at the last minute, the piece never 'came off' on stage. I was devastated.

Cheryl and Janet suggested that I needed more time and space for my piece than the 'anthology' format could offer and if I developed it into a full script, they would try and organize a rehearsed reading of it. This lifted me from an unbearable depression - an over-reaction no doubt in retrospect - and in August 1988, while on holidays in Greece, I started *'ITHAKA'*. It was to be a journey of self-exploration for the main character and *'Journey'* was indeed its working title. I kept only a few lines and some ideas from *'Convict'*.

I didn't go back to the workshop for that and the next term but Cheryl and Janet put me in touch with Ruth Ben-Tovim, who was to direct the reading. By December, I had written the first act and showed it to Ruth who liked it. She had in the meantime become Artistic Director of the Corner Theatre (now the Hen and Chickens) and said that we might be able to put it on there. This never actually happened in the end for a number of reasons, but at the time it gave me confidence and encouraged me to carry on. I finished the first draft sometime in March and discussed it with Ruth, Cheryl and Janet, all of whom made useful suggestions. I produced the second draft by May. The reading at Riverside went very well but also pointed to the need for some changes, especially in the third act which was overlong. I worked on those and finally finished the play in August 1989.

'ITHAKA' refers to a poem by Kavafi by the same name and means that freedom, knowledge, 'home', whatever it is you are heading towards, is actually to be found in the quest for it. The journey is the end. Interestingly, as a friend pointed out to me recently, the Greek word for freedom, eleftheria, actually means 'going towards something'. You never actually obtain freedom as it is always ahead of you.

THE CHARACTERS

Actors can double roles.

SULA: A young, Greek woman, early twenties. Withdrawn and passive with bursts of passion. A dreamer.

SHADOW: A woman with SULA'S build. Harsh and ruthless but also cool and wise.

LENNA: SULA'S friend from home, two years younger. Gregarious, loyal to a cause, philosophically minded. Moderate.

SULA'S MOTHER: Big and bolshy.

SULA'S FATHER: Scraggy and pathetic.

SULA'S BROTHER: Spoilt brat/clever arse, nineteen years old.

DEBORA: A classical pianist of Hungarian origin in her forties. Attractive and calm but vulnerable.

LOUISE: A theatre director in her thirties. Full of vigour and energy but somewhat callous.

CUSTOMS OFFICIAL

The play spans seven years, 1974 to 1981, corresponding to a particular period in Greek history.

ACT ONE

SCENE ONE:

A poor-looking and chaotic living room.

(SULA walks on stage from the right. She comes in reading an extract from Antigone. She is completely absorbed in it. Her parents are at the opposite end of the stage, both in cement or some such like material, up to their necks. They look dead.)

SULA: So to my grave. My bridal-bower, my everlasting prison. I go to join those many of my kinsmen. Who dwell in the mansion of Persephone. Last and unhappiest, before my time.

(SULA walks towards her parents while reciting, without having seen them and first trips on her mother, shocked)

MOTHER: *(pretty casually)* Get me out of here, your father's gone off his head; he tried to kill me and then buried me alive.

SULA: And why did he do that?

MOTHER: Why? Because he's a bloody lunatic, that's why.

SULA: Did you do anything to him, mum?

MOTHER: Yeah. I boiled his egg a minute too long. Now get me out of here.

(SULA moves towards unburying her mother when her father's frantic screams stop her.)

FATHER: Don't. Don't let her out. She's mad. She's lying, lying through her teeth. She buried me and then went and buried herself.

SULA: And why did she do that?

FATHER: Because she's barmy, that's why.

SULA: *(reproachfully)* Did you do anything to her dad?

FATHER: No, nothing at all.

SULA: Nothing?

FATHER: Well, you know your mother, I just said the wrong thing that's all.

SULA: And what was that?

FATHER: I just said "You useless good-for-nothing fat slob"

SULA: Is that all?

FATHER: Yes, that's all I swear. Now get me out of here.

(SULA starts moving towards unburying her father. Her mother starts shouting.)

MOTHER: What on earth are you doing? You believe him? He'd say anything to get out of a spot. He tried to strangle me I tell you, and because I didn't let him, he buried me alive. Then he went and buried himself for an alibi.

(SULA stands looking very confused not knowing who to believe. Then decisively)

SULA: I'll tell you what. I'll get you both out. All right?

(The parents look at each other half shame-faced, half accusing. SULA starts unburying her mother

130

when her brother walks in.)

BROTHER: What are you doing? Are you crazy?

SULA: *(exasperated)* And why am I crazy?

BROTHER: Because they're corpses. And people don't go around digging corpses out of their graves. It's just not on.

SULA: But they're alive.

BROTHER: *(in roaring laughter)* Alive? Why are they in graves then?

SULA: Because they play silly-buggers with each other, that's why. Now will you give me a hand and stop being clever?

BROTHER: *(nodding at her to go close to him)* I'll let you into a secret if you promise to help me.

SULA: What are you talking about?

(Cries are heard from the parents. SULA turns to help them. Her brother stops her.)

BROTHER: You know Takis?

SULA: The immigrant who just came back from Germany?

BROTHER: Yes, him.

SULA: What about him?

BROTHER: Do you like him?

SULA: Like him? He seems OK.

BROTHER: He's a hard worker.

SULA: Good for him.

BROTHER: He was there for fourteen years, working day and night making money. He's brought lots of it back.

SULA: Ah. Bravo. His mother must be pleased.

BROTHER: Aren't you?

SULA: Me? Why should I be? I got nothing to do with him.

BROTHER: You could, you know.

SULA: What's this? Is my young brother trying to match me up with a boyfriend?

BROTHER: Who said anything about a boyfriend?

SULA: What are you on about?

BROTHER: He's asked to marry you.

SULA: That ugly, bald mass of flesh? He must be joking.

BROTHER: No, he's not. He's come back to find a wife and when he saw you, he made up his mind straight away, so he sent his mum over to ask for your hand. He doesn't want any dowry either. He's a walking miracle sis.

SULA: I see. And what kind of help do you want?

BROTHER: Sis, if you marry him, you save me. He promised, amongst other things, to educate me, to help me go to University in Germany and become an engineer. If I stay here, all I'll end up doing is my Army Service and then work like a dog for the rest of my life like dad. I'm a sensitive soul, sis, I'll probably end up either topping myself or committing murder.

131

You're my only chance of breaking out and getting a better life.

SULA: What else did he promise?

BROTHER: He's going to set dad up with a shop so that his father-in-law won't stand out in the streets behind a stall any more. And mum with every modern domestic appliance a woman could want. And the house with television, hi-fi and furniture to be proud of. And brand new clothes for all. He's mad about you sis. He'd do anything to have you.

SULA: And when did he ask to marry me?

BROTHER: Three days ago.

SULA: And why wasn't I told?

BROTHER: I'm telling you now.

SULA: And what did dad reply to him?

BROTHER: He said he was honoured and sure that his daughter would be too. Takis will come with his mum in four days for the final arrangements.

SULA: For the ...what? In four days! *(suddenly making a decisive movement towards the door)* I'm going to be at Lenna's for a while. I'm off.

(The parents instantly get up and run towards her. They get hold of her and try to get her back in the room. SULA resists at first but then gives in. They make her sit on a chair and all three circle around her.)

MOTHER: Sit down, my daughter. We got to talk to you.

FATHER: Yes, yes. About important things.

BROTHER: I've broken the news to her.

FATHER: Well done son. I'll give you a Turkish delight later.
Listen to me my child. You know I only want what's good for me, sorry, for you I mean. Now, Takis is a good lad. He'll be a good husband and later a good father. He knows how to take care of things. Look how clean he keeps his lorries. And the one he drives himself, God Almighty, what shine, what show.

BROTHER: Fancy sis. You can ride to Europe with him and come and visit me when I study. The truth of the matter is you have no dowry. You have no hope. You'll end up a spinster selling socks like dad. You can't get any lower than that.

MOTHER: Why don't you shut your mouth and show some respect for your father? What's wrong with selling socks?

BROTHER: *(mockingly)* Nothing. It's a noble occupation.

MOTHER: That's right. It's better than sitting around cafes all day, killing flies. Or leaning against walls all night, whistling at the girls.

SULA: Leave him alone mum. He'll grow up.

MOTHER: When? He's only a year younger than you and look at him. You'd think he was still eleven the way he goes on. Huh! You upset me now and I've lost my thread.

BROTHER: You weren't saying nothing.

132

MOTHER: I was thinking it.
Listen to me Sula. Listen to your mother. Your mother's heart bleeds for you and she does what she does because she knows what it is to be a woman. And that's all to do with getting married and having kids. This is a woman's destiny, her purpose in life. But should she accept any old fool? No! She should be choosy. Pick someone good and strong and healthy who will provide for her and her kids. And this is what I want to tell you. Good men are hard to come by. Look at this miserable sock-seller I ended up with. All yellow and wasted, ugly like a curse. But looks aren't important. Who cares about appearance when what's inside is rich and hard-working? And this lad, Takis, never does anything but work. What a good husband he'll make! And he wants you! No dowry, nothing. What luck has struck us. You should be on your knees praying to God and thanking him.

(Silence. The three look at SULA expectantly who finally speaks slowly, deliberately as if talking to children.)

SULA: You're all forgetting one thing. I want to go to Drama School.

(All three laugh.)

BROTHER: Drama School! Do you know anybody from this town to ever go to a Drama School? You are funny sis.

SULA: But I'm serious. You all know I've been working for two years, making and selling ceramics just so that I could go and try my luck.

MOTHER: But your luck has come and knocked on your door, my girl. You don't have to go and look for it!

FATHER: And what luck this is! For all of us. Three trans-continental lorries! Ah, that will shut the mouths of all those clever dicks who laughed at me and pitied me. I'll parade down the square with a brand new double-vested suit, smoking a cigar and they won't dare to even spit in front of me. Ahah! Justice at last. My son-in-law with three lorries to his name and my son at University in Europe. They'll all go green with envy and beat their daughters for not getting there first.

BROTHER: And I'll be an engineer and then I'll come back and build bridges and new roads and turn this town into something to be proud of. People will admire me and then they'll vote for me when I stand for Mayor.

MOTHER: And I'll have a house I can invite people to and not be ashamed of. And I'll buy new dresses and do my hair up. And for the first time in my life I'll feel like a lady. I'll walk down the streets with my head held up high. My daughter married and married to a rich man. Ah, dear God, with what good fortune you blessed us at last! I knew you'd remember us after all we've been through. Thank you, thank you for your kindness and generosity.
(She crosses herself three times)

SULA: *(in the same tone of trying to speak rationally to children or imbeciles)* But I don't even want to get married.

(All three jump as if hit by a

bomb.)

FATHER: What did I hear? It's my ears. I'm getting old.

MOTHER: It's the heat. It's too hot in here. Open the window. She needs some fresh air.

SULA: I want to be an actress.

FATHER: What? Actress? My daughter wants to become a whore? What does she mean by that?

MOTHER: Ah, young dreams! I wanted to be a singer once. I've got a voice like a canary, I do. *(She gives out a little melody.)*

BROTHER: She's only saying this to test us.

FATHER: Test what?

MOTHER: Test whether we love her enough to persevere with what is good for her, of course.

BROTHER: Test to see how strict we can be.

SULA: No, no. You're all wrong.

(SULA makes to get up from the chair but the other three jump and sit her back down again.)

BROTHER: I know. I know. You're a modern girl. You don't believe in marriage?

SULA: Well?

BROTHER: I'm a modern boy too. But I'll get married when my time comes. And you should too, when the time comes and that's now. Because you'd be crazy to say no. I'm a realist, sister, and I'll talk to you on the level. You've got to marry this guy for three good reasons.
One: It's a unique chance for you to do the most important deed in your life, to help your family rise from poverty and misery.
Two: You won't have to worry about earning a living for the rest of your life.
Three: You'll get a lot of respect from society. It's perfect. How can you refuse?

MOTHER: But she's not refusing! How could she break her mum's heart? Her mum who sacrificed her life for her. Her mum who'll surely die if her daughter doesn't accept this God-sent gift. Because who else is going to marry her without a dowry? People here are poor. Getting a dowry from their wives is often their only hope. And these days, the immigrants go and marry foreign women, shame on them. But not this one. This one's come back home to find a wife, just like he should. And my daughter is the lucky one. So, how could she refuse?

FATHER: No, she couldn't! She loves her old dad, she does, Sula. She'd want him all set-up in business and smart-dressed walking down the street with a hat on. I remember she used to tell me when she was little how sorry she felt for me slaving away the way I did and how she wished she could help. Well, she'd be all too glad to now, wouldn't she? No, she couldn't refuse.

(SULA has gone very silent. She seems to be in deep conflict. She recites something from 'Iphigenia in Tauris.')

SULA: Friends, here's another truth which I have just perceived. The

134

unfortunate, meeting those still more unfortunate, think of their own hard fate and feel no sympathy.

(They all stare at her, then at each other. They signal to each other and gather at the end of the stage in a conspiratorial circle, a tight cluster.)

FATHER: You don't think she is... *(makes a gesture to say she is going mad.)*

BROTHER: Yep. I think she is losing her marbles.

MOTHER: Oh, my poor girl. Oh, my poor girl, crackers. *(She crosses her hands in despair.)*

FATHER: *(full of self-important paternalism)* Crackers or not, she's family. We should take care of her.

(They look at each other, nodding frantically, then focus on SULA again. Just then, a woman walks in and stands behind and above SULA's left shoulder. She looks like SULA as much as possible, at least in body shape and stance, wears black long clothes and a black scarf wrapped around her head which hides most of her face. Or she could be wearing a mask. She is SHADOW. From here to just before the end of the play she is situated behind SULA's shoulder hovering/ hissing/ standing still and hard/ running in and out/ talking confidently and wisely but harshly/ semi-circling SULA from the back and to the left side; depending on what else is happening)

SHADOW: Damned be the meek! How inert and pathetic you look. Bowing your head to fate like a lamb to the slaughter.

SULA: What else can I do? It's my duty. I'm the only one who can change these poor creatures' bad fate.

SHADOW: Who the hell do you think you are? Jesus Christ?

SULA: But who else will save them? If I desert them, that will be the end of them.

SHADOW: So what? Turn your back on them.

SULA: But how could I? They're my family.

SHADOW: They're nothing but squabbly rats. Let them tear each other to pieces. Let them sink in the sewer. Let them run around in circles, caught in their own traps.

(In the meantime the cluster of MOTHER, FATHER AND BROTHER is twitching about very nervously.)

FATHER: I can hear two voices.

MOTHER: Me too. But I don't see anybody else there.

FATHER: Neither do I.

BROTHER: She is bewitching us. She wants to drive us insane and have us all locked away. Then she'll be free to go.

MOTHER: *(full of conviction)* She wouldn't do that to her mother! *(Pause. Then in horror)* Would she?

FATHER: She wouldn't turn her back on her father, would she?

BROTHER: Let's tie her up. Then she'll have to stay and see sense.

135

(The other two look at each other in doubt at first, then they nod emphatically. They start tiptoeing behind SULA who is lost in her thoughts and pounce on her. The BROTHER runs to the other room and brings some rope. They tie her up. SULA jumps at first, struggles for a while and finally resigns to it, in disbelief. The other three all tiptoe backwards and then run out of the room.)

SCENE TWO:

SULA is still tied up in the chair. She's got a blanket over her body. LENNA, her friend, comes running in, full of anxiety. She doesn't seem to notice that SULA is tied up.

LENNA: Has your brother gone mad? He came around and I couldn't make out heads or tails from him. All he kept saying was how could Sula be so heartless and selfish to abandon us like this. He was crying like a baby. I didn't know what to do.

SULA: You should have given him a dummy.

LENNA: Well? Is it true? Are you leaving us?

SULA: Yes. I'm off. Off and as far away as possible. To a foreign country.

LENNA: Ah, now this is madness. Emigrating! *(horrified)* A young woman alone! You just can't do that. You mustn't! You'll land in terrible trouble. You'll be murdered, you'll kill yourself, you'll end up in an asylum or become a prostitute or a junkie.

SULA: But you know how careful I am. Don't you trust me?

LENNA: I do, I do. But it's not you. It's the big city. It just swallows you up like a whale and then you are just not there any more. You are just in this big whale's belly and you can't breathe, you can't move, you can't do a thing. So in the end you rot and you die.

SULA: And what happens here? You rot and you die in a dog's belly. I'll never get what I want here.

LENNA: And what is that?

SULA: Freedom, that's all. It's as simple as that.

LENNA: *(laughs)* Freedom! Sula, you are past twenty, you should know by now that life is nothing but an Obstacle Course. And living it is learning how to overcome them. What would you do without obstacles Sula? You'd be bored stiff. Freedom! Freedom would dull your brains away.

SULA: You already have a lot of freedom I can only dream of.

LENNA: Are you telling me that if you had what I've got you'd be happier? Educated parents, money, coming from the city?

SULA: No, but I could lay my mind on other things.

LENNA: Like what?

SULA: Like acting.

LENNA: But you can do acting here. It's ideal. You can play the good girl, the dutiful daughter, the self-sacrificing sister, the faithful wife, the abiding citizen. Need I go on? There are roles a plenty. And ample applause. And a living.

SULA: So you do know what they want me to do?

LENNA: Confirm it.

SULA: Marry me off.

LENNA: Well, well. Just as I said. Here is your chance to play all these grand life roles.

SULA: Bravo! But be serious. Don't you see I would go mad if I got married?

LENNA: You are dramatic! It's no big deal. Everyone does it. You get married, you shut everybody's mouth and then you can do what you like.

SULA: Like what?

LENNA: Like having clandestine affairs full of tormented passion, thanks to the obstacle of marriage.

SULA: Do you know what happens to a woman who commits adultery in this town?

LENNA: No, tell me.

SULA: They stand here in the middle of the square and everybody passes and slaps her in the face.

LENNA: That's bad. I wonder what's in her mind when all of this is happening. I wonder if she is still thinking of the pleasure she had and whether she'd do it again.

SULA: She probably either curses the moment she did it or wishes she lived some place else. Besides, adultery is not my idea of freedom. I just want to get out of here.

LENNA: Where would you go that was better?

SULA: England. It's the place for me. Everything there is so much freer than here.

LENNA: Ah, but people there are so cold and unfriendly I hear. Very uptight and suffering from a massive superiority complex. They'll treat you with contempt or even worse, ignore you completely. Oh, you'll be lonely.

SULA: I might but I'll be free. And the people there can't be any worse than these malicious gossipers over here. It's because I can't stand their gossip I never step out of the house, except to visit you. You're the only thing that makes this town bearable.

LENNA: (getting serious) Then stay for me. Don't go. England will ruin you. She will break you.

SULA: And if I stay here this backward little country of ours will.

LENNA: Don't talk like this. Anyway, now that the junta fell, things will change.

SULA: What things? Civilian dictators will replace the military ones. Besides, the changes I want are in people's heads and that will take a long time. I can't wait.

LENNA: Oh, stay with me. Stay!

SULA: (Pause) There is something about me you don't know, Lenna.

LENNA: *(faltering and looking very confused and embarrassed)* I don't know what you mean.

SULA: That's precisely it. You don't. And you are my best friend.

LENNA: But I thought we had no secrets from each other.

SULA: *(melancholically)* There are some secrets you can't even tell your best friend in this town, in this country, in this world.

LENNA: *(shifts uncomfortably)* I don't want to know. I do want to know. Oh, let's forget about secrets. The thing is, why must you go?

SULA: *(dramatically)* To search for my Ithaka.

LENNA: You picked a strange place to look for it. And what shall I do without you?

SULA: You'll soon have University and you'll forget all about me.

LENNA: I never will. I'll write to you. I'll come and see you. I'll come and get you back! *(She embraces her.)*

SULA: I'll miss you the most. You are my only regret. But I must leave. And you must help me.

LENNA: What do you want me to do?

SULA: First of all, untie these ropes.

(SULA makes the blanket slip. LENNA jumps and looks at the ropes very surprised. She starts moving towards SULA but suddenly stops and moves away.)

LENNA: Who did this?

SULA: My dear family.

LENNA: But why? *(Pause. Reflects.)* Come to think of it, I would have probably done the same.

SULA: Lenna, you're my friend, not theirs. You are my only hope!

LENNA: *(thinking fervently)* Then, you should stay!

SULA: Oh, no!

(SULA slumps her head in despair and resignation. LENNA slowly turns her head and looks at SULA. She begins to soften and walks towards her. She strokes SULA's hair and then slowly unties her. SULA jumps up full of relief and starts moving about in fast movements.)

SULA: Thank you Lenna. Now, I want you to do one more thing for me.

LENNA: What is it?

SULA: Tell my brother you've persuaded me to stay. Then go and get a night train ticket to Athens for me. Can you do this?

LENNA: Yes, yes. Alright. *(Worried but resigned to the fact that SULA is going.)* We'll never lose touch. You promise?

(They embrace and LENNA leaves. SULA makes a decisive movement as if packing a suitcase.)

SCENE THREE:

In London

(An empty space in the middle of the stage. A booth on top of which there is a neon light saying 'ALIENS'. Behind it stands an OFFICIAL wearing an exaggerated Suit. He is making mechanical, repetitive movements of checking passports, looking people up and down and letting them in or turning them away.
SULA is queuing in a very long queue. This doesn't seem to bother her. She looks very excited, full of enthusiasm and is beaming. Every now and then she picks up her suitcase and shuffles along as the queue moves very slowly. Eventually she reaches the OFFICIAL. She smiles at him but is met with a cold stare. He is an Automaton at first and changes into nauseating familiarity at the end.)

OFFICIAL: Passport please.

(She hands it over. He peruses it, then examines her, unnerving her. Puts the passport aside.)

OFFICIAL: Money please.

SULA: Money?

OFFICIAL: Yes, that's right. How much money have you got?

(SULA tries to smile but her smile freezes on her face when she sees the OFFICIAL's expression.)

OFFICIAL: Your purse please.

(She reluctantly hands over her purse. The OFFICIAL grabs it, goes through it, empties it, picks up a single £10 note and looks at her with a sneer. Puts it aside.)

OFFICIAL: Suitcase.

SULA: Suitcase?

OFFICIAL: Yes, my dear. Suitcase. Hand it over.

(SULA slides it along, totally uncomprehending. The OFFICIAL goes through it, picking up various items, examining them and then throwing them back. At the same time looking SULA up and down with a permanent sneer. She looks very embarrassed and offended. He pushes the suitcase aside with contempt.)

OFFICIAL: Purpose of visit?

SULA: Many reasons really.

OFFICIAL: Tourism? Work? Study?

SULA: Study. Study and work.

OFFICIAL: You can either study or work, you can't do both.

SULA: *(mistaking this as a doubt of her abilities)* Oh, no. I can. I know I can. I'm sure I can. I can study in the day and work in the evening or the other way around.

OFFICIAL: When I say you can't, I mean it's not allowed, it's illegal.

SULA: *(very puzzled)* You mean it's illegal for people in this country to both work and study?

OFFICIAL: *(smugly)* For people here, no, but for you, yes!

SULA: *(uncomprehending)* For me yes? But why?

OFFICIAL: *(becoming very impatient)*. I haven't got all day, you know. In there.

SULA: What for?

OFFICIAL: *(indifferently)* To be searched, just a routine matter. In there now please.

(SULA doesn't move. SHADOW runs in.)

SHADOW: Kick him in the balls!

SULA: He'll send me back!

SHADOW: Spit at him!

SULA: He'll have me arrested!

SHADOW: Scream at him!

SULA: My voice has gone!

(SHADOW exits.)

OFFICIAL: You said something?

SULA: No, nothing.

OFFICIAL: *(as if talking to a dimwit)* Now, go in there my dear and do as you are told. There is nothing to be afraid of. In there please.

(SULA still doesn't move. He gets off the booth, grabs her and pushes her as if a dummy). In there now please.

(Quick change of light and SULA is back looking very distressed.)

OFFICIAL: *(complete change of tone)* Now my dear. What shall we do with you? Let me think. Oh, yes. We could let you in for a while to do some of our shit jobs. *(checking himself)* I beg your pardon. I mean some of our essential, socially useful jobs in industries that would crumble without you foreigners. Yes! I mean what other sucker would work for next to nothing in jobs that nobody wants? I do beg your pardon. What I really mean is that these are very demanding jobs that require a particular kind of skill found amongst people like you. There! *(he smiles satisfied)* I'll be generous. I'll give you one month's visa.

SULA: *(almost desperate)* But one month isn't enough!

OFFICIAL: Plenty of time. Plenty of time. And count yourself lucky. Were your skin a little darker I'd have sent you back where you came from. Ha, ha, ha, *(he grabs SULA and draws her close to him to tell her a secret in a conspiratorial tone).* Only an hour ago *(chest swells)* I had this Paki girl here getting all dignified with me and telling me she is married just so as to sneak into the country. Now, I know a virgin when I see one. *(salivating lecherously).* Ha. So, in there we took her and checked her good we did. I watched, making sure there were no tricks. Getting proud with me, the little whore. You should have seen her face then! I showed her who's on top around here. *(he violently pushes SULA back again).* Now, off you go my dear. And remember, the first thing you do is report yourself to the ALIENS' Police. Off you go now, and I'll be watching you, watching you good.

(SULA walks away, dragging her suitcase, head and shoulders bent. She goes around a few circles, puts down her suitcase, looks around, admires London, livens up. Then a physical enactment of her first three years in London doing menial, repetitive cleaning and serving jobs, also showing the

sexual harassment and humiliation that comes with them. Metallic music sounds should accompany her movements. The OFFICIAL stands around in various pompous poses and watches her approvingly and full of self-satisfaction. SULA's body language becomes gradually harder.)

ACT TWO

SCENE ONE:

A smart living room and bedroom with velvets, silks, laces and mirrors.

(Three years later, SULA is obviously older. She is hardened, less idealistic. She is being interviewed for an au-pair/maid job by DEBORA SPENCER, her prospective employer. Both women examine each other while the other isn't looking. There is an erotic charge between them, increasing as the scene progresses.)

DEB: Well Sula, tell me a few things about yourself.

SULA: What would you like to know? *(nervous laugh)*

DEB: How old are you?

SULA: I will be twenty-three in March.

DEB: *(wistfully)* Such a young thing. *(change of tone)* Now! I don't like formalities at all. I don't really want this to be an interview as such... but more of an introduction to each other. I'll tell you things about me and you about yourself and we'll see if we suit each other. Agree?

SULA: I do.

DEB: I'll start. Shall I? I'm a classical pianist. I go on tours a lot, so I'm not actually in the house that much. There are no children to look after, I live here on my own. They did say that to you at the agency I hope.

SULA: Yes they did.

DEB: And you don't mind?

SULA: No, not at all. I am relieved. *(Both laugh)*

DEB: Good! And what about you? Where do you come from?

SULA: I come from Egypt but I'm Greek.

DEB: Oh, that's interesting. How come?

SULA: It's a long story.

DEB: I love stories. Do tell me.

SULA: *(dreamily)* Well... My father was a merchant seaman you see, trading in silk. His travels often took him to the Middle East and Egypt in particular. One summer he found himself in Alexandria. A fortune-teller had told him to stop working for three whole days because something important was going to happen to him. The third night of the third day had come and nothing had happened. So he went to one of Alexandria's many bars to while the hours away. It was very smoky and very noisy. Suddenly, all sound stopped and on the stage appeared a dark woman of mesmeric beauty, singing the most plaintive of songs. That was my mother. An Egyptian by birth and a Greek by origin. My father gave up everything, just to be with her. They got married and settled in Alexandria which is where I was born. We went back to Greece when I was eleven.

DEB: Fascinating! I also have a mixed background. My parents were both Hungarian but they disappeared mysteriously in one of their travels to Bulgaria, when I was seven. No trace of them was ever found. I was adopted by an English diplomat, a close friend of my mother's. She brought me to London, put me in a school, found me a guardian, settled my finances and off she went again. So why did you come to England?

SULA: I didn't want to get married.

DEB: *(pleased)* Don't you believe in marriage?

SULA: I'm not cut out for it. *(getting bolder)* How about you? Have you ever been married?

DEB: No, never. I'm not cut out for it either. *(Both laugh)*

DEB: Have you been here long?

SULA: Three years.

DEB: And what have you been doing all this time?

SULA: Working, working and working.

DEB: Nothing else? I mean, don't you have any interests?

SULA: I've been a dedicated member of an amateur theatre company.

DEB: *(full of interest)* Do you act?

SULA: *(full of self-deprecation)* Yes,

it's a hobby I have. A passionate hobby, let's say.

DEB: *(enthusiastically)* Oh, I have a theatre director friend. Her name's Louise. She's away now. You must meet her. *(checking herself).* Well, if everything goes well that is and we both like each other and you take the job. Shall I fill you in on your duties here? See if they're acceptable to you?

(SULA agrees)

DEB: First of all I'd like to say that I don't want a formal employer and employee situation. I want us to be like friends; to have conversations and dinners together and perhaps also go out sometimes. That's it, if you agree of course. *(tentatively)* And if you're not very busy with your friends.

SULA: I haven't really got any friends here.

DEB: *(relieved)* Oh! Well in that case, there should be no problem. *(Pause)* I could perhaps teach you the piano if you're interested?

SULA: Thank you very much but I'm not... *(Pause)* I'd love to hear you play it though.

DEB: I'd love to play it for you. Especially Bach. Are you familiar with his music?

SULA: No, not really.

DEB: It doesn't matter. You definitely will be if you stay here... As I said earlier, I live alone. I don't see many people. I am not a very sociable person. You could have the basement flat to yourself and the rest of the house too when I am not here, if you wish. You could certainly use this living room whenever you like.

(SULA looks pleased)

DEB: What I would like you to do is hoover, dust and polish the furniture. Keep the house clean whether I am here or not. And when I am here *(tentatively)* I would like you to serve me breakfast and lunch in bed.

(DEB checks SULA's response. SULA is a little surprised but intrigued.)

DEB: You won't even have to prepare it. I will get up, prepare it and go back to bed. I would simply like you to come in, open the curtains, bring the tray to me and say : "Good morning Debora, how are you today?". I would then like you to sit and talk with me while I have my breakfast. When I finish I want you to get my bath ready and be around to hand me over the towels and bathrobe. That's all. How does this sound to you? Difficult? Eccentric?

SULA: No, no. It's fine.

DEB: I should add one more thing: I have a habit of waking up at nine in the morning. I have breakfast, a bath, go for a long walk, practice and then go back to bed until midday. I then want my lunch and another bath and I would like you to repeat the morning duties. You will then be free for the rest of the day. How does this sound? Hard?

SULA: Sounds good. Not hard, not hard at all.

DEB: Well, what do you say? Would you like to work for me?

SULA: Yes, I would.

DEB: Good! And please, call me Debora.

SCENE TWO:

DEBORA's bedroom

(SULA is lying in bed. DEBORA walks in with a tray in her hands wearing a maid's uniform. She carefully places the tray next to SULA, draws the curtains and returns.)

DEB: Good morning madam. It's a lovely day today.

SULA: Oh, good morning Debora. You are up early. Are you going out?

DEB: With your permission madam, yes. I have some business to attend to.

SULA: Business? You? Would you care to tell me about it?

DEB: Please allow me to keep it a secret. I can assure you, you won't be disappointed when you find out.

SULA: Ah, a surprise!

(She sits up properly and sets to her breakfast eagerly. She nods to DEB. to sit near her. They are playfully sexual with each other and SULA occasionally feeds DEBORA. SULA suddenly puts aside her breakfast and gets up.)

SULA: Time to begin the day's work. Debora!

(DEBORA dashes across the room alarmed.)

SULA: You have no grace Debora. Go back and answer my call like a well trained maid.

(DEBORA repeats the movements slowly and with self-control.)

SULA: *(Arrogantly)* That's better, much better. Have you prepared my props for today's rehearsal?

DEB: I have indeed.

SULA: And have you typed out my lines carefully?

DEB: Very carefully.

SULA: Good! Have you found me an agent?

(DEBORA blushes and begins to tremble.)

DEB: I'm.. I'm terribly sorry madam. I... I haven't been able to. I... have been busy.

(SULA becomes very strict and stern)

SULA: Busy? Did I hear you say busy? My maid is too busy to look for an agent for her mistress? *(indignantly)* What about that? *(slowly and gravely)* This is a grave error. A serious slip...

DEB: I apologise humbly madam... It was just that your friend, Miss Spencer, the pianist, demanded some of my time and I couldn't refuse her.

SULA: Miss Spencer has no right to interfere with my maid and my time. In the future you will simply have to learn to say no to her. You belong to me Debora, not to Miss Spencer. You understand?

DEB: I do indeed madam. Please forgive me.

SULA: I appreciate your modesty and your readiness to see your faults. I forgive you. But now it's time for my bath. You have run it, haven't you?

DEB: Oh, no! I'm terribly sorry. I was just about to, Sula.

SULA: Sula? We are getting familiar, aren't we? Not only are we becoming lax in our duties but we are forgetting our position. If this misconduct happens again, I shall have no choice but to dismiss you.

DEB: *(panic-stricken)* Oh, no! Please don't do that Sula. I beg your pardon, madam. I promise, I absolutely promise this will never happen again.

(DEBORA bows and goes to run the bath. SULA smiles and sits in front of the mirror dreamily. DEBORA returns.)

DEB: Your bath will be ready in two minutes, madam.

SULA: Come and comb my hair now.

(DEBORA obeys. SULA turns around, they embrace and kiss passionately. A very quick change of light and DEBORA takes off her apron. They are both sitting up against the bed.)

SULA: You know Debora, you make me feel free. I feel I can be whoever I like with you and still be accepted. That's rare.

DEB: Perhaps that's what love is.

SULA: Yes, yes that's it. You make me feel loved.

DEB: *(laughing)* Don't sound so surprised. After all, we are lovers! And what sort of lovers would we be if we didn't make each other feel loved?

SULA: The sort that uses and abuses each other. And that means everybody.

DEB: Such a young woman, such cynical views!

SULA: Sometimes I think that people keep their worst malice and viciousness for their lovers. Have you noticed?

DEB: I've had lovers who were less than pleasant to me but no, not outright vicious.

SULA: You're lucky. Or maybe you just went for very particular types, very civilized. *(Both laugh)*

DEB: Well I hope you're not planning to get vicious with me.

SULA: Who me? No. I couldn't be vicious if I tried. But I do often have dark, primitive thoughts. I'm a Barbarian, see?

(DEBORA embraces her. They are silent for a few seconds in their tenderness. Then, complete change of mood.)

DEB: Now, my lovely one, what would you like to do today?

SULA: Now, let me see. The weather is bad. So we don't want to go out.

DEB: No, we don't like it out there, do we?

SULA: No, we want to stay in. Always in, where no-one will disturb us. Where no-one will check us. Where no-one will control us.

DEB: Where we can be divinely free to do as we please.

SULA: Where we can dream and play.

DEB: Where we can be anyone we like with anyone we like.

(They embrace with joy. Freeze.)

SCENE THREE:

The living-room

(SULA is sitting down reading a letter and listening to Greek, Eastern sounding music. LENNA's voice reads out extracts from the letter.)

LENNA: In June I shall be the proud holder of a Philosophy degree. And so what, I hear you say. So you can join the thousands of jobless graduates crowding the pavements? But not me! No, never me. There is so much political work to be done. There is an upheaval going on. The junta keeps rearing its ugly head, even from behind bars. But they don't stand a chance. Their support is minimal. As for the Conversatives, they're on their way out. People are through with them. They want to change, they want socialism. Spirits are high. The movement's growing fast. I can see the beginning of a new era in our country. Aren't you dying to take part in all this? It doesn't touch me I hear you answer. But how do you manage to cut off like this? Detach yourself from such important events in the history of your country? My country's exiled me, I hear you say. Why should I care? I find your letter disturbing. You never tell me what you do. I wish you would. Have you found what you were looking for? Are you ever thinking of coming back? I very much want to come and visit you. Maybe in a year or two. I'll try my best. Please write more often. All my love to you, your

145

Lenna.

(SULA slowly sinks into melancholy. She is unaware of DEBORA walking in enthusiastically.)

DEB: Oh, there you are! *(her face drops when she sees SULA in that state. She acts a 'not again' and goes near her).* Something wrong?

SULA: No, no. I was just reading my friend Lenna's letter.

DEB: What sort of a friend is she to bring you down like this? She can't be good for you. Don't get in touch with her again!

SULA: But she's the only friend I've got.

DEB: *(With contained anger)* She puts pressure on you to go back all the time. You don't need friends like this. Stop writing to her.

SULA: But she's my only contact with home.

DEB: I thought you hated home.

SULA: I do but I can't help wanting to hear news about it.

DEB: *(dismissively)* Buy the newspaper and find out that way, Look. That home is in the past. Forget about it. It only causes you pain. Your present is here with me. I'm your home now. *(She embraces her.)*
There, that's better. Now close your eyes. I've got a surprise for you. *(She gets up and almost talking to herself she goes and changes the music)* Now, let's try something more... uplifting. *(She makes a gesture, puts on Bach and goes back to SULA.)* Open your hands.

(She puts a small box in SULA'S hands who now looks very excited; she loves gifts and eagerly opens it. She gives out a cry and lifts a small silver or gold cage with a beautiful, multi-coloured bird in it.)

SULA: It's lovely!

DEB: It's to celebrate a special event.

SULA: What?

DEB: A year and a half since we met.

SULA: Oh, Debora, you're spoiling me. *(She begins to cry)*

DEB: Sula, Sula, my little one. What's the matter?

SULA: I don't know what's wrong with me. I feel lost.

DEB: Lost? Lost where?

SULA: Lost in this house. Lost in my head. Lost.

DEB: *(uncomprehending)* What have you lost?

SULA: I don't know if it's a case of what I've lost or what I haven't found. I just feel like I'm nowhere.

DEB: *(pained and puzzled)* How can you call this nowhere?

SULA: This? What?

DEB: This. *(She embraces the whole room with a gesture. Then almost desperate).* This, here, everything. You, me, our love, this house. What do you call this?

SULA: (seems upset at seeing DEBORA desperate and makes a move towards her to comfort her. She then changes her mind and becomes very playful and sexual) I call this... Let me think. I call this a lost little girl without a mummy.

DEB: (DEBORA sighs with relief, smiles and begins to think intensely) But you are not as little as you feel. How old are you?

SULA: I'm sixteen. But my mummy left me when I was six.

DEB: Oh, and where did she go?

SULA: She came here to Paris. That's why I'm here now. I've come to look for her.

DEB: In a theatre café?

(They both move simultaneously and sit as if in a café.)

SULA: You see my mother is an actress. She left me and my daddy because we stood in the way of her career.

DEB: And what makes you think she'll want to see you now?

SULA: I heard she wants her little girl back very badly.

DEB: I had a little girl once. But my husband kidnapped her from me, leaving me a note saying I wasn't fit to be a mother. I lost all trace of them. What's your name?

SULA: Sophie. I was called something else when I was little but daddy changed it. What do you do?

DEB: I'm a playwright.

SULA: (excited) Oh, really? I want to be an actress. Like my mother. She's very beautiful you know.

DEB: This coffeehouse is very smoky. Would you like to go someplace else?

SULA: I'd love to. But where?

DEB: We could go to my house. I only live two blocks away.

SULA: Yes, yes. And you could show me some of your plays and I could act them out and you could tell me how I was doing.

DEB: Why not? That could be fun.

(They get up from the tables, walk out of the cafeteria, down the street and into DEBORA'S apartment).

SULA: Oh, I do love your place. All these velvets, silks and laces. And your mirrors. Ah! (She looks coquettishly into one of the mirrors, draping herself with a cloth of velvet).

DEB: (very radiant) You can come and play here whenever you like.

SULA: Will you write scripts for me?

DEB: It would be my pleasure.

SULA: And I'll become a great actress?

DEB: Great as great can be.

SULA: And will you, will you let me lean on you?

DEB: You can lean on me, lie with me, live with me.

(SULA whirls around happily and

falls into DEBORA's arms.)

SULA: *(in a whisper)* Mother!

(A magical moment. Very sensuous. They begin to kiss.)

SCENE FOUR:

The living-room

(SULA is on the floor writing furiously. DEBORA walks in, looking at her full of curiosity. SULA is unaware of her presence. When she sees her standing above her she starts and tries to hide what she has been writing.)

DEB: What are you doing?

SULA: Nothing.

DEB: What you were doing just now, Sula, didn't look like nothing.

SULA: Oh, I was just scribbling away.

DEB: *(suspiciously)* To whom?

SULA: *(surprised)* No-one.

DEB: You mean you were writing to nobody?

SULA: *(innocently)* Yes, why? Is that so strange?

DEB: *(Becoming vexed. Feeling fooled).* What's the point of writing if you aren't writing to somebody?

SULA: You could be writing to yourself.

DEB: That's ridiculous. Why would anybody want to write to themselves? Surely they can bypass the mail and speak to themselves directly?

SULA: Perhaps writing's easier than speaking for some.

DEB: Ah. Well, can I see it?

SULA: *(going very shy and embarrassed)* I'd rather you didn't.

DEB: *(affronted)* But surely we have no secrets from each other!

SULA: It's not really a secret. It's just something I'd rather keep to myself.

DEB: *(becoming agitated but trying to control it)* But you can't! Let me have a look.

SULA: No!

DEB: *(play-fighting and grabbing it off SULA's hands and reading it)* Well, well. Is this what all the fuss was about? *(With a slight mocking in her voice).*

SULA: *(extremely embarrassed).* It's just a try. Please, give it back to me.

(DEBORA hands it back mockingly)

SULA: I wanted to act my own lines. I thought it would give me more confidence. I was going to show it to Louise to get her professional opinion. She said she'd be glad to read it.

DEB: *(becoming very suspicious).* And why wasn't I informed about these grand plans? Has Louise been using her theatre work to seduce you behind my back?

SULA: Debora! Louise is your best friend. Don't you trust her?

DEB: (seems beside herself with jealousy). For once in my life I find the woman I want and everybody tries to snatch her away from me. Best friend. Ha! (Thinks. Calms down.) Yes, I'm sorry my love. You really want to become an actress, don't you? I am sorry, I neglected your dream my little one. I was wrong. I've got my piano, you'll have your acting. Yes, you will.

SULA: (very excited) You'll help me get into a Drama School?

DEB: Drama School? What do you want to go there for?

SULA: I need professional training.

DEB: That's exactly what I have in mind. I'll pay for a private tutor to come here, to you!

SULA: (somewhat disappointed) Oh, thank you Debora.

DEB: You don't sound very excited.

SULA: It's just that all I ever hear is Bach.

DEB: I'll devise a whole new repertoire for you. How's that?

SULA: That would be lovely. But... (she begins to tear her draft in shreds absent-mindedly) I need to see some other people. I want to go out into the world again.

DEB: Whatever for? It's so ugly out there. Full of harsh metal, steel and concrete. But here? A world of satin, velvet and lace that you adore, you adore, remember?

SULA: How can I forget? I'm sorry, I just feel all... alone.

DEB: But I'm here nearly all the time. How can you feel alone? You're with me! I've stopped touring to spend more time with you. I've limited my London concerts to the absolute minimum. I've turned down offer after offer. I've even stopped practicing as much as I used to. But if you want me to limit what's left, I will.

SULA: Oh, Debora would you? I just feel all shivery and shaky when I'm alone. I can't stand it. I become convinced I suffer from a terminal disease, and I've been banished to isolation for punishment. I can't move, I can't breathe, I think I'm going to die. I'm taken over by little demons tearing my guts to pieces and laughing, laughing, laughing.

DEB: Sula, Sula. Why didn't you tell me before? Maybe you should see a psychotherapist.

SULA: (jumping with sudden vigour) No! I want you. Here with me, day and night. Never leaving me for a second.

(She clings to DEBORA desperately, who strokes her bewildered).

Ah, I feel better already. That's it, gone. Everything's gone. I'm free now. Free and happy. Here with you. All to myself. Oh, Debora can I ask you one last big favour?

DEB: (overwhelmed) Anything!

SULA: Could you stop playing the piano?

DEB: But why? Oh, Sula please. Anything but that!

SULA: But Debora listen! So far you've had your piano and me. And I've had nothing but you. But now I could have acting and you and you could have nothing but me. Celestial equality. This will be

149

the proof of your love for me, Debora. Total sacrifice!

DEB: No, no! This I can't do.

SULA: *(decisively)* Then you don't love me. *(Sulks. Body slumps. Head hangs down.)*

DEB: Please, Sula. Ask me something else.

SULA: Nothing would make me happier than this.

DEB: *(in turmoil)* Are you sure?

(SULA on seeing that DEBORA is considering it, jumps up and gets almost manic, eyes burning, very intense.)

SULA: Do this Debora and I will be yours forever!

DEB: You promise me no more depressions?

SULA: Yes, yes!

DEB: Total surrender?

SULA: Total as total can be.

DEB: Very well. So be it!

(SULA gets ready to run to DEBORA with outstretched arms, full of joy, while DEBORA stretches her hands to welcome her but both freeze half way through).

SCENE FIVE:

The living-room

(SULA looks as if she is going towards the left of the stage. DEBORA enters from the right, walks behind her and covers SULA's eyes with her hands. SULA starts and brings her hands to DEBORA's hands. They stay like this. The whole encounter between them is playful with impending danger.)*

SULA: Oh, it's you.

DEB: Of course it's me. Who else could it be?

SULA: No-one.

DEB: No-one naturally. And where were you going, may I ask?

SULA: *(casually)* For a walk.

DEB: Without me?

SULA: Would that be so bad?

DEB: Bad? Bad is not the word. It would be unprecedented. *(Pause)* We aren't rebelling are we?

SULA: Why would we do that?

DEB: Because we're restless? Because we want to hurt someone? Because we crave attention?

(SULA denies all three by turn.)

DEB: Perhaps we want to cause a reaction.

SULA: What sort of reaction?

DEB: A reaction that says "You're stepping out of line, girl. You need some discipline and failing that some punishment".

SULA: What are we? Some sort of Judge or Jailer?

DEB: No, no. We want no judges around. A jailer yes, that's

different. But a Jailer cannot exist without a prisoner. Therefore we are both.

SULA: *(whispers)* Both. A Jailer and a Prisoner. *(She turns around to kiss DEBORA. DEBORA holds her off, pulls SULA's hands behind her back and holds them there.)*

DEB: Trust me?

SULA: With my life.

DEB: Close your eyes and don't move.

(DEBORA gets some silk scarves, comes back and ties SULA's hands behind her back.)

SULA: *(laughing)* What are you doing?

(DEBORA reassures her smiling. She then takes SULA and makes her sit on a chair. She ties her ankles to it. SULA is completely willing. DEBORA blindfolds her, stands in front of her, full of satisfaction, smiles and tiptoes out the door.)

SULA: *(playfully)* Debora? Where are you? Deb! Are you hiding? I can't come and look for you! *(anxious)* Where are you? *(more and more anxious)* Debora! Oh, where are you? *(she slumps)* She's gone! *(full of despair)* How could she? I trusted her! This is not fair, not fair at all. *(almost shouting).* It's not fair!

(LOUISE walks in all chirpy.)

LOUISE: What's not fair? What are you shouting about?

SULA: Oh, Louise!

LOUISE: How're you princess?

SULA: *(with a mixture of anger and shame)* I'm... I'm not well.

LOUISE: Oh, what's wrong?

SULA: Well, nothing specific really. Just an overall feeling of being tied down.

LOUISE: So you are. Who did this?

SULA: Debora. She was only playing.

LOUISE: Well, shall I untie you or leave that to her?

SULA: Oh, no. You do it. My hands and feet really hurt.

(LOUISE unties her, looking bemused. SULA shakes her feet and hands but stays in the chair.)

LOUISE: There you are. A free woman!

SULA: That I'm not.

LOUISE: Oh? And who is?

SULA: You are.

LOUISE: And you're not?

SULA: *(dramatically)* I'm a prisoner of love.

LOUISE: Count yourself lucky.

SULA: But you're all work, travel, and adventure! I wish I were like you.

LOUISE: Like me? It wouldn't suit you. You need a home, a loyal lover. I think you and Debora are really well suited. It gives me comfort to see you together. You make me feel I've got a family.

SULA: A family! I hate families! I ran two thousand miles to escape mine.

LOUSIE: Let's stop talking about problems shall we. It's not my forte. Listen, I've got a small part for you.

SULA: Seriously?

LOUISE: Yes! That's why I came.

SULA: Louise, you're great, and what's the part?

LOUISE: You'll play the maid of an old, eccentric lady. You'll be good at it.

(SULA's face drops and she sits down again. LOUISE ignores this.)

LOUISE: We're starting rehearsals in seven days. Here's your script. *(She throws it on SULA's lap.)*

SULA: *(flatly)* Thanks.

LOUISE: You're welcome. Now, lift that long face of yours and get to work. I don't know what your problem is but work is your answer. I've got to go now. Ring me on Monday. Ciao bella and get reading!

(LOUISE exits. SULA picks up the script, rolls it up, thinks for a while, then sticks it in a vase and goes to look for DEBORA.)

SULA: *(all softened up)* Deb! Where are you? *(playfully)* Come out or I'll come and get you!

(SHADOW enters.)

SHADOW: This is the end, don't you see?

SULA: *(panic-stricken)* The end? The end of what?

SHADOW: Of you and her of course.

SULA: No way! This is just a bad patch. This love will never end. She's my lifeline. She gives me all I want. She is me and I am her. We are one.

SHADOW: What useless deceptions, fit for brains that don't dare to think.

SULA: Debora! Please come out!

SHADOW: Don't waste your breath. She's gone out.

SULA: But why?

SHADOW: Just to prove what a worthless little object you are. To be used and discarded at her pleasure. You must make her pay for this. Make her regret it bitterly. Make her crumble. Make her beg for forgiveness she'll never get. You must leave her. Now!

SULA: What? Leave without even saying goodbye? It would kill her.

SHADOW: So much the better.

SULA: But what shall I do without her? And who can I be without her? And how can I live without her? *(SULA is in turmoil.)*

SHADOW: Hurry! Hurry!

(SULA picks up the script, a couple of scarves, lifts them to her cheeks tenderly, hesitates.)

SHADOW: Run!

(SULA begins to pack feverishly. SHADOW gives out a horrible, sardonic laugh.)

ACT THREE

SCENE ONE:

A cell-like bed-sit. On the floor are drawn a circle and a linear line. Stage is dark. Lights only on the person/s speaking.

(SULA walks a semi-circle, stops, goes back. Draws over it very deliberately with the chalk and walks back on it balancing very carefully. Repeats in the opposite direction. All this she does very ritualistically. She then suddenly jumps on the line very energetically. Stops and turns to the audience.)

SULA: I'm free at last. For the first time in my life I'm free. I don't have to do anything, please anybody, work at anything. No one can catch me, pin me down, put me in a little box. No, no. I'm free. Free like nothing. What can be freer than nothing? Happier and lighter than nothing? Ah, that's what I've reached: a superior plane of being. Don't you envy me? I'm only twenty seven and I've already found my Ithaka, my Land of Dreams. It's right here, in this very room. All I have to do is stare at this wall and... magic! Anything can happen!
(conspiratorially) I'll tell you a secret. I have a kingdom. I am a Queen. A Queen, with dutiful subjects. I'd love to show them to you, but they only come when I'm on my own, you see. They come and fill the room, these strange half-human, half-animal creatures strutting around, lying about, sitting up straight, drinking the nectar of the Gods and talking in a hundred languages. And we form circles, we dance, we sing and we pray. And it's just heaven. *(she roars with laughter)* I'll tell you something else. You should try and stay awake nights on end. The things you'll see and hear. You'll never want to sleep again. *(Pause)*
So, here I am in this Wonderland where nothing can hold you back because you are nothing yourself. Nothing and everything at once. So I'm free and happy. Happy happy, so happy.

(SHADOW enters)

SHADOW: Happy to be a coward and free to run from one safe, little hole to the other. You're a long distance runner on an endless marathon, that's all you are. Somebody pulls the trigger and off you go. Always reacting, never acting. Always running.

SULA: *(she slumps on the floor)* Happy? Who's happy? Only fools are happy. I don't want to be happy anyway.

SHADOW: You can't even think. You just hover around in circles or hop along to and fro, to and fro. You plunge ahead blindly or plod along sheepishly. You have no idea of the simple facts of mean and measure. You just sit, stand or lie there all siezed up inside. You're not even dead. You can't even get it together to commit suicide. You just rot here instead. You rot and you stink. You stink do you hear?

(SULA gets up mechanically and starts obsessively to tidy up the room and to draw and redraw the circle and the line.)

SHADOW: To and fro, to and fro.

(SULA stands dead still and terrified for a few seconds, then turns to the audience apologetically

and conspiratorially. SHADOW withdraws.)

SULA: The people you end up with sometimes. Fancy, me, being stuck in here with her! She never leaves me a moment's peace. She goes on and on and on. Always telling me unpleasant things. Scary things. She has no respect for my feelings at all. I don't even know who she is. And she won't go. What would you do in my place? I ask you. She follows me everywhere. And it's very embarassing to have someone like her around when you go out. Truth be told, she is the main reason I avoid going out. She has no idea how to behave in public. She insults everybody and gets me into trouble. So I stay in. *(Silence.)* *(Then suddenly she decides to go out towards the right and sees LENNA rushing towards her excitedly. They embrace and whirl around.)*

SULA: Lenna! You are manna from Heaven!

LENNA: Am I glad to see you again! Well, how's my runaway friend?

SULA: Looking for a way out of this!

LENNA: I've come just at the right moment. I've come to take you back.

SULA: *(delighted)* Back home?

LENNA: Yes, back where you belong. Away from this cold and dismal city, where people look half-dead. Where machines do their thinking for them.

SULA: Where to love means to torture. Where to be free is to live in a cell.

LENNA: To a country where there's still hope.

SULA: To a country where there's still life and laughter.

LENNA: Where people fight for change not conquest.

SULA: Where people have dreams and ideals.

(They embrace again full of exuberance.)

LENNA: This is it Sula. A noble cause to fight for and win. A chance to make history. To breathe in an air full of possibilities. To be part of a revolution. New ideas, new situations, new freedoms. To join with people in the streets. You've got to see it to believe it. Masses and masses of them, all united against the conservatives. All ready to take control of their lives.

SULA: It must be exciting!

LENNA: It's feverish. Just imagine. The whole country taking part in a massive play that the people themselves wrote. Theatre in its true meaning. You'll love it.

SULA: And will we storm the palace?

LENNA: Well no, there's no one there now, but impotent officials. This is going to be a revolution through parliament. Through the ballot. No bloodshed. Imagine! For the first time ever, the socialists in power!

SULA: We'll be heroines!

LENNA: We'll win!

(They embrace again and freeze. SHADOW enters.)

SHADOW: The triumph of compromise and sell outs. Pfu! A revolution through parliament. Ha!

You know what this means? The same old suit worn inside out. That's all. And worse. Desperate fools like you, dying for something to get hold of, will be lulled into a stupified oblivion. As for people united. Well! Heard that one before. Oh, they'll be all lovey-dovey while they fight the common enemy alright. But as soon as they win, out will come the knives especially sharpened for the back stabbing. Out will come the wagging fingers. As for her. Trust her to join a movement that will sell everybody down the drain. Does she look like a revolutionary to you? An idealist? No! All she's thinking about is a good position in the Government. And you're only part of her recruiting campaign. Socialism. Pfu! All the likes of her want is a bit of the pie for themselves. Nothing more. You lick their arse? You'll be alright. You show your teeth? Forget it. So, what's new? She's just a despicable opportunist. She got her degree, looked for a career and found one: in socialism! Ha!

SULA: (sarcastically) "And what shall we do without Barbarians? Those people were some sort of a solution". (Changes tone) So, you've been sent here to recruit me?

LENNA: No, of course not. What's got into you?

SULA: (recoiling from her friend) And I thought you were my friend.

LENNA: (looking very puzzled) But I am your friend!

SULA: Don't. Don't mention that word. I know now. I can see everything clearly.

(She covers her face in despair. LENNA goes to touch her but she shrinks back.)

SULA: Ulterior motives, hidden purposes, foul intentions.

LENNA: Sula?

(LENNA is trying once more to touch SULA and calm her down.)

SULA: Get away from me. Get away. (she begins to shiver). Go, go, get out.

(SULA pushes LENNA out. LENNA looks totally bewildered and keeps trying to comfort her but SULA is beyond herself and keeps pushing her out calling "Out, out". LENNA exits totally uncomprehending. SULA returns alone still shivering. She slowly stops shivering, composes herself, smiles and starts walking towards the opposite side of the stage. LOUISE walks in from there, full of energy.)

SULA: (Full of joy) Louise! It's so good to see you.

LOUISE: Princess! How are you?

SULA: I'm fine, fine. I was coming to visit you actually.

LOUISE: Yeah? Well, here I am and guess why?

SULA: (teasingly) To ask me to marry you.

LOUISE: Don't be silly. Try again.

SULA: Debora's sent you!

LOUISE: This girl has no idea. I'm looking for a heroine.

SULA: Oh?

155

LOUISE: A heroine, a protagonist for my new play.

SULA: And you're looking for her here? *(Looking around confused.)*

LOUISE: *(very amused goes and ruffles SULA's hair patronizingly).* I want you!

SULA: *(can't believe her luck)* You serious?

LOUISE: Under one condition. No moods and tempers with me. OK?

(SULA agrees emphatically.)

LOUISE: And I'll coach you. *(full of self-importance)* I'll shape you up, don't you worry. *(manhandles SULA in various positions)* You keep our agreement and I'll sort you out.

SULA: Oh, you must, you must. Tell me, what's the play about?

LOUISE: It's about a young Turkish woman who, after serving a long sentence escaped and emigrated here. But then she developed an obsession that she was still a prisoner. So, she locked herself in her room, nailed shut the windows, put a padlock on her door and near starved herself to death. She recovered later when a friend had the brilliant idea to pose as a Jailer and gain her confidence. It's a true story.

SULA: Do you think I'll be good?

LOUISE: You'll be ideal.

SULA: *(getting carried away)* I'll be brilliant. My time has come at last. Oh, I'll stun them! I'll have them all running after me, crying out for contracts. Begging me while I brush them aside. Louise! You're a true friend. Let me kiss your hand.

(She bends to kiss LOUISE'S hand, who is all swollen up with self-satisfaction and they freeze.)

SHADOW: Look at you, crawling up Miss Director's bum. So is this what you want to do? Be at the mercy of people like her? A Director! Did you ever ask yourself why did she choose this job? She is a powermaniac that's why. She likes to order people around. Telling them what to do and what not to do. Torturing them. Humiliating them. That's what she's doing with you. She never intends to give you a part. She's just mocking you. Or else she'll stick you into a poxy little production somewhere, prop you up on a rotten, old stage, give you a few meaningless lines to mouth that no one cares to hear and off you go. An actress. Pleased? Happy? Why don't you go and do something useful in your life? You don't even know why you want to act. What's the point of acting if you don't know what you're acting for? What a spectacle you are! What a ludicrous specimen. On your knees! If only you could see yourself in a mirror!

SULA: So you think I'll be good as a prisoner?

LOUISE: Very good indeed.

SULA: You also thought I'd be good as a maid.

LOUISE: And you were!

SULA: You like me being down and out, don't you? Makes you feel good.

156

LOUISE: How dare you!

SULA: How dare I strip your mask?

LOUISE: What?

SULA: You heard me. Take your crumbs and your power games elsewhere, Miss Director. Go!

LOUISE: *(exiting furiously)* You'll regret this Princess. But just for old times sake I give you another chance. Ring me if you change that upside down mind of yours. But not later than Sunday.

(SULA bows ceremoniously, raises her head and points to the door majestically. Then stands in the middle of the stage for a few seconds triumphant. Her expression gradually changes to one of horror and putting both her hands on her temples, she starts running out. Lights on DEBORA who stands at the exit towards which SULA is running. She is still as a ghost, very drawn, very bedraggled.)

(Shocked silence.)

SULA: Debora!

DEB: May I come in?

SULA: Of course.

(SULA takes DEBORA and makes her sit down. She strokes her almost protectively. A moment of incredible tenderness.)

SULA: The pleasures we had together...

DEBORA: The journeys we made...

SULA: How we played...

DEBORA: How we loved each other...

(Silence)

SULA: And now we're separated. *(she laughs)*

DEB: *(hurt)* And we shouldn't be.

SULA: But we can't stay together for ever!

DEB: Why not?

SULA: I need to be free.

DEB: What is freedom worth without love?

SULA: And what is love worth without freedom?

DEB: But don't you see? We need each other. We're both falling apart. I need to be with you.

SULA: And I need to be alone. You see your need is impossible to satisfy but mine is not. Besides... you got a lot.

DEB: But all I want is you.

SULA: Be appreciative! You got music, friends, money, a name.

DEB: But it's as if I have nothing without you. I can't do a thing since you left. I can't move. I'm paralysed. Half of the time I can't even wash myself.

SULA: That's disgusting.

(SULA's face, instead of softening on hearing this, is getting harder and harder.)

SULA: And what do you want here?

DEB: I came to see how you were.

SULA: And now you've seen me, you can leave.

157

DEB: Sula, you can't do this to me. Don't send me away like this. I'll... I'll... I'll kill myself. I beg you.

(DEBORA falls on her knees. SULA looking at her full of contempt, tries to make her rise but DEBORA resists.)

SULA: Get up. Have you no pride?

DEBORA: Please come back, I love you.

SULA: Love? You call this love? If you really loved me, you'd be happy with my happiness.

DEBORA: But you're dreaming. This is all a joke. Oh, please tell me it's a joke and a dream, a bad dream.

SULA: No it's not, it's real. And you should encourage me to go further. But you! What do you do? You try to draw me back to your silver cage. No thanks. Look at you *(she shoves a mirror at her)*. You really let yourself go. You look pathetic. You look like everything I despise. A drunken, whimpering slut on all fours.

DEB: Oh, take pity on me.

SULA: How can I feel pity for what repulses me?

DEBORA: Oh, but you loved me once. You were happy with me.

SULA: *(softens)* While I still had hope. But the years passed and I saw my dreams getting further and further away from me. That's why I had to leave you. To try and catch up with them.

(She hardens again and pulls away)

SULA: So, here I am. My Ithaka now is this room. And you have no place here. So leave!

(DEBORA staggers up from the floor, pulls a dagger from her coat pocket and goes to stab herself. SULA in a flash grabs it away from her. DEBORA exits. SULA stands like a statue, expressionless, holding the knife she grabbed from DEBORA. Then very abruptly she starts moving manically up and down the line. Stops.)

SULA: I've got rid of everybody at last. No-one can ever hassle me again. I've escaped all those long arms stretching out to get me and claim me as their own. What am I? A pair of socks to be used for somebody else's need?
(pauses and then looks around. She carries on in a Don Quixotish tone)
Who sent them here is what I want to know. There was one motive behind every one of those witches. To catch me, hold me and squash me into a pulp. But did they succeed? No, of course not. I'm strong, stronger than any of them. I'm free like the wind and even freer. Because nothing can stop me. Not now that I've got to where... *(slows down)* where I am?

(She slumps on the floor. She then crawls across it fatalistically and buries herself under the same material her parents were buried under. She lies as if she is dead. Her PARENTS walk in from one end of the stage, clinging on to each other for life, looking around in amazement, pointing at things and talking to each other but soundlessly. They come across SULA but don't seem to recognise her. SULA hears them, lifts her head up, rubs her eyes in disbelief, stares in shock and horror, covers

her face with her hands, looks at them again and falls back flat on her back. They walk, all across the stage, and go out the opposite way they came. SULA rises again, looks around, confirms her PARENTS are gone, sits up. She remains very still and silent for a few seconds, head bent. She then slowly raises her head. Her expression is one of utter despair)

SULA: Oh, my God. What have I done? Like a hungry hyena, I turned on the only people who give a damn about me... But why? What got into me? What happened? I don't remember. It wasn't me. It can't have been me. Maybe I dreamed it all. Maybe none of them ever came. Yes, yes that's it. Of course. Just a dream. *(shows relief, then agony)*. Or maybe they did come and I turned on them just to make myself feel better. Oh, what a lowly human I am. What a disgusting, loathsome vermin I am. A rat in a rathole. That's me. *(philosophically)* I'm scum and I'm just where I belong. In the muck.

(SHADOW enters)

SHADOW: Spitting venom at yourself will get you nowhere.

SULA: I'm only here because you pushed me and I loathe this place. *(getting hateful)* You know something? It's you. It's all your fault. Everything began with you around. *(she begins to circle SHADOW very threateningly)* I've gone from one trap to another and who led me there? You!

SHADOW: And who followed? You!

SULA: I want freedom, you understand? And all I end up with is you!

SHADOW: Freedom from what and to do what?

SULA: Freedom from constraints. *(full of menace and circling around SHADOW faster and faster)* And guess who's my biggest constraint? You! I've got to get rid of you!

(She pounces on SHADOW and goes for her throat. There is a struggle. Lights go on and off. When the lights are on again, SULA collapses on the floor exhausted. SHADOW stands unscathed and with a knowing smile. SULA is panting and sweating. She raises her head towards SHADOW and faces her for the first time.)

SULA: Why do you push me where I can't go?

SHADOW: Can't? And why not?

SULA: Because I get dizzy. I think I'm going to fall. I've been falling for a long time and I never reach the end. I just hang there. I can't pull myself up and I can't reach the bottom either. I just live in fear. It's all I feel. It's who I am. I am fear. There's nothing else.

SHADOW: Nothing else?

SULA: *(optimistically)* Is there?

SHADOW: All extremes contain within them their opposites and can easily transform into each other.

SULA: *(looks delighted, as when you have a sudden, important insight)* Who are you?

SHADOW: I'm the one you can't run away from. I'm Shadow.

SULA: Tell me what Shadow is.

SHADOW: Shadow is the edge of time, is the crack of dawn. Shadow is a depth where you can only hang suspended, never reaching the end.

Shadow is thoughts never formed in words, dreams that won't go away, poems that refuse to be moulded. Shadow is the law of desire and passion, the Realm of the Underworld, the world of misfits, outcasts and rebels. Shadow is the time when every moment reveals a new possibility. Is the darkness that defines light, the hell that heaven is marked with.

Shadow is the eyes that couldn't see, the lives that couldn't be, the chains that were never broken.

SULA: Pleased to meet you *(Shakes hands. Pauses. Turns to the audience)* And what shall we do today, my friend?

Lights down

FORCED OUT

Jean Abbott

FORCED OUT began in the summer of 1988 when we were preparing for the second *Attic Work* evening for the Women Writers' Workshop. Cheryl Robson was surprised that no-one had submitted anything to do with Clause 28, then under discussion in Parliament. As a result I wrote the last scene of the play which eventually became *Forced Out* and the scene which is now Scene Two but which was then intended as the opening scene. I started with the final scene because I had a very strong image in my mind of a woman leaving the country because her life had become intolerable, and at that stage Ros went on her own.

After a script development session and some re-writing these scenes were performed as part of *Attic Work* 1988. During the following months I wrote the rest of the play, again with the support of a script development session. In the summer of 1989 a reading of the whole play was given, directed by Anna Birch, as part of the *Attic Work* season. Further re-writing followed and early in 1990 Claire Grove read the play, encouraged me to write a radio version and decided to give this version a reading as a joint venture by the Women's Theatre Group and Women Writers' Workshop. This reading took place in May 1990 at the Oval House Theatre, in Kennington.

The script published here is a stage version which incorporates many of the dialogue changes made for the radio version, but restores some scenes such as the present Scene One, which are largely visual. The headteacher was originally male, so that the play could be performed by three actors; the change of sex gives the part more impact but entails the use of a fourth actor. Other differences from the earlier versions include constant re-working of what is now Scene Thirteen and changes to the last scene to give a more positive ending. I find a constant conflict between my wish to present positive images of lesbians and the realities which we face in our daily lives. I am appalled by the increasing narrow-mindedness I see around me.

I would like to thank all the actors and directors who have worked or commented on the script, particularly Claire Grove for her stimulating combination of encouragement and criticsm.

CHARACTERS:

ROS CROWLEY,	a schoolteacher, 30s
JAN,	a systems analyst, Ros's lover
MRS McKENDRICK,	Ros's Scottish headmistress
MR CROWLEY,	Ros's father
MAN ON BOAT	
FOOTBALL HOOLIGAN	

The male characters can all be played by one actor, but the last scene is more effective with two.

The settings should not be naturalistic.

SCENE ONE:

A disco. ROS and JAN are dancing to "I want to dance with somebody" by Whitney Houston. At first they dance energetically but they end in each other's arms. A series of coloured lights on the floor flashes on and off, throwing large jerky shadows of their dancing onto the back wall.

End of scene.

SCENE TWO:

JAN is singing while she prepares the evening meal in the kitchen of the house she shares with ROS in a London suburb.

ROS enters.

JAN: Hi.

(ROS puts a pile of exercise books on the table and a bag on the floor.)

ROS: Hi!

JAN: Watch where you put your rubbish, I need that space.

ROS: That's 4F's essay on "Twelfth Night."

JAN: Like I said, rubbish.

ROS: True. Most of them can't even spell the title.

JAN: Or the author.

(Pause)

JAN: What's the matter?

(She switches off the radio.)

ROS: Nothing, why?

JAN: You look dreadful.

ROS: I'm just tired. What's the great gastronomic delight tonight then, for which you need all this space?

JAN: Only lasagne but I need the room to dish up. You leave those books on the table and I'll probably spill sauce on them and the kids won't like that, will they? The pages all stuck together so they can't read them.

ROS: Or better still, so I can't read them! Hey, gimme that cheese sauce.

JAN: *(grabbing her)* You just leave my cheese sauce alone. I'm not having it wasted on a load of manky kids. *(she turns ROS round in her arms and kisses her.)* What's up?

ROS: They'd probably prefer cheese sauce to the filthy cat paw-marks they got last week, after Cleo had been out in the rain.

JAN: Will you stop evading the issue and tell me what's the matter?

ROS: I need a drink, that's all. Is there any of that plonk left or have you used it all to liven up the lasagne?

JAN: *(standing in front of the fridge door)* I'll let you have some wine when you tell me what's bothering you.

ROS: That's blackmail.

JAN: Yes, what are you going to do about it?

ROS: It's immoral.

JAN: So are lots of things but that doesn't stop people doing them.

ROS: It's not fair.

JAN: "But Miss, it's not fair." Will you stop lying to me!

ROS: I'm not.

JAN: You bloody well are. You don't seriously think I can't tell after all these years?

ROS: I'm sorry.

(Pause.)

JAN: Here, have a large glass of plonk and sit down.

ROS: Thanks, I.....

JAN: *(putting her arms round her)* Come on.

ROS: You know Tracey Williams?

JAN: The terror of 5E?

ROS: She handed this in today.

JAN: She did some work?

ROS: It's no joke.

(JAN takes the piece of paper and reads.)

JAN: "Did you have a nice time at the disco on Saturday night? I saw you leaving with your friend. She looks nice. You wouldn't have thought she was one of those filthy lessies. Not like you, I've always thought there was something the matter with you. Like you always wear trousers even in the summer. I watch you at the front of the class and you've got ever such small tits and short hair, just like a bloke. I've often wondered why you don't do something about it, and then when I saw you coming

out of the club with all those butch women it all fell into place."

JAN: The little sod.

ROS: That's not all. She stayed behind at the end of the lesson.

JAN: Shit.

ROS: She asked if the other staff know I'm a lesbian.

JAN: And?

ROS: Would I pay her £500 to keep quiet.

JAN: I hope you clouted her.

ROS: I want to keep my job for god's sake.

JAN: So what did you say?

ROS: I said no, so she said she'd have to go and see what the head said about it. Or she might be able to get more than £500 from a newspaper.

JAN: The little bugger.

ROS: So I said that I'd have to think about it and anyway it would take me a couple of days if I did decide to pay her.

JAN: That sounds as if you were admitting you were in the wrong.

ROS: *(angry)* What the hell was I supposed to do? I wasn't exactly thinking straight. I was shaking from shock.

JAN: I'm sorry. So she did go away?

ROS: In the end, yes, there was another class coming in. She said she'd see me again tomorrow. I set

163

the class a boring comprehension, went to the bog and threw up.

JAN: And then you went to the Head.

ROS: No.

JAN: Why ever not?

ROS: I don't know how she'd react.

JAN: She's hardly going to condone the blackmail of one of her staff by a pupil.

ROS: No, but I don't know how she'd take me being a lesbian. And I wanted to think through all the implications and discuss it with you.

JAN: Oh yeah. You refused to talk about it when you came in, remember. I had to drag it out of you.

ROS: I wanted more time to sort it out for myself first, how it might affect you, especially it if got into the press at any stage. After all, you haven't exactly proclaimed your sexuality all over the office, have you?

JAN: No.

ROS: We ought to consider the consequences if I tell the Head.

JAN: You haven't any alternative.

ROS: I don't want to discuss it with her, my sexuality's none of her business.

JAN: A fifteen year old blackmailer is her business. What else can you do, fork out the money?

ROS: If I tell Mrs McKendrick, I could lose my job.

JAN: *(thinking)* Yes.

ROS: Thanks for the support.

JAN: Can they sack you?

ROS: Probably. I don't know, it depends on the governors. Gay's a dirty word. We're not exactly encouraged to talk about lesbians in school these days, let alone turn out to be one.

JAN: I thought the authority was an equal opportunity employer.

ROS: Staff are appointed by the governors now, I don't know how far my status is protected. I should have chosen a more trendy and less respectable borough to work for.

JAN: You've been there years, look at all the time and effort you've put into the place, surely they'll give you some support. And you're in the union for god's sake.

ROS: Big deal. All the officials are men, they'd be a fat lot of use.

JAN: So don't tell the head, don't pay Tracey either. Then what? She goes to the papers? Is that what you want? I'm bloody sure I don't.

ROS: It won't get into the papers.

JAN: Oh won't it.

ROS: They're not going to believe a fifteen year old.

JAN: Who're you kidding? Probably take her mum with her, won't she? You said she's just as bad.

ROS: Worse.

JAN: There you are then. On the front page. Reporters on the doorstep. Won't take them long to find out where you live, and who with. Will it? Where does that leave me?

ROS: I don't want to put you in that situation.

JAN: You don't have any choice. You've got to tell the Head and take what happens.

ROS: Suppose Tracey gets there first?

JAN: You just make sure you see Mrs McKendrick the minute you get in. I bet Tracey's usually late.

(Pause)

ROS: I'm not sure.

JAN: You can't let the kid get away with it. What do you want for god's sake, pay the kid her five hundred? Then what happens?

ROS: She comes back next week for more.

JAN: And the week after that, and the week after that. You'd never feel safe, you'd always wonder when she'd decide she could get more from the tabloids.

ROS: I shouldn't have tried to hide it.

JAN: I'm in no position to criticise.

(Pause)

ROS: Pots and kettles.

JAN: We shouldn't have to hide, it shouldn't matter.

ROS: *(ironic)* You can't have people like me corrupting the youth of the country, encouraging them to love each other.

JAN: Instead of beating each other up.

ROS: *(ironic)* Boys will be boys.

JAN: The rough and tumble of school does them good.

ROS: Or the occasional thrashing.

JAN: It's all part of growing up.

(Pause)

ROS: I feel sick. I don't think I'm going to be able to manage any of that lasagne.

JAN: Me neither. Do you think it'll freeze? We ought to eat something if only to soak up the wine.

ROS: Suppose I get the sack?

JAN: You won't.

ROS: Even if I don't they could make things pretty unpleasant for me.

JAN: For us.

ROS: I know. I couldn't face it at all without you.

JAN: You don't need to, we'll face it together.

(They embrace.)

The coloured lights flash on as at the disco. The chorus of the song plays very quietly.

SCENE THREE:

Night-time

ROS: I am afraid. I fear the unknown knock on the door, waking us in the night. I am afraid of the men who want to tear us apart, who follow me in the street, who rape me with their eyes. I am afraid that without thinking I will hold your hand in the street and the men will turn on us and cast us out. I fear the questions I can't answer, I fear the ordinary because I can't be part of it, I fear the unusual because I might draw attention to myself. I hide like a snail under my stone but in fear lest a casual passer-by picks it up and finds me underneath or steps on it without thinking and crushes me.
(Pause)
I build walls around me with bricks made from the straw of my fear and the mud of my sweat but they blow away in the first breeze and leave me naked and exposed. I used to love the dark which I shared with you, finding you more fully through touch alone but now I daren't turn out the light for fear of what might be hiding in the dark corners.

JAN: I am afraid of losing you.

One line of the song "With Somebody who loves you".

SCENE FOUR:

The headmistress's study. Next day.

Mrs. M^cKENDRICK is Scottish.

HEAD: *(incredulous)*. A disco?

ROS: Yes.

HEAD: You went to a disco?

ROS: Yes.

HEAD: I thought it was the children who went to discos.

ROS: It's not a crime.

HEAD: No. *(Pause)*. No. *(thoughtfully)*. What was Tracey Williams doing outside a disco?

ROS: Does it matter?

HEAD: Possibly not. She just happened to be standing outside this... disco when you came out. I presume you were not alone?

ROS: There were about a hundred women coming out of the club.

HEAD: I find it strange that a lady of your years should patronise such an entertainment but I don't quite see why it should constitute grounds for blackmail.

ROS: It was a lesbian disco, Mrs McKendrick. *(Pause)* Look, do the details matter? It's not me who's committed the crime, it's Tracey.

HEAD: I must ascertain all the facts before I can decide on an appropriate course of action. Tracey Williams saw you and... a friend leaving a lesbian disco on.... Saturday night?

ROS: Yes.

HEAD: And you allege that as a result she yesterday tried to blackmail you.

ROS: Yes. Here's her note.

HEAD: I see. *(She reads it)*. It says nothing here about money.

ROS: She's not so stupid she'd give me written evidence.

HEAD: *(She starts writing).* And did she mention any particular sum?

ROS: Five hundred pounds.

HEAD: And if you fail to produce this money?

ROS: She would tell the papers.

HEAD: Well I can assure you, Miss Crowley that I am as anxious to keep this out of the papers as you are.

ROS: I don't want my private life all over the front page.

HEAD: I certainly don't want this school over the front page. We've got enough problems with falling numbers as it is, without any unwelcome incidents like this. *(Pause)* I'll see Tracey straight away and put a stop to it.

ROS: I see.

HEAD: I can't have this sort of thing getting out, I've the name of the school to think of.

ROS: But what will you do to Tracey? Blackmail is a criminal offence.

HEAD: Surely you don't want to involve the police? The tabloids would have a field day.

ROS: What's the alternative? Shut her up and do nothing? She just sits in the back of my class with a knowing grin on her face.

HEAD: I'll move her to another set, of course.

ROS: And what do you think she's likely to tell her friends?

HEAD: I'll have to make sure she doesn't tell them anything.

ROS: If I know Tracey Williams she's probably told them already. She's got one of the biggest mouths in the school.

HEAD: You think that even if we stop her going to the papers it's likely to spread round the school anyway?

ROS: It seems very likely to me.

HEAD: So that it could get out to parents and so on? We must stop that.

ROS: You could call in the police.

HEAD: Surely you don't want to go to court?

ROS: *(angry)* No of course I don't, and I'd be very reluctant to see a girl of her age face such serious charges, but the police could make her see that it was serious and give her warning, so she'd be less likely to try anything again.

HEAD: I'll think about it, Miss Crowley but I'd really rather the whole business didn't go beyond these four walls. We have to consider the effect it would have on the other children.

ROS: What effect?

HEAD: The effect it will have on them if they learn of your.... lifestyle.

ROS: What do you mean, my lifestyle?

HEAD: Well no-one had realised....

ROS: That I'm a lesbian?

HEAD: Quite.

ROS: Why should it make any difference? I've taught here for nine years, most of the pupils know me pretty well by now.

HEAD: Yes but they and indeed the staff were not aware.....

ROS: That I'm a lesbian? What difference does that make to my teaching ability? They can't take away the three grade A's my A Level set got last year, can they? If that's how you measure success. Or the fact that my bottom set can now read well enough to cope with an unemployment form?

HEAD: I don't dispute your teaching record, Miss Crowley.

ROS: I haven't suddenly become a different person you know. Lesbians aren't monsters with two heads, we're just ordinary people like you meet in Tesco every week.

HEAD: Please don't shout, Miss Crowley. This whole business is rather awkward.

ROS: It's more than that. Why does my sexuality suddenly matter? I'm still the same person. You don't go round telling everyone you're heterosexual, do you?

HEAD: Of course not, but with recent legislation....

ROS: It doesn't say lesbians shan't be employed as teachers does it?

HEAD: No, but the parents....

ROS: So you're going to abandon an experienced member of staff to pander to the prejudices of the more vocal parents? I'm finding the whole situation very distressing, Mrs McKendrick and I had hoped to receive more support.

HEAD: There's no question of abandoning you, Miss Crowley, it's simply that I have to consider all the ramifications of the situation. I can't help thinking that your reticence on this subject up til now hasn't been entirely helpful.

ROS: You'd rather I'd been entirely open about my lesbianism? Brought my partner to staff socials?

HEAD: Well, perhaps not flaunting it quite so openly.

ROS: Flaunting it! If I can't bring my partner to enjoy the wild dissipation of a staff social, are you surprised I spend my Saturday nights in a place where I can dance with my arms round my lover without creating a scandal? Make up your mind, Mrs McKendrick. If I'm going to be open about my lifestyle as you call it, then I've got to be accepted by my colleagues.

HEAD: If I'd had some idea how things stood I might have been more prepared to deal with this situation.

ROS: Can you honestly say that if you'd known I'm a lesbian you'd have treated me in the same way? Promoted me? If you find it hard to stomach the idea of meeting my lover how can I be sure it wouldn't affect your whole attitude towards me? It's a risk I haven't felt able to take.

The women look at each other. Noise of children shouting and playing.

SCENE FIVE:

The noise of children fades to a few isolated shouts. The park. Evening.

JAN: I used to come here as a child with my mother. We'd bring a picnic, egg sandwiches were my favourite, wrapped in greaseproof paper. We'd watch the dogs running across the grass and the kites in the wind.

ROS: The past is over, it's the future that counts.

JAN: We're tied to the past as those kites are tied to the ground.

ROS: I want to cut the string and fly free.

JAN: Do that and you disappear, out of sight and out of control.

ROS: But free.

JAN: Lost.

(ROS picks up a stick and holds it like a club.)

ROS: I'd like... I'd like...

(They laugh.)

TOGETHER: Violence is not the answer.

ROS: It is for some people.

JAN: How would violence help you now?

ROS: I might feel a lot better if I could beat hell out of Tracey. Or better still, the Head. I keep telling myself Tracey's only another victim of the system but I don't feel convinced. The Head, now, she's part of the system. She is the system. But....

JAN: But?

ROS: The system says, right, that staff stick together. Never back a kid against the staff, even when the teacher is blatantly wrong. Group solidarity.

JAN: Yes.

ROS: So why's she believing her story? That it was all some kind of joke and she 'won't do it again, miss, sorry miss. '

JAN: Because you've put yourself outside the group. And the group is much harder on one of its own.

ROS: But I'm not outside the group, I've played the game by the rules.

JAN: No. You're much more dangerous because you're the enemy within who's been hidden all these years. They thought you were one of them but by your very nature you're not. And they feel betrayed.

ROS: This is stupid, the staff don't even know yet. Some of them at least will be more supportive than the Head has been.

JAN: The Head 's being one of the group.

ROS: She's being a fool. Tracey's denied demanding money and Mrs prissy-faced McKendrick's just told her to come back tomorrow. *(Pause)* I know what I'd do if I were Tracey.

JAN: She wouldn't!

ROS: Why not? What's she got to lose?

JAN: She'd be expelled, wouldn't she?

ROS: Come off it Jan, what's that to the likes of Tracey? She can't wait to leave school. I should think the prospect of being expelled would be an incentive. That and the money.

JAN: So she'll be off to Fleet Street. Wapping.

ROS: Presumably.

JAN: She wouldn't really?

ROS: What would a fifteen-year old do in her position? Why'd she write the note in the first place? Why's she got it in for me?

JAN: That's a lot of questions.

ROS: With no answers.

JAN: Power? Jealousy?

ROS: Jealousy!

JAN: Perhaps she fancies you herself?

ROS: Come off it! She's the sort who's really into boys. Bags of make-up, eyes done so heavily it looks as if she hasn't had a decent night's sleep in weeks. Never does any work, though she's much brighter than she lets on. She couldn't possibly fancy me.

JAN: Don't you be so sure. I bet she's got a reputation for knocking round with lots of boys.

ROS: Sure. You should see what they say about her on the toilet walls.

JAN: There you are, then. I don't suppose she's enjoying it very much. So she's taken a fancy to you on the sly.

ROS: Don't be ridiculous. If that's the case, why's she trying to get me sacked?

JAN: It's all in her subconscious?

ROS: Balls. She's just a nasty, smutty-minded little shit-stirrer.

JAN: So where does that leave us?

ROS: In the shit with her.

JAN: You mean, there could be a reporter sitting on our doorstep when we get home?

ROS: Possibly, though it's a long way from Wapping to Hammersmith.

JAN: What the hell are we going to do?

ROS: There's nothing we can do. Unless you have faith in crossing your fingers.

JAN: I see, you're just going to walk home, give a quick interview to the bloke on the step, pose for pictures and go in for an early night.

ROS: Don't be stupid.

JAN: We've run out of time, what are we going to do?

ROS: We could take a plane to Greece and go and live on Lesbos.

JAN: Will you bloody-well grow up?

ROS: I can't take the hiding and the hypocrisy any more. Looking over my shoulder all the time, watching every word, keeping my mouth shut in case I give people ideas. Listening to them shooting their mouths off about gays and not daring to respond in case they guess. Feeling I ought to have the courage to be open. I don't know what to do. I can't think.

JAN: There's no point in us going home together. We'll go round to Jennifer's and you can wait there while I go home. If the coast is clear I'll give you a ring and you can come back.

ROS: And if the coast isn't clear?

JAN: You have to decide whether you want to come home at all tonight or in the future.

ROS: I'm not going to be driven out of my own home.

JAN: It would only be temporary.

ROS: It's ludicrous! Of course I've got to go home, all my stuff's there.

JAN: Well, we might be clear for tonight. I've no idea how long it takes them to respond to this sort of thing. I suppose it depends what else is happening. Let's hope for a riot or a disaster. *(Pause)* Come on.

ROS: Can't we stay and watch the kites for ever?

JAN: No.

ROS: *(running)* Someone just cut my string.

(JAN catches her hand and stops her.)

JAN: You don't get away that easily.

(The Whitney Houston song plays softly. They hold their position while the coloured lights throw their shadows on the back wall.)

SCENE SIX:

The classroom. Children's voices, taped, then quiet as ROS walks in. Each voice is different. All are male.

ROS: Good morning. Please sit down.

VOICE: Been to a disco lately, Miss?

ROS: Get out your copies of "Twelfth Night" and turn to Act Five.

VOICE: Viola's a lezzie, isn't she, Miss? Dressing up like a bloke.

VOICE: Just like you, Miss.

VOICE: What about Olivia then? She's fallen for a woman.

VOICE: Bender!

ROS: Turn to Act Five and let's have some quiet.

VOICE: Is it all true, Miss?

ROS: You don't want to believe everything you hear.

VOICE: There's no smoke without fire.

(Laughter.)

ROS: We're not talking about fire, we're discussing "Twelfth Night".

171

VOICE: You like us to notice things, Miss.

VOICE: Take an interest in the world around us.

ROS: Try taking an interest in "Twelfth Night". Now, Linda, could you please tell us how Shakespeare draws the different strands of the plot together in this scene.

VOICE: Shakespeare was a poofter, wasn't he, Miss?

VOICE: They were all bent in those days.

VOICE: We shouldn't have to read things written by a load of benders.

ROS: You read things that are on the syllabus.

VOICE: I bet a load of benders wrote the syllabus.

ROS: Turn to Act Five and be quiet. Whatever's on the syllabus you won't pass if you don't pay attention.

VOICE: Doesn't matter if I don't pass lit. It's just a load of stupid books.

VOICE: By a load of poofters.

ROS: You may not care whether you pass, Robert, but there are others in the class besides you so just shut up and give them a chance.

VOICE: I don't want to read about a load of benders.

ROS: Any more interruptions and you'll be in detention.

VOICE: What do you do in bed, Miss?

ROS: Stand up, Robert. What do you do in bed Robert? Have a good wank?

(Silence.)

ROS: You don't like being asked personal questions, do you? It's rude, isn't it? Well I don't like being asked personal questions either. It's rude. Got it?

VOICE: Yes.

ROS: What have you forgotten?

VOICE: Sorry Miss.

ROS: Sit down then and let's hear what Linda's got to say.

SCENE SEVEN:

ROS and JAN'S house. That evening.

ROS: After that they shut up. And they were my good set. The others were worse. I'll probably have Robert's dad up the school tomorrow complaining about my language.

JAN: He wouldn't have the nerve to tell his dad, would he?

ROS: Of course he would. His dad probably put him up to it. But the worse bit was at the end. Karen, the little quiet one, came up and said, "I don't like boys either, Miss." What the hell can I say to her? If I brush her off I'm not helping her and if I help her I'm promoting homosexuality.

JAN: What did you do?

172

ROS: 3C came rioting in at that point and by the time I'd finished shouting at them, she'd gone. So I had a temporary escape. I don't know what I'll say. Poor kid.

JAN: She's got guts though. I'd never have dared say that to anyone when I was fifteen.

ROS: I can't imagine that, you not having courage. You always seem so positive, so sure of yourself.

JAN: I've built it up over the years. When I was fifteen I was appalled at the things I was feeling. They weren't the sort of thing I could ever imagine discussing with anyone. I was too busy covering up, pretending to be like everyone else. I didn't know there were other people like me around.

ROS: You went to an all girls school, though, there must have been others. Staff, surely?

JAN: Oh yes. Everyone knew about the P. E. teacher. At least we all talked about it, but I never really believed it. I thought it was just the sort of thing girls said about unmarried teachers. I didn't imagine for a moment it might be true. In any case she was a heroine, totally unapproachable. And it was one thing to suspect some distant figure of being a lesbian but it didn't seem to have much to do with what I was feeling.

ROS: I know.

JAN: I grew out of it and became what you see today. *(laughing)* Calm, confident, well-adjusted! But I feel sorry for that kid, you'll have to try to help her.

ROS: Look, pastoral care is all very well in its place but my priority right now is getting me out of the shit.

JAN: I'm sorry, I'm not being much help, am I?

ROS: Hold me. When I'm next to you nothing else seems to matter. I can lose myself in the feel of your arms and the smell of your hair. I love you so much it hurts.

(The phone rings. They break.)

ROS: You don't think....

JAN: I don't know. Shall I?

ROS: Ok

(JAN picks up the phone.)

JAN: Yes? Who is it? Oh, hi Sue!

(ROS collapses into a chair.)

ROS: Thank god for that.

JAN: Look I'm sorry if you're stuck but we really can't commit ourselves to the helpline this weekend. We've got a problem of our own..... no, I'd rather not discuss it just yet, it may all calm down... yes, I'll give you a ring in a day or two... thanks.... bye. I didn't fancy going into all the details here and now.

ROS: No. Though she'll probably find out all too soon.

JAN: It might be alright.

ROS: I've just got this feeling, a sinking in the pit of my stomach.

JAN: I know, I've got it too. Shall we go out? Anything's better than sitting around here waiting for the

173

phone to ring.

ROS: I've got marking to do.

JAN: You've always got bloody marking to do! Can't you give it a rest and behave like a normal human being for one night?

ROS: Its only third year poems, it won't take long. You shouldn't have shacked up with a teacher if you couldn't take the hassle.

JAN: It's every bloody night. You're either late back from some meeting or you spend the whole evening slaving over all that drivel. I'm sick of watching telly on my own. I shacked up with you, as you so elegantly put it, because I wanted to share more than the bed with you.

ROS: The pissing marking has got to be done, right? It goes with the job, like all the long holidays everyone's so jealous of. If I don't do it the kids will moan and they're quite enough problem at the moment as it is, without giving them even more ammunition. I'm not giving anyone at work any excuse for throwing more shit at me and I could do without it at home too.

JAN: I'm only trying to help. Get you out. Give you a break. And you just shout at me.

ROS: You started it.

JAN: I bloody didn't.

ROS: For god's sake, shut up! We sound like a couple of five year olds. I don't want to fight with you. *(Pause.)*

JAN: I'm sorry.

ROS: Me too. *(Pause.)*Look, it's really not much tonight, just half an hour or so, and it'll make life much easier tomorrow.

JAN: You get stuck in then, and we'll go out when you've finished.

(The phone rings. Pause. JAN picks it up.)

JAN: Yes? Who's speaking please? I'm sorry, I only speak to people who identify themselves.

(She puts the phone down.)

ROS Was it them?

JAN: I don't know. Maybe. He asked to speak to you. Could have been selling double glazing, I suppose.

ROS: They usually tell you the name of their grotty company.

(The phone rings again.)

ROS: I reckon it was them.

JAN: Shall I?

(JAN picks up the phone.)

JAN: Hello? Who is it? I won't talk to you unless you give me your name. I don't understand what you mean. I don't think you've got the right person.

(She puts the phone down.)

ROS: This is stupid. Take the phone off the hook.

(The door bell rings.)

JAN: I'll go.

ROS: I don't think you should.

JAN: It could be anybody. I'll put the chain up.

(She goes. The phone rings. ROS picks it up.)

ROS: Who is it please? I'm sorry, I think you've got the wrong number.

(She cuts off the line but doesn't replace the receiver. JAN returns.)

JAN: I'm afraid it was...

ROS: I know. That was them on the phone. I cut it off. How many were there?

JAN: Just the one at the door and another at the gate.

ROS: Shit.

(The door bell goes again.)

ROS: Pity you can't hang up on the doorbell.

JAN: I can bloody well disconnect it, though. Where did you leave the screwdriver?

ROS: In the kitchen drawer, where it should be.

(JAN goes. After a pause the doorbell stops. She returns.)

JAN: I'd better check the back door.

ROS: They'd have to go through the gardens.

JAN: Better safe than sorry.

(She goes again. ROS looks out of the window. She moves quickly away. JAN returns.)

ROS: There's a photographer out there, he may have caught me when I looked out just now.

JAN: Keep well away from the window, then. I'll pull the curtains in a minute.

ROS: You don't think they might have seen us....

JAN: I think we were well away from the window.

(Someone starts banging on the front door.)

JAN: We could surely get out past two blokes for god's sake. They're not allowed to use force, are they?

ROS: No, but they'd get our photos.

JAN: They've probably got those anyway, you at the window, me at the door.

ROS: I just don't want to go out there.

JAN: We could get through the back, there was no sign of anyone there.

ROS: And if they got a photo of us going over the fence? That'd look really good.

JAN: You fucking well suggest something then, it's you they're after. They don't even know who I am.

ROS: You're on the electoral register, aren't you?

JAN: They can hardly go and check the electoral register at this hour of the night.

ROS: I'm sorry I've landed you in it like this.

JAN: It's not your fault people can't

175

accept a few gays about the place.

ROS: You make us sound like gnomes in the garden. Get your gays here. No home is complete without one.

JAN: Fool.

ROS: Corrupter of words.

JAN: What?

ROS: "the lady Olivia has no folly.... I am her corrupter of words. "

JAN: You and your bloody Shakespeare.

(More banging on the door.)

JAN: I'll pull the curtains.

ROS: Make them think we've gone to bed. Get their filthy minds working. No, don't put the light on, they might see through the cracks.

JAN: Are we going to sit here in the dark all night?

ROS: If we have to.

JAN: Well let's put the telly on then.

ROS: No. It covers up sounds.

JAN: That's the idea.

ROS: I want to know what they're up to.

JAN: Let's go to bed then.

ROS: Could you take your clothes off and get into bed, let alone go to sleep, knowing that lot are on the doorstep? Probably looking through the letterbox?

JAN: No, but I'll go and pull the curtains across the door so they can't see in.

(She goes. There is a loud bang. JAN re-enters.)

JAN: I shut the letterbox on his fingers.

ROS: Great. Are they going to stay there all night?

JAN: I suppose so.

(The banging on the door starts again.)

ROS: What are we going to do?

JAN: I've no idea.

The lights come up full, very white and bright. They then fade to just a white light on the floor, throwing their shadows onto the wall. The Whitney Houston song plays very loudly.

SCENE EIGHT:

The lights start dim but become harsh and glaring during the speech.

ROS: I used to like it here. I still do, really. A nice safe house in a row of houses all the same, in a street just like all the other streets. Old ladies who've lived here all their lives, people like us who're getting the first place of their own. Not too many kids, the houses aren't big enough. A bit of garden to sit in in the summer. Thick walls, keep you warm in winter. Do the place up a bit; make it your own. Things are changing. Young people can't afford these places any more. Going up-market. Nice pad for someone in the city. And now the

176

thick walls are a trap, stopping us from getting out, barely keeping the newshounds at bay. The cosiness has become a cage and we're the animals on display. Look at us, trying to live like ordinary people, pretending we're normal, just like everyone else. Who do we think we are?

(By now the lights are full. They snap to dim. Long silence.)

I want to stay in my nice cosy house, in my nice safe street, living my ordinary life like any ordinary person.

SCENE NINE:

The headmistress's study.

HEAD: "Gay Miss Shock". The governors will not like this, Miss Crowley.

ROS: I don't like it.
Mrs. McKendrick how do you think I feel with reporters hammering on my door all night?

HEAD: It will be most distressing for you.

ROS: Very.

HEAD: However difficult this may be for you personally, I have to consider the interest of the school as a whole and all this publicity can only create the wrong impression for prospective parents.

ROS: Thank you for your support, Mrs McKendrick.

HEAD: You're not going to do your case any good by being bitter.

ROS: Bitter!

HEAD: Or angry.

ROS: I have every reason to be angry. My privacy is being invaded, my professional status threatened, and you expect me to keep calm about it.

HEAD: We must avoid being over-emotional.

ROS: I'm not being over-emotional, I'm trying very hard to keep calm when my whole identity is being attacked.

(Pause.)

HEAD: I wonder whether the best thing might not be for you to take some sick leave and go away for a rest. Until it's all blown over.

ROS: Try to push it under the carpet. Keep a low profile and hope it will all go away? I'm not playing that one either. It's time some of us started supporting the policies of equality to which this authority is supposedly committed.

HEAD: If it were only up to me, Miss Crowley, but I'm afraid that the increased powers of the governors may take matters out of my hands.

ROS: If I was being hounded because of my colour it would be illegal, wouldn't it?

HEAD: Yes.

ROS: My sexuality is just as much a part of me as my colour, I can't change it. To persecute someone for their sexuality is just as offensive as to persecute them for their colour. Any sort of persecution is evil. What kind of example is that giving the children?

HEAD: Persecution is rather a strong word.

ROS: What other word would you use to describe what's been happening to me over the last few days? My picture all over the front pages, nauseous innuendoes about my private life, I'm unable to go home, there's reporters hanging round outside the school all day and instead of supporting me you suggest I run away.

HEAD: I think that your absence might relieve some of the pressure on the school, which as I'm sure you appreciate is making life rather difficult for us all.

ROS: It's not my presence which is making life difficult, it's the presence of the press.

HEAD: I'm simply looking at the situation from a practical point of view. The sooner we can get these people off our backs the sooner we can get back to normal.

ROS: I can't do that, can I? Everyone knows now. To pretend to be something I'm not would be even more dishonest.

HEAD: The situation is obviously going to need very careful handling. Are you certain that you'll not take sick leave? It would make everything much simpler.

ROS: Oh yes, it would get them off your back, but what about me? They're perfectly capable of following me, for the time being at any rate. No, Mrs McKendrick, I'm staying put.

HEAD: Well, don't be surprised if the governors take an interest. I've already had several parents change their minds about sending their children here in September. Falling rolls will mean cuts in staff, you know.

ROS: And I'll be first on the list?

Lights down

SCENE TEN:

A room at SUE'S. The same evening.

ROS: *(angrily).* Why can I be firm and decisive with her and not with you?

JAN: You used to be.

ROS: When did I change? Have I changed?

JAN: If you live close to someone you don't always see them changing. I still love you, even the changed you.

ROS: I'm glad. *(Pause.)*I don't know what I'd do without that.

JAN: Graham called me in to Head Office today.

ROS: And?

JAN: He's taken me off the project.

ROS: He's sacked you?

JAN: No, not as bad as that, though I'll lose bonuses and travel expenses. They're going to keep me at Head Office until "things have died down a bit. The publicity might damage our relationship with our client." I thought I'd been getting some funny looks, but they don't know me well enough to say anything to my face. Graham knew

178

it was me as soon as he saw the article.

ROS: I'm surprised Graham reads that sort of paper, I'd have thought the "Financial Times" was more his line.

JAN: I dare say someone told him. Offices are just as much hotbeds of gossip as schools, you know.

ROS: I'm sorry, it's all my fault.

JAN: For Christ's sake - what could you have done to stop it?

ROS: Taken the sick leave?

JAN: *(half-joking)* I could fancy a fortnight in Greece. Blue sea, empty beaches. Cheaper this time of year. Nice to go in term time.

ROS: You think I should run away?

JAN: You should do what you think is right.

ROS: You're as bad as Mrs McKendrick. Take the easy way out. Don't rock the boat. Anything for a quiet life.

JAN: There's a lot to be said for a quiet life. We liked it when we had it, remember? It was more fun than this! Camping out in someone's spare room, scared to go out. How long can we go on doing it?

ROS: As long as we have to?

JAN: Weeks? Months? A year? How should I know?

ROS: So what do you want? One minute you tell me to do what's right, the next you're telling me to sell out.

JAN: I'll help you as much as I can, but I can't make up your mind for you

ROS: It's O. K. for you, isn't it? No one's going to sack you, you're too bloody valuable. English teachers grow on trees.

JAN: You'd feel better about everything if I lost my job too? Thanks very much.

ROS: I'm glad you're not going to lose your job.

JAN: I'd never have guessed.

ROS: I'll probably have to resign anyway. Every time I walk down the corridor I feel the eyes in my back. My classes give me hell. My sixth form give me funny looks and change the subject when I walk in the room. I can't teach anybody anything. I daren't go in the staffroom. But if I go, they've won.

JAN: Stick it out then.

ROS: I don't think I can. Help me!

JAN: Talk to Sue, go to the helpline, counselling, marriage guidance, but don't expect me to make a choice for you.

ROS: You already have.

She slams out of the room. The Whitney Houston song plays very loudly.

SCENE ELEVEN:

ROS'S father's house.

FATHER: You've got a nerve walking in 'ere like this. Bold as

179

brass. Dunno how you can show your faces.

ROS: Nice welcome dad.

FATHER: 'ave you seen the papers?

ROS: I told you not to read rubbish like that.

FATHER: Rubbish is it? Can you deny it?

ROS: Deny what? That Jan's my lover? So? The rest of it's a load of balls.

FATHER: You just watch your language. What would your mother have said?

ROS: Sorry.

FATHER: How do you think I feel, opening me paper one morning and finding all that about my daughter?

JAN: You'd rather she'd told you all about it years ago?

FATHER: I don't want to know anything about it, it's disgusting. Ought to be locked up.

ROS: You want them to lock me up?

FATHER: If they'd locked them all up years ago you'd never have met that Jan. Never had the opportunity. Settled down and got married like your cousins.

JAN: Why have I suddenly become "that Jan" as if I wasn't here?

FATHER: You don't have to be here. I didn't ask you.

JAN: You were glad enough to see me when I was helping sort out the garden.

FATHER: If I 'ad my way she'd have nothing more to do with you.

JAN: I'll see you outside, Ros.
(JAN leaves)

ROS: How dare you talk to her like that after all she's done for you?

FATHER: I never asked her to do anything.

ROS: No, because Jan's not the sort of person you have to ask.

FATHER: If you hadn't gone away to college you'd never have met. This is what comes of giving you an education.

ROS: She wasn't the first. I'd have been like it anyway, even if I'd never left home. Why do you think I didn't have many boyfriends?

FATHER: What you need is a good bloke to sort you out. Show you what's what.

ROS: I've never met a man I could begin to feel about in the same way I feel about Jan.

FATHER: I don't want to know.

ROS: As long as everyone's the same as you it's OK. If they're the slightest bit unusual, god help them. What is this normality you keep going on about? Sharing a bed with a woman for forty years, fucking her quickly in the dark every Saturday night without stopping to consider what she wants? That's normal is it? What's so wonderful about that?

FATHER: I'm not going to sit here and have you talk about your mother like that. Just you get out of my house.

ROS: When I was a kid I used to look up to you, respect you. I beat up Bobby Radford because he said

180

you were a miserable old git, and you thrashed me for coming in with a black eye. I thought you could solve every problem. I loved going out with you, even just down to the shops. I remember the day you took me down the river to Greenwich, you telling me about the sights and the ships , as if we were going on a voyage of discovery. Do you remember?

FATHER: Yes.

ROS: I didn't know then that Bobby Radford was right.

FATHER: Think you can wheedle your way round me like you did when you were a kid? Forget it . I don't need you.

ROS: Throw me out, then you really will be on your own, you really will have done it then. First Richard, then me. I often wondered why he went quite as far as Australia, but at least you still get letters from him. There'll be nothing from me. No-one to write to the council and sort out your housing benefit, no-one to sort out your fuel bills and get your loft insulated. But at least you'll have the satisfaction of knowing you've done the right thing.

FATHER: Just get out, you bloody little pervent.

SCENE TWELVE:

Outside ROS'S father's house.

ROS: Hold me.

JAN: Here in the street?

ROS: I don't care any more.

(They embrace.)

SCENE THIRTEEN:

The classroom. Children's voices.

VOICE: Still here, Miss?

VOICE: Thought you'd have gone days ago.

VOICE: Haven't you had enough of us?

ROS: Page forty-three.....

VOICE: Good picture of you in the paper, Miss.

VOICE: And of your friend, Miss.

VOICE: Yeah, I could really fancy her.

ROS: No...

VOICE: It's disgusting, wasting her on a woman.

VOICE: My dad says you should get the sack.

VOICE: And mine. It shouldn't be allowed.

ROS: I said page forty-three.

VOICE: You shouldn't be allowed to corrupt people like us.

VOICE: I don't know why you bother, Miss.

(Lights change. ROS is having a nightmare. SUE'S house.)

VOICE: Ruining the youth of the country, you are.

HEAD'S VOICE: I worry about your influence on the children

FATHER'S VOICE: It's unnatural. What would your mother have said?

HEAD'S VOICE: We have to maintain standards.

VOICE: You're not part of society.

FATHER'S VOICE: You're not normal.

VOICE: Stop pretending you're like everyone else.

VOICE: Hiding in your ordinary house.

VOICE: Shopping in Sainsbury's.

VOICE: Trying to melt into the background.

HEAD'S VOICE: What gives you the right to question our values?

FATHER'S VOICE: What makes you think you've got any rights at all?

VOICE: You should be grateful.

VOICE: You've got a job, haven't you?

VOICE: You've got somewhere to live, haven't you?

VOICE: You've got enough to eat.

(The voices becomes louder and faster, building to a climax .)

VOICE: What about the starving millions?

VOICE: Prisoners.

VOICE: The oppressed.

VOICE: The homeless.

VOICE: The sick.

(ROS wakes, shouting.)

JAN: What is it? What's the matter?

ROS: Nothing. Dreaming.

JAN: Tell me.

(Pause)

ROS: I've handed in my notice.

JAN: You did what?

ROS: I couldn't go on living a lie. I couldn't go on pretending I wasn't affected by their stupid standards, that all this didn't matter.

JAN: What about a job? You can't just live on air.

ROS: I'm not going to sponge off you, if that's what you're worried about.

JAN: Don't be stupid. You know I'll do everything I can for you.

ROS: I'm going to go to France. Get myself a job.

JAN: Running away ? Leaving me to face the shit on my own? Where's all our sharing gone?

ROS: You told me to make up my own mind.

JAN: How can you destroy everything we've buillt up over the years?

ROS: When I'm out of the way the pressure will die down. It's me they're worried about. You only talk to computers, they can't be corrupted like children.

JAN: But-

ROS: We're trapped here in Sue's room, only going out to go to work. What sort of a life is that?

JAN: Better than a life apart.

ROS: It's no life at all. You've got your job, you'll be alright.

JAN: I'm not the problem. Don't run away from me.

ROS: You told me to make my own decision

JAN: Do you want to be on your own? Look at me.

ROS: I want to be strong

JAN: Be strong but don't be stupid

ROS: I have to go.

Lights down

SCENE FOURTEEN:

The deck of a cross channel ferry. ROS is leaning on the rail. Noise of football chants in the distance.

ROS: *(ironically)* And the white cliffs of Dover, glowing pink in the sunset, gradually fade into the distance. Not a bluebird in sight.

(A man comes and stands and looks over the rail beside her.)

MAN: Pleasant evening. *(Pause.)* Going on holiday? *(Pause.)* On your own?

ROS: Piss off, will you?

MAN: I was only passing the time of day.

(He goes. The noise of chanting grows louder. JAN enters with two plastic beakers of tea.)

JAN: Make the most of your last cup of proper English tea. From a stewed pot with plastic milk.

ROS: Are you sure about this?

JAN: I'm certain.

(They drink and look out.)

ROS: I don't want to swap my dirty English pub and glass of bitter for a French café and a glass of wine. Even though it'll cost less. I want to be with my own people, in the place where I was born.

JAN: I know.

ROS: I want to be able to walk down the road on a Saturday and buy books in my language and think in the language I speak every day. I want to drive on the left and watch Channel Four.

JAN: Listen to the cricket on a summer afternoon.

ROS: Watch the kites in the park.

JAN: I want to feel free.

ROS: Together.

(One of the football supporters staggers onto the deck. He is wearing faded jeans and a Union Jack T-shirt. He sings the last line of 'Rule Britannia' and gives a nazi salute. ROS and JAN laugh.)

Lights down.

183

FAIL/SAFE

Ayshe Raif

I knew I'd written a draft of *FAIL/SAFE* by 1984 because I'd found it in one of my files. But having moved house three times since then, I must suppose that I disposed of all the notes and previous drafts I'd written. This presents a problem in describing the process of writing the play, but I must assume I'd begun sometime in 1983 because I have a vague recollection of a number of previous drafts.

I know that this play was a mish-mash of my own experiences, which may have been rather hum-drum, but which I'd used as a base to start from. I have a close relationship with my mother, although I suspect we rely on each other too much. I'd done a little market research, but only over the telephone. However the motivation for writing the play initially came without doubt from my acquaintance with Lulu, (who also featured in my first play *CAFÉ SOCIETY** - the character of DOLLY was partly based on her). I used to run into her regularly when I lived in Hackney and I knew her for some years. She was in her 70's, widowed with no children, surviving in appalling conditions with only her cat to live for. I can't remember how or why I first came to visit her flat. It could be that I'd helped her home one day. She was a big woman who had difficulty getting about, although she insisted on a daily walk to the bottom of the road, turn right, and up to the top of the street where the shops were, stopping at the three cafés on the way.

Anyway, rather like JO, I found myself regularly and systematically cleaning the flat. It was a mammoth task, and to my shame, I left off when only half-way through. I'd told Lulu on a number of occasions that I was going to move and couldn't come any more but I don't think she ever really took it in. Or rather, she chose not to. The last I heard of her (a year or so ago) she was still alive and had been moved into a home for the elderly. She stayed on my mind, perhaps because I'd had no luck in securing her a home help, perhaps because it must have seemed that I'd just abandoned her (which I had) and I felt guilty, angry and sorry for her. The play came together around her, and the other issues that concerned me at the time.

I was, and still am, interested in how we shape our own lives. How we establish patterns that make us miserable, presumably because we get some comfort or satisfaction from them. So, when we see JO making return weekend visits to her mother, we know she'll never break away - no matter how much she feels she should - because GWEN and everything to do with her, is JO's anchor and her fail/safe mechanism for when real life gets too tough.

185

Finally I was intrigued at how greatly sisters can differ from each other, yet how strong, if in unequal measures, the bond between them can be.

First produced at the Soho Poly Theatre, London. 1st-31st May 1986, with the following cast:

JO	JANETTE LEGGE
GWEN	GABRIELLE BLUNT
MAVIS	HELENA McCARTHY
ELLA	SHEILA BURRELL

Directed by SUE DUNDERDALE
Designed by ALEXANDRA BYRNE

CAFÉ SOCIETY is published by Samuel French Ltd.

NICHOLAS DE JONGH (THE GUARDIAN)

"Ayshe Raif's Fail/Safe is a most disturbing lament for the way that some family ties becomes chains from which there will never be escape... The play brims with sharp, humorous and authentic impressions of old age ...a compelling vignette of family wretchedness."

CAROLE WODDIS (CITY LIMITS)

"Ayshe Raif captures unflinchingly the power struggles, guilt trips and cruelties between mothers/daughters/sisters ...with dialogue that is unerringly accurate and shafted with bitter humour."

CHARACTERS:

JO	42	
GWEN	70	Her mother
ELLA	68	Her aunt
MAVIS	80	An acquaintance

TIME:
The present

SET:
An ordinary living room a bit faded, somewhere in Hackney.
A smaller set on stage of a dirty cell-like room.

ACT ONE

SCENE ONE:

The curtain rises on JO sitting at the table, drinking tea. GWEN enters with toast. She puts it on the table and surveys the breakfast.

GWEN: It's just that you said nine.

JO: *(butters toast)* You don't have to take everything I say as gospel you know.

GWEN: *(sits, pours herself some tea)* I had the tea ready. I was worried.

JO: That makes a change. You shouldn't have waited up Mum.

GWEN: Why couldn't you have come earlier? *(shakes out a napkin and puts it over JO'S lap)*

JO: I told you, I was working. *(shoos her off)* Stop it.

GWEN: Till so late in the evening?

JO: Some of it is evening work. Most of it is evening work. Look do we have to have an inquisition?

GWEN: I don't like you working nights; it's dangerous.

JO: Not nights. Evenings.

GWEN: There's some strange people about.

JO: Especially in Wapping. *(does a mad tick and hunchback).*

GWEN: *(ignoring this)* You should look for another job. What about an office job?

JO: *(taps typewriting on table)* Twelve letters before lunch - ting!

- six reports before five - ting!

GWEN: Perhaps you could find one round here? When you get here so late it gives us no time at all.

JO: *(salutes)* Message received and understood.

GWEN: Perhaps you just don't wanna come home at the weekends.

JO: *(eating)* I don't.

GWEN: You know I live for my weekends. Since your father died I -

JO: I know.

GWEN: I know, I should've had more children -

JO: I know, I know! Don't go on Mum, the same things over and over! *(Coughs and splutters. GWEN jumps up and pats her on the back. The coughing passes and JO pushes her away. Sips tea, recovers.)* Alright. *(sighs)* I can't bear to be away from you Mummy; I can't wait to rush here every weekend to watch the telly Mummy.

GWEN: Oh didn't I say? It's not working.

JO: Oh no! *(she goes to see for herself)* Why didn't you get it fixed?

GWEN: It's too expensive.

JO: Don't be stubborn. You won't last out.

GWEN: I suppose not. It's the only company I have in the week.

JO: You probably talked it to death.

GWEN: I don't!

JO: You've been doing it for years.

GWEN: *(firmly)* I do not talk to the television.

JO: Yes Mum *(she returns to the table to finish breakfast)* I'm glad I brought my records.

GWEN: Can't you do without them for a day?

JO: Mm-mm. *(meaning no)*

GWEN: *(tuts, pause)* Shall we go to see your Aunt Ella tomorrow?

JO: The weekly pilgrimage from Hackney to Walthamstow is the highlight of my week.

GWEN: We don't go that often.

JO: Every Sunday for fifteen years.

GWEN: She hardly ever comes here.

JO: Wonder why?

GWEN: She should. I'm eldest.

JO: Yes Mum.

(Pause. The bus passes. This is a regular occurrence. It rumbles by slowly and shoots a neon glare at the window. The bar of neon light can be seen even when the curtains are drawn. It can be a maddening or comforting familiarity, depending on your mood.)

GWEN: Did I tell you the neighbours are having new windows put in? I heard it'll cost £2,000.

JO: Ooo!

GWEN: I don't know where they've found the money because he's only a milkman and she doesn't work. He goes to work ever so early. I hear him leave. *(Pause)* I don't sleep so well these days.

JO: *(clearing table)* You should tell the doctor.

GWEN: I can't get used to being alone Josie.

JO: You should take a lover.

GWEN: Behave.

JO: Why not? *(takes tray to kitchen)*

GWEN: I've already got two in the upstairs cupboard.

JO: *(returning)* Only two?

GWEN: You don't want too many strange men in your home do you?

JO: Your home Mum. Have as many men as you like.

GWEN: And your home. Even if you're not here in the week, your room's still your room, any time you want to come back.

JO: *(sighs)* We had this conversation last week. *(Goes to sofa and lies on it. GWEN deliberately comes and sits in the armchair facing JO who, sensing a plea, turns over and puts the cushion over her head.)*

GWEN: You'll wanna come back one day won't you Josie? It's all very well playing at being independent in rented rooms but you'll get fed up of it. You will. Josie? *(as she's not getting through she goes to her shelf of ornaments and dusts them)*

GWEN: Look at the Lloyd's daughter. "There I was running two

188

jobs, making myself ill, and what for? Just to pay the rent on a flat I was never in." That's what she said. "My room was empty and waiting for me at home, no rent, no -"

JO: Carol Lloyd is a nit-wit. *(turning around)* She's the type who brings her Mum to her first job interview.

GWEN: That's sweet.

JO: *(lisps)* Yespth.

(Slight pause. GWEN decides to let it go.)

JO: *(watching her)* Why don't you throw those out Mum?

GWEN: These? They could tell the whole history of this family.

JO: They only gather dust.

GWEN: From my engagement to your first job.

JO: But they're -

GWEN: What?

JO: They're - *(wants to say cheap and nasty, but checks herself)* - so fiddly.

GWEN: I don't mind. Anyway - you collect.

JO: Art Deco Mum. Not alabaster doggies.

GWEN: Right, now - *(turns back, finishes)* Will you come shopping?

JO: Haven't you been?

GWEN: I was hoping -

JO: You know I hate shopping.

GWEN: It's heavy to carry Josie.

JO: I bought you that trolley.

GWEN: It's awkward to steer.

JO: You'll have to learn then.

GWEN: Get 'L' plates eh? *(They laugh. GWEN goes to kitchen for carrier bags)* It's just nice having company. Like old times. *(returns with carriers)* Remember?

JO: All of a month back? Nah. *(sits up, scratches her head)*

GWEN: Josie.

JO: Hmm.

(They look at each other as GWEN tries to summon up courage, but fails)

GWEN: Let's have a picnic tomorrow.

JO: A picnic? We'd be bored silly after ten minutes. Oh alright.

GWEN: Now where's my bag? *(fetches it from sideboard and checks contents carefully)* I don't know why you won't come. I don't know what you're going to do here all morning. *(goes to hallway and returns with coat)* Oh Josie, will you help me to change the curtains later?

JO: Oh Mum.

GWEN: They need a wash, you can see. We should've taken them down last week really.

JO: Oh I'm tired.

GWEN: Not now. Later'll do. Well, I'll be going.

189

JO: Mum? *(she goes to the record-player and puts on a record -Louis Armstrong 'Body and Soul')*

GWEN: Hmm?

JO: Can you bring me a paper back please?

GWEN: Of course I will. *(exits)*

The bus passes. JO sits back and listens to the record. Halfway through she stands and switches it off. She grabs her coat and exits.

SCENE TWO:

MAVIS sits in her chair. There is a loud knock on the door. She exits to open the door, leaving her seat empty.

JO: *(off)* Good afternoon, I'm from Brown and Willis Research Agency, we're an independent market research company and a member of the Market Research -

MAVIS: *(off)* Oh, are you going to ask me questions?

JO: *(off)* Just a few if you don't mind.

MAVIS: *(entering)* Well you'll have to come in.

JO: *(off)* We don't usually. *(peeps her head round the door)* Actually I'd rather -

MAVIS: *(making her way to the armchair)* I can't stand for too long. You'll have to come in. Close the door behind you please.
(She sits. JO enters uncomfortably and approaches MAVIS, looking around the room as she does so, obviously taken aback by the filthy condition of the place.)

MAVIS: Don't you want to sit down? *(sees the expression on JO'S face)* I can't manage it. I haven't invited my friends here in months. I'm almost 80.

JO: *(sits on edge of chair)* Haven't you got a home help?

MAVIS: They won't send me one. I don't know why. I was always kind to old people when I was young. I fetched their shopping, cleaned for them and cooked their meals. I thought nothing of it. Things change. I'm out of tea I'm afraid.

JO: Oh no, that's alright. Um, well the survey is among pet owners. I see you've got a cat - that's the first question. *(marks it down)*

MAVIS: My Suzie, yes she's all I have. She's twenty you know. If anything happened to her I wouldn't want to live.

JO: What brands of catfood can you think of?

MAVIS: Oh, she'll only eat Paws.

JO: Yes. *(writes)* Good. Er, can you think of any others?

MAVIS: Kitten-Cat. No, that's all.

JO: And do you buy Paws regularly?

MAVIS: Oh yes, she won't eat anything else, I told you.

JO: Which varieties do you buy?

MAVIS: Only the liver. She's not keen on the others. She used to eat Kitten-Cat but I bought a tin of Paws once and that was it. She wouldn't touch anything else after that.

190

JO: *(writes hurriedly)* ...wouldn't touch anything else after that.

MAVIS: *(sees she's writing this down)* I know they put something in it.

JO: *(writes all she says)* What do you mean?

MAVIS: Something addictive.

JO: What do you like best about Paws Liver?

MAVIS: I don't eat it my dear. It's too expensive.

JO: What do you dislike about Paws Liver?

MAVIS: I've told you - it's too expensive. Do listen.

JO: I'm sorry but I have to ask all the questions.

MAVIS: Damn silly if you ask me.

JO: Yes. Well, that's all the questions, thank you very much, now if I could just have your name please.

MAVIS: Miss Mavis Russell.

JO: I have the address, now occupation of head of household, retired. What was your previous occupation please?

MAVIS: You sound like a recording.

JO: I have to ask the questions as they're written. They're quite strict about that.

MAVIS: Do you do this all the time?

JO: It feels like it.

MAVIS: Oh?

JO: No I mean there's a lot of evening work and it just feels like I do this all the time.

MAVIS: What do you do during the day?

JO: Nothing much. Laundry, library. I go to Camden Passage on Wednesdays.

MAVIS: Where?

JO: Angel.

MAVIS: Oh.

JO: Um, could I ask your previous occupation please.

MAVIS: Actress.

JO: Oh - a professional actress?

MAVIS: Of course. Do I get a free sample?

JO: What? Oh no, I'm sorry. Well, that's all then. Thank you. *(puts clipboard away)*

MAVIS: You don't need to rush off do you? I mean, it's such a chilly day outside.

JO: Well, I must press on.

MAVIS: *(looking round)* I can't manage it. Everytime I bend my head goes round. Suzie's always knocking things down and I can't pick them up again. Naughty girl. She teases me, hides for hours and I can't find her. *(Pause)* Oh well, I suppose you're anxious to leave. Everyone is.

JO: It's not that, it's just...

MAVIS: They're so busy. No-one has a few minutes to spare. What a dreadful way to live.

JO: Yes, I suppose it is. *(shamed into making conversation)* That's interesting, that you were an actress I mean.

MAVIS: The profession's all changed now. No style. I spent many years with the Appledown Touring Company. I often took the leading role. I remember one play we had in our repertoire - 'Black Roses' by Dorothy Grant - have you heard of it? Never mind. I played the role of Amelia Benson, whose lover's cowardice reduced her to a life on the streets. *(acts from her chair)* "Is this all there will be for me? Every step lower than the one before, until - what? What could be worse? Could there still be more, waiting for me, forever waiting for me?" *(she pauses. JO claps.)*

MAVIS: I'll always remember. I have some photographs somewhere, would you like to see them?

JO: I'd love to.

MAVIS: Would you really?

JO: Oh yes.

MAVIS: But they're in the bedroom somewhere and it's such a mess. I could look them out for you if you can come again.

JO: Well, I don't know.

MAVIS: You wouldn't come again would you? No, of course not. No-one does. I wouldn't have said, but I thought you wanted to see my photographs.

JO: Oh I do.

MAVIS: You'll come then?

JO: Well, yes I could I suppose, one day.

MAVIS: When? When would suit you?

JO: Well, I'm not sure.

MAVIS: *(downhearted)* Oh.

JO: *(ashamed)* I could manage Thursday morning. Would that be okay?

MAVIS: I'll be in all day Thursday.

JO: *(rising)* I'll pop in then. For a few minutes.

MAVIS: I'll look out the photos.

They face each other as the lights go down.

SCENE THREE:

GWEN sits alone at the table. Finally we hear a door slam upstairs and JO coming down. GWEN is stony-faced. JO enters with a towel, wiping her face.

GWEN: *(stands)* I'll get lunch ready. *(exits)*

(JO hangs the damp towel on the back of a chair. GWEN is banging about in the kitchen.)

JO: I said I'm sorry.

GWEN: *(off)* I don't know why you had to go.

JO: I enjoyed myself! For a change.

GWEN: *(off)* Just like that. There one minute - gone the next. You left me with all the shopping to carry back. I don't know why you bothered to come at all.

JO: You're so dithering - I couldn't stand it. "Shall I get apples or

192

pears? One pound or two? Which spuds look the nicest?" Why don't you make a list before you go? That's what I do. I check all the cupboards, go directly for what I need and return home not even tired. Quick, simple, clean. *(Pause. GWEN doesn't respond)* I can't bear the court-marshall over whose stall has the best carrots. *(Pause.)*

GWEN: *(enters)* You didn't even tell me. I didn't know where you'd gone.

JO: Your fault for leaving the harness behind.

GWEN: I was worried.

JO: I've only been to the pub Mum - not a trans-world expedition.

GWEN: On a Saturday. Only men go to the pub on Saturday mornings.

JO: Perhaps I've changed sex then without noticing. *(picks up newspaper)*

GWEN: It wouldn't make much difference, the way you dress.

JO: Wicked! *(they chuckle)* Have you ever been to the pub on a Saturday morning?

GWEN: No.

JO: Have you ever been in a pub?

GWEN: Of course I have.

JO: I've never known you to. I can't imagine you having a drink in the Clapton Tavern.

GWEN: You didn't go there?

JO: Dum-daram-dum!

GWEN: Oh Josie!

JO: What?

GWEN: They have - dancers.

JO: Strippers Mum.

GWEN: Oh Josie, how could you?

JO: I didn't get up on the stage mother.

GWEN: But you could've got accosted.

JO: Not very likely. The four minute warning wouldn't distract their attention. You should've seen how serious they were. I could've laughed. Almost. I only stayed a few minutes.

GWEN: Thank goodness for that. I hope nobody saw you. *(exits)*

JO: Then I went for a walk over the old ground. The school, Dad's factory, the park. I was trying to get something into focus but it didn't happen. *(Pause)* Being serious is hard work; I had to go and have another drink after. *(Pause)*

GWEN: *(off)* Lay the table Josie.

(The bus passes. Lights dim to show the passing of time - an hour. Both women sit relaxed. JO burps.)

GWEN: I expect you're not used to eating decent meals anymore.

JO: Mmm.

GWEN: You look thinner as it is.

JO: I'm wasting away.

GWEN: *(after a while)* I'll have to do the washing-up in a minute. Did you notice the price of onions? Tomatoes were fifty-eight a pound.

The cucumber was only forty-two because I got it off the end stall. I should get all my veg off him really but I can't help buying before I get that far. Have to carry it twice the distance that way. I wouldn't mind but I get this pain. *(Pause)* Terrible pain down my left arm. *(Pause)* I bought some curtains. They'll look lovely up. *(stands)* I thought we could put them up this afternoon, eh?

(She exits to hallway)

JO: Mum?

GWEN: *(off)* Hmm?

JO: I told you last week to go to the doctor about that pain.

GWEN: Oh - I went.

(JO waits for her return. The bus passes with its familiar rumble. GWEN returns with the package of curtains.)

GWEN: I haven't really looked at them yet. Ready-mades. Could've run them up myself really. Do you remember the dresses I used to make for you? There. *(She shakes them out over her lap like a blanket. JO gets up and lethargically removes old curtains. GWEN begins to put the rings in the new curtains.)* I thought they'd cheer the place up. Did I tell you I broke the blue and white teapot? Handle slipped. Then I lost my knitting needles. This was all last week. And then I defrosted the fridge -

JO: What did he say?

GWEN: I forgot to take the food out and it was all ruined.

(JO removes the curtains in silence.

Drops them in a pile by the wall. Then she helps GWEN to hook up the new ones.)

JO: Well?

GWEN: It's not my arm. I get out of breath sometimes and this other pain. You do like these curtains don't you Josie? *(Pause)* It's angina.

(GWEN waits for JO to react but she doesn't. They finish in silence and JO begins to hang the new curtains.)

JO: That walk I had. I was thinking - twenty years today. *(GWEN becomes tight-lipped)* I had a celebratory drink to Ruth's freedom. I wonder what she's doing now. She was gutsy for nineteen wasn't she? Straining at the leash, determined to have her own life. I was only 22 - I should've gone with her. But I thought I'd hang on and see you over the crisis. Didn't know I'd hang on for twenty bloody years though. *(Pause. She finishes)*

GWEN: *(choked)* There. The room looks so much brighter.

JO gets down and puts the record on. She listens to a few bars then begins to mime with actions to the song. GWEN ignores her. After a moment she leaves the room. JO stops miming.

SCENE FOUR:

MAVIS is sitting alone on stage.

MAVIS: You've made a lovely job of this room Josephine. Hasn't she Suzie? She's hiding again. *(JO enters, wiping sweat from her face, sits on arm of chair.)*

JO: Well, now at least you can invite your friends round.

MAVIS: Oh if the kitchen weren't so dirty. I've pinned a note on the wall there, can you see it? *(JO gets up and looks)* If anything happens to me, or if I go into hospital, I want Suzie put to sleep.

JO: You don't mean that?

MAVIS: I couldn't bear to think of her alone, not loved or cared for, in strange places with strange people. Poor Suzie. And if she goes first I won't want to live. She's all I...

JO: *(rolling down her sleeves)* I'll have to go now.

MAVIS: I can't sleep at night. Will I see you next Thursday then?

JO: Well, like I said, I am a bit busy just now. I'm still settling into my place and there's things I have to do.

MAVIS: I am grateful for what you've done you know. You didn't have to Nancy.

JO: Pardon?

MAVIS: Sorry?

JO: You called me Nancy.

MAVIS: Oh.

JO: Never mind. Well look, I'd better..

MAVIS: I'm sorry about the photographs. Next time perhaps.

JO: Oh don't trouble.

MAVIS: I was rather looking forward to next week. I think too much when I'm on my own. It's just that it's my birthday. But it doesn't matter. Never mind.

JO: *(unenthusiastically)* Oh your birthday? It's not is it? *(MAVIS simply stares at her)* Oh well, in that case, perhaps I could.

MAVIS: It would be so nice.

JO: *(submitting)* Yes of course I'll come. We'll celebrate.

MAVIS: But you mustn't buy me a present. Is that understood?

JO: Yes, alright then.

MAVIS: Thank you my dear.

JO: Now I really must be going.

(She picks up her coat, ready to say goodbye)

MAVIS: I'll show you my photographs of the Appledown Touring Company. You'll see Dotty in lots of them. She was my best friend. Although she was a little jealous of me because I was a better actress and often got the leading roles. But then I was a little jealous of her because she was better-looking. She flirted too much with Robbie. I haven't told you about Robbie yet have I?

JO: I'm sorry Miss Russell, I'd really love to stop and listen but I have to go to work soon and I mu..

MAVIS: Off you go then. You don't have to stand on ceremony with me.

JO: Right. See you next week.

MAVIS: I'll wait in. Goodbye my dear.

JO hurries out.

SCENE FIVE:

GWEN is fiddling with the curtains. She closes one, looks, decides to close the other and switches on the light. Surveys the effect.

GWEN: I wasn't sure about the colour. What do you think?

JO: *(off)* I met a man. I didn't tell you.

GWEN: Oh?

JO: *(enters, sits)* Paul. He works at the zoo. Says he loves animals but kills baby chicks. He smashes them on the ground before he feeds them to the eagles. Says it's humane.

GWEN: Oh how dreadful.

JO: He's always laughing, like nothing bothers him, but then he doesn't care very much. *(Pause)* Has he given you anything?

GWEN: Who?

JO: You know.

GWEN: I've got tablets. I put one under my tongue if - if I have a turn. It takes a few minutes then I feel better.
(She sits, toying with her knitting.)

JO: *(flatly)* That's alright then.

GWEN: It's not that serious as long as I keep my tablets within reach. You'd never know. Josie, the doctor agreed that if you wanted to come back...

JO: *(cutting in)* You should've got the television fixed. What are we gonna do all evening? *(Picks up the newspaper and pretends to read. GWEN is hurt by this, but when she can speak)*

GWEN: It's just that I wouldn't be a burden. I wanted to tell you. *(GWEN begins to knit erratically. JO puts on a record, listens tensely to a few bars, takes it off, and sits taking up the newspaper.)* Did I tell you they're gonna plant trees in our road? They've sent a letter and we all have to contribute something but I think everyone will don't you? I asked next door and they will. They seem to be able to afford anything anyway. I don't know how because he's only a milkman and she doesn't work. They're having new windows put in, did I tell you?

JO: Oh don't keep on Mum.

(JO flings the paper down and exits to kitchen. GWEN looks crestfallen. She puts the knitting down as we hear a key in the door and ELLA enters. GWEN stands to greet her.)

GWEN: Ella!

ELLA: Is the kettle on?

GWEN: Did you come alone?

ELLA: Frank's picking me up later.

GWEN: Josie's here. *(goes to door)* Josie, your Aunt Ella's here.

ELLA: *(hanging her coat in the hall)* I thought I'd have a break today. *(returns, sees knitting)* What are you knitting?

GWEN: A jumper for Josie. Do you like it?

ELLA: It's lovely.

GWEN: It's a simple pattern really, only you've got to - *(JO enters)* Oh Josie, make your Aunt some tea - there's a good girl.
(JO curtsies cutely to GWEN)

196

JO: Hello Aunt Ella.

ELLA: Hello Jo. Lord, you look awful.

JO: Thanks.

GWEN: I told her.

JO: Once or twice. Great for my confidence. *(exits)*

ELLA: So, how's everything?

GWEN: I broke the teapot Ella. The blue and white one.

ELLA: Oh what a shame.

GWEN: I didn't grip the handle properly and it slipped. I've had it for so long too.

ELLA: Oh well, never mind Gwen.

GWEN: I know, but first I lost my number six knitting needles, then the sink got blocked the other day. And on Thursday I switched off the fridge to defrost and forgot to empty it. Everything was ruined.

ELLA: That's not like you.

GWEN: I was upset about the teapot. It was such a nice shape.

ELLA: I broke a crystal vase last week.

GWEN: You break things on purpose when you lose your temper.

ELLA: No, this was an accident. Anyway Gwen, these things don't really matter. Do they?

GWEN: *(seemingly mollified)* How have you been? How's Karlly?

ELLA: He's got a bit of a cold, otherwise he's okay. But we'll have to stop calling him Karlly. Says he's too big for that and we have to call him Karl.

GWEN: He's only twenty-seven.

ELLA: Twenty-eight.

GWEN: And Katherine and Barry? How are they?

ELLA: Oh full of beans as usual. She rang me last night. They're preparing the childrens' birthday party.

GWEN: I bought Jamie's card. He is seven isn't he?

ELLA: Mmm.

(JO enters with the tea tray)

JO: And how's uncle Frank?

ELLA: In good spirits at the moment.

GWEN: Has he found a job yet?

ELLA: He's got one lined up.

GWEN: There what did I tell you? You hear Josie, your Uncle Frank's got another job.

ELLA: What about you Jo? How are you getting on in your new place?

GWEN: I wish you wouldn't call her Jo; it sounds so masculine.

JO: Don't forget I'm changing sex mother.

ELLA: What?

JO: Nothing. I'm still settling in.

ELLA: I suppose it takes time.

JO: Spending my weekends here doesn't help. I've still got lots to do.

197

GWEN: I don't know why you keep saying that. She leaves Sunday afternoon. She's hardly here any time at all. *(looks at tea tray)* Oh Josie, you've forgotten the biscuits.

JO: There weren't any.

GWEN: Oh. I'll nip to the corner and get some.

(GWEN gets her coat from the hall)

ELLA: It doesn't matter. Gwen.

GWEN: Won't be a minute. *(has gone)*

JO: *(pouring tea)* So he got it.

ELLA: Yes.

JO: The job Barry arranged?

ELLA: Gwen doesn't seem to understand, but I should've expected that.

JO: Mum's quite good at not listening to what she doesn't want to hear. *(hands her the tea)* Do you have to go?

ELLA: We want to.

JO: It'll be nice for you I suppose. *(Pause. They sip their tea)* Oh Aunt Ella, why did you have to marry such a young man?

ELLA: I'd recommend it Jo.

JO: If he'd been your age you could've retired nicely together and stayed put. Gardening and crocheting.

ELLA: Please! *(Pause)* So, how is it in your place? I didn't have a chance to ask last week.

JO: It's okay.

ELLA: No really, tell me about it.

JO: I got a lot of pleasure from everything at first. I stared at the trees in the street. I smiled a lot. I even felt young and new in the world. Pathetic really. Now I feel like a gate-crasher at someone else's party. Not entitled. *(Pause)* I've got a local. I go there nearly every night. See the same people. Some of them go from the dartboard to the fruit-machine and back again. Afraid to talk. Others tell you everything but switch off when you start. I go in on my own but no-one's heavy. I drink till I'm nearly blotto then I go home. You'd think someone'd wanna take advantage of me wouldn't you? No such luck. *(Pause)* My records still give me pleasure. At least that hasn't changed. You have to have pleasure. The more difficult it is the more pleasure a simple thing will give you.

(She looks at ELLA who avoids her gaze, embarrassed. JO continues with a note of harshness in her voice.)

JO: Let me tell you about my street. It's a cul-de-sac. There's this dishevelled old house on the corner. The woman stands at the gate all day. She asks me the time whenever I pass. She asks everyone. The time's all we give her. If it's raining she sits at the window and calls to you. You can pretend not to hear. She's not old, just dirty with those eyes that seek you out. And a scrawny neck. Sagging and dirty. *(calmly)* I'd like to wring it for her.

(Awkward pause. GWEN returns.)

GWEN: I'm back. *(removes her coat and enters with biscuits, talking)* I bought some new curtains Ella, did you notice?

ELLA: Oh yes. *(goes to inspect them, GWEN follows)* Where did you get them from?

GWEN: A stall in the market. They're seconds but I can't see anything wrong. They're not faded.

ELLA: They're nice.

GWEN: They make quite a difference really don't they?

ELLA: Yes. *(the bus passes)* Oh Lord, that bus! Doesn't it drive you mad?

GWEN: I hardly notice it anymore. *(ELLA turns back)* I wasn't sure about the colour.

ELLA: *(a little weary)* It's a good choice Gwen.

GWEN: *(pleased)* Oh well, come and have your tea. *(She trails ELLA back to her seat, as she seems forever to trail behind ELLA)* Josie put them up didn't you Josie?

JO: You make me sound like a performing seal. Why don't you ask about Uncle Frank's job?

ELLA: Wait a minute Jo.

GWEN: Why? *(she nervously opens biscuits and puts them on tray)*

ELLA: Well Gwen you see, it's the one Barry was trying to get for him.

GWEN: But that was in Exeter.

ELLA: Yes.

GWEN: That's stupid Ella. A printer's a skilled job. He can find work if he keeps looking. You're

just panicking that's all.

ELLA: Even if he could, that's not all.

GWEN: Of course he could. He's only been unemployed three or four months - that's nothing these days. *(She stares at ELLA who slowly smooths down her skirt.)* You're not really going are you?

ELLA: I've been trying to tell you for the past two months we might.

GWEN: But I didn't think... What about Karlly? Karlly won't want to go.

ELLA: He's staying on in the house.

JO: You're not selling it then?

ELLA: There's no need and I want to know Karlly's alright. *(to Gwen)* You must've known we were serious.

JO: When will you go?

ELLA: It could be six weeks.

GWEN: So soon? It's hardly any time at all. So that's why you came?

ELLA: He had confirmation yesterday.

GWEN: I thought it might be a special occasion to bring you here.

ELLA: I wanted to come earlier so that we could do some shopping, but Karlly... *(trails off, feeling miserable)*

JO: So where will you live?

ELLA: With Katherine and Barry.

(Pause)

199

GWEN: What about me?

ELLA: Do you want to come too? *(hastily in case GWEN thinks it's an offer)* It's not far on the train.

JO: Four adults and three kids; it'll be like Spaghetti Junction.

GWEN: Don't joke about it Josie.

(Awkward pause. JO goes to the window and stands there, her back tense. Suddenly she flings open the curtains as the bus rumbles by. She makes grotesque frantic postures at it.)

GWEN: Josie! Stop that!

JO: *(calm again)* Why? Do you think any of those tired faces even noticed me? Just another bus load passing through. Two dozen tiny minds focussed on themselves.

GWEN: Just don't do it again.

JO: Do you care what they think? They're really nothing to do with us you know.

GWEN: Oh stop it. I hate these moods.

JO: What moods?

GWEN: 'Me and the world out there' moods.

JO: *(hurt)* Do you know what day it is Aunt Ella?

ELLA: What?

JO: Twenty years today - since Ruth's flight to freedom.

ELLA: *(disinterested)* Really?

JO: *(disconcerted)* Mum doesn't like to be reminded but Ruth could be dead and buried for all the mention she gets in this house.

ELLA: Mightn't it be better if she were?

JO: Who for? You?

ELLA: It would suit me perfectly.

(JO exits)

GWEN: Don't bait her Ella.

ELLA: I'm fed up of this annual memorial to a selfish little brat.

GWEN: Don't speak about her.

ELLA: Her one claim to fame was to have run off with the guitartist of a fifth-rate rock band.

GWEN: Whatever Josie says, just ignore it.

ELLA: No Gwen. She extracts the maximum amount of guilt and wretchedness she can from you. I won't allow it.

GWEN: Perhaps she has to. Besides she's not the only one to have made me feel wretched today.

ELLA: Gwen -

GWEN: Just bite your tongue. For my sake.

(JO returns flushed with a framed photograph in her hands. She sets it down on the T.V. It is a photograph of a young lank-haired girl, made up in the false-eyelashed dolly style of the mid-sixties.)

GWEN: *(sharply)* Where did you get that?

JO: You thought she took it didn't you? It's been upstairs in my wardrobe ever since she left. Today it can stay down here.

GWEN is visibly upset. ELLA, shaking with her anger, exits to the kitchen. GWEN watching her with frightened eyes, gets up and follows her out. JO puts a record on and sits listening and staring at the photo. The lights and music fade into the next scene.

SCENE SIX:

MAVIS: *(standing)* Won't you come and sit down now? Nancy? *(turns away and sits)* I was just the same. Could never sit still for too long. Even so. Oh Nancy, really dear, don't cross me like this. Come along. *(a moment later JO enters, puzzled)*

JO: You're getting me confused with someone.

MAVIS: What?

JO: Nancy. Who is she?

MAVIS: No-one. I'm sorry. *(Pause)* You don't have to do the kitchen today you know.

JO: Birthday present. Although I did think it was today?

MAVIS: What dear?

JO: Your birthday. You led me to believe it was today. Not that it matters, not really.

MAVIS: But I told you it was Monday.

JO: I don't think so. Anyway now the kitchen's done you can invite your friends round.

MAVIS: What friends? All my friends are dead. They were good people. Marvellous fun. Theatricals always are. My best friend was a

girl called Dorothy. Dotty. She was a terrible flirt. Wouldn't leave Robbie alone. Have I told you about Robbie?

JO: Did you find the photos?

MAVIS: I've got masses. In the bedroom somewhere. It's such a mess.

(Pause)

JO: Miss Russell?

MAVIS: Yes dear? Call me Mavis.

JO: I enquired, about home helps.

MAVIS: Oh, will they send someone?

JO: Well, you have to get a letter from the doctor first, then go on the waiting-list. It may be some months but you'll get one eventually.

MAVIS: But I'm 80 years old.

JO: There's no priority, not just for housework they said. They said it was the cuts.

MAVIS: The cuts?

JO: So if you go to the doctor...

MAVIS: No. I haven't been to a doctor for 30 years.

JO: But if you don't go -

MAVIS: You'd love my photos. Marvellous people. Me on the stage! I was a pretty girl then. You'd like to see them wouldn't you?

JO: *(wearily)* Yes.

MAVIS: It's just I'm not sure where they are. It's so untidy in there and so dark. Would you change the light bulb for me?

JO: Yes.

MAVIS: I don't like to ask.

JO: It's nothing, really.

MAVIS: Then perhaps I can find them. There's one of me as Amelia Benson. That was my greatest role. "Is this all there will be for me? Every step lower than the one before, until - what?"

JO: Miss Russell?

MAVIS: "What could be worse?"

JO: Miss Russell. *(MAVIS looks at her)* Is there a new light bulb?

MAVIS: I'll fetch it. *(is about to finish her speech)*

JO: Tell me where it is and I'll get it.

MAVIS: Now let me see. Suzie? I've even got some of Robbie. Have I told you about Robbie?

JO: Yes. I'll have to make a move soon, so...

MAVIS: He was my - friend. I was a flapper when we met you know. A bright young thing - skinny and poor but he fell in love with me. I must have had some charm, I was only twenty after all. He was much older but we were so much in love.

JO: Miss Russell.

MAVIS: I think I loved him first because he was so much like a father to me. My own father died when I was ten you see. He was married of course, but we managed to see quite a lot of each other and

I don't think she ever found out. We were quite happy really and I had my career.

JO: *(in her impatience to get away)* How did you manage in those days before the Pill?

(MAVIS stares at her for a moment.)

MAVIS: Tut, what am I thinking of? You wanted to go five minutes ago. You young people - always so busy. *(stands)* Suzie? *(to JO)* Well it didn't go too badly did it? I have enjoyed this afternoon.

JO: *(guilt-ridden)* Yes, so have I. Er - shall I change the light-bulb now?

MAVIS: If you don't mind. I am grateful.

(MAVIS fetches the light bulb and a torch. She gives the bulb to JO who exits, followed by MAVIS who remains in the doorway shining the torch.)

MAVIS: I'm sorry about that. I don't mind if you step on them. They fall out of the wardrobe and I can't pick them up. They need a good clean. I used to be so clean. Changed my clothes twice a day. So you won't be able to come next week?

JO: *(off)* I may be a bit busy.

MAVIS: Of course you will. Young people these days, always have so much to do. I'm more than pleased with what you've done Nancy. It's quite lovely to sit in a tidy room, makes us cheerful, me and Suzie. *(looks again into the bedroom, clouds over.)* I'll make a start in here myself. Use the broom handle to pick them up. Clear a path to the window. I'll get there in the end. Yes, I'll make a start tomorrow. Ready? *(She switches on the light. A spotlight hits her face. She is joyous.)* Oh marvellous Josephine! Thank you! Oh thank you so much!

The spotlight fades.

SCENE SEVEN:

GWEN and ELLA sit close by shelling peas. They work on in silence for a while.

GWEN: Did I tell you there's a new shop in the market? Fancy goods. It's lovely to walk around. All bright lights, crystal glasses and pretty colours. Quite expensive though. You'd be surprised at the prices.

ELLA: Everything's dear nowadays.

(Pause)

GWEN: You shouldn't have said that to Josie you know.

ELLA: It's the truth. As far as I'm concerned there is no Ruth. She only exists in Jo's memory.

GWEN: It hurt me too.

ELLA: It's true.

GWEN: I know.

(Pause)

ELLA: Why does she still go on about her?

GWEN: It's like a stab in the back to me. You should've kept quiet.

ELLA: I tried. I stood in the kitchen and gritted my teeth.

GWEN: You always let your temper get the better of you.

ELLA: It's so morbid. Still, I wonder what she is doing now.

GWEN: The same as all the other groupies and flower children. She'll have an ordinary life. Mortgage, husband, children.

ELLA: Oh, that's awful.

GWEN: What is?

ELLA: To think you've got grandchildren who won't know you.

(Pause)

GWEN: I've got a headache.

(Pause)

ELLA: What do you think she's up to?

GWEN: Probably going through Ruth's old things.

ELLA: You haven't kept them?

GWEN: Josie - *(Pause)*

ELLA: It's not only morbid, it's macabre. You don't think Jo's, you know, going a bit -

GWEN: No.

(They shell peas in silence. The bus passes by outside.)

GWEN: Oh Ella, I can't get used to her being away.

ELLA: It'll take time Gwen.

GWEN: It seems so strange. Josie sitting alone in one room, me sitting alone here - I can't see the point. And she's paying out good money.

ELLA: Perhaps she needs time on

her own.

GWEN: But she could go to her room any time she liked to be by herself. I wouldn't interfere.

ELLA: Oh Gwen!

GWEN: When I was a girl I never even thought of leaving home.

ELLA: Things were different then.

GWEN: You left when you married and even then, like as not, you landed up in the next street. I don't understand it. I looked in on Mum every day, right up to when she died. I wanted to.

(ELLA pats GWEN'S hand)

ELLA: Let's have some coffee.

(They have finished shelling the peas)

GWEN: There isn't any.

ELLA: No coffee?

GWEN: It's too expensive.

ELLA: You'll turn into a miser.

GWEN: I have to be careful.

ELLA: But you just bought curtains.

GWEN: Because I economise. *(stands)* I can nip down to the shop on the corner.

ELLA: Never mind. Sit down. Look Gwen -

GWEN: That new Indian grocers is wonderful. They never close before nine and the lady there is ever so nice, always has time for a chat.

ELLA: Gwen -

GWEN: Did I tell you she's got a lovely daughter who helps in the shop? She's getting married soon. It's been arranged by her parents but she doesn't seem to mind.

ELLA: Have you finished?

GWEN: They're a lovely family.

ELLA: What did you mean, you have to be careful?

GWEN: *(a little ashamed)* I don't know what you think I live on Ella.

ELLA: You've got your pension, and your savings.

GWEN: The pension's not much. I pay the bills from my savings but there's only a couple of hundred left and I don't want to spend it all. It used to be alright when Josie was home. Her little bit made all the difference. Now she gives a fortune in rent to some stranger.

(GWEN gasps. ELLA turns to see what has startled her and is herself taken aback. JO enters. She wears RUTH'S old clothes, too tight for her. Skirt and blouse circa '65, and shoes. She has let down her own lank hair, badly bouffoned and most grotesque of all, she wears the false eyelashes and make-up of the day copied from RUTH'S photo. She looks a cross between 'Baby Jane' and a man in drag. GWEN and ELLA are horrified. JO strides into the centre of the room and strikes a Twiggy posture, hand on one hip.)

JO: Look at this! Ring any bells? Now tell me she doesn't exist. These are Ruth's clothes. She lived here. She came through this house like fresh air through a churchyard. Ruth's was a free spirit. *(postures and mimicks)* "Hey man, a gig in

Brighton? Sure I'll come. Hitch down and stay the weekend. It'll be groovy". "Let's have some music. Music is my life man. I've got to have music and love. Love is life man". "Hey, there's a party tomorrow. I'd never miss a party. Life's too short man". *(she laughs)* And it bloody well is, isn't it?

(Pause. ELLA and GWEN can only stare. JO begins to feel uncomfortable. She puts on a record - 'The Free' or 'Ten Years After' and begins to dance.)

JO: I could've gone. I could've had all that; more fun in six months than I've had in 42 bloody years. Parties, travelling, popping pills, sleeping around. I could've done all that. I could've lived in that world.

(She turns up the music and dances, more and more energetically. She shakes her hair and her limbs. At one point frustration takes over from dancing, and she almost looks as if she is having a fit. GWEN and ELLA watch. At its height, simultaneously the action freezes, the music stops and lights brighten.)

Quick blackout.

End of Act

ACT TWO

SCENE ONE:

MAVIS sits alone on stage.

MAVIS: I'd have been a great grandmother by now. I knew she'd be a girl. Beautiful. Dead. They wrapped her in newspaper and put her in the dustbin. I would've liked to hear her laugh. Nancy. She'd have had children. Now she'd be living nearby and popping in every day. Or, I like this best, we all live together and I tell stories to make the children laugh. And when Nancy asks about her father I tell her. What a wonderful man he was and how much he loved her - more than anything in the world. *(Pause)* Everyone said ... I did what they told me. But I didn't know it was you Nancy, there like that already. God's paying me back. Robbie didn't understand. He thought I was upset because there'd be no more. But it was you. I couldn't bring you back could I? Not you Nancy.

(She picks up the beautiful sequined shawl from her lap as JO appears)

MAVIS: Here.

JO: No, I couldn't.

MAVIS: It's just to say thank you. You'll have to have it cleaned of course.

JO: It's beautiful.

MAVIS: No good to me. Only Suzie matters now.

JO: Thank you, I love it.

(JO gazes at the shawl and tries it over her shoulders, not listening to MAVIS.)

MAVIS: I live for Suzie. If she didn't need me to feed and care for her I wouldn't bother anymore. Isn't it strange the way we keep on. Waking up every day. Sometimes I think I'll live forever. When I hear of someone dying, someone young or half of a couple,

I wonder, why couldn't it have been me? He wakes me up every day. To punish me Nancy. *(looks to see if she's there)* Nancy?

JO: You've called me Nancy again.

MAVIS: Did I dear? I'm sorry.

JO: I wish you wouldn't. *(stands)* I can't stay any longer.

MAVIS: Oh!

JO: I'll finish next week.

MAVIS: Sit down please. You're just like Robbie, won't let a job go till it's finished.

JO: What does that mean?

MAVIS: *(regardless)* He was so stubborn. Portly and stubborn, but he was very charming. Not good-looking you know but so charming all the girls loved him. Dottie couldn't leave him alone. That's why we stopped being friends. She would flirt and she was prettier than me and I'd get so jealous. Jealous. I can't remember how that feels now. It was a shame really because I liked her. I wonder if she's still alive?

JO: I'll come back next week to finish the bedroom.

MAVIS: It's 30 years since Robbie passed away.

JO: Thank you for the shawl. *(turns to go)*

MAVIS: Did I tell you about Robbie?

JO: A few times.

MAVIS: It's hard to lose someone. All I have now is my Suzie. I live for Suzie and she lives for me. Can you see that note on the wall?

JO: *(flatly)* Yes.

MAVIS: I pinned it there in case something should happen to me. If I go first I want her put to sleep.

JO: When I finish the bedroom next week the whole flat will be clean and tidy. Won't that be lovely?

MAVIS: I wish I could keep it that way. This room gets so untidy in between your visits. I do try but Suzie knocks things down. I get dizzy when I bend. Suzie? You're such a naughty girl.

JO: I have to go now.

MAVIS: Stay a few minutes more Nancy.

JO: I'm not Nancy!

MAVIS: Did I -?

JO: Yes. *(she turns to go)*

MAVIS: Josephine. Don't go.

JO: I really am pushed for time. I've stayed too long already.

MAVIS: Did you come across the photographs?

JO: No.

MAVIS: Don't go yet.

JO: I must.

MAVIS: Please.

JO: Really I must. Thank you for the shawl. Goodbye Mavis. *(exits)*

MAVIS: Goodbye my dear. See you next week? See that Suzie? Always rushing, just like her father. Where are you girl? Come to mummy. Suzie? Suzie?

Sits back in her chair, exhausted, and closes her eyes.

SCENE TWO:

GWEN knits nervously. ELLA studies the newspaper.

ELLA: She's taking her time over that washing up, small wonder.

GWEN: *(hastily)* I've always hated washing up.

ELLA: I still can't believe my luck when I can clean a non-stick pan in one go.

(Pause)

GWEN: Do you remember the public baths?

ELLA: What on earth made you think of that?

GWEN: I don't know. Sometimes you used to skip your turn, I remember.

ELLA: We were the only ones in our street silly enough to spend money on baths. I hated the big oak doors and marble everywhere. All that steam. Women murmuring their complaints over the cubicles. I used to imagine a morgue would be like that.

GWEN: I liked it. The cold, that must've been the worst thing when we were small.

ELLA: You used to put your icy feet on me in bed.

GWEN: No I didn't.

ELLA: You did!

(Pause. The bus passes.)

GWEN: It was such a different life then. We were forever popping into each other's houses. Even when you upped and went to Walthamstow, the best of my week was Wednesdays and Saturdays when we had our dinner at Mum's.

(ELLA looks at GWEN for a moment.)

ELLA: You spend too much time here Gwen.

GWEN: What do you mean?

ELLA: Well -

GWEN: What?

ELLA: I don't know. How about Bingo? Meet people. You'd like that.

GWEN: Bingo?

(JO enters from kitchen)

ELLA: Josie might go with you sometimes.

(Gets up and exits past JO to kitchen)

GWEN: Where are you going? *(gets up)*

JO: Clickety-click, sixty-six. Gawd in heaven, number seven!

GWEN: Oh Josie. *(goes toward door)*

JO: You can't gad about to Bingo if you have angina.

GWEN: Shh! *(pulls her away from kitchen doorway)*

JO: I know. Why haven't you told her?

GWEN: She doesn't need to know. Anyway I could go to Bingo if I wanted.

JO: *(mimics)* It's too expensive.

GWEN: You've changed in some very unpleasant ways since you left Josie, and I don't like it, not one bit.

JO: Yes maam. You'd better rap my knuckles maam. *(hears ELLA returning)* I'll go for the coffee.

(She grabs her jacket and exits. ELLA enters eating the last of a biscuit.)

ELLA: She scared me rigid this afternoon.

(GWEN sighs and sits down. ELLA sits)

GWEN: I don't know what sort of life she's been leading. She doesn't tell me anything.

ELLA: You shouldn't expect her to.

GWEN: I was thinking - we could swap rooms. I don't need the big bedroom.

ELLA: What are you talking about? She won't come back.

GWEN: You don't know.

ELLA: Ask her yourself.

GWEN: You can't understand.

ELLA: Don't you see?

GWEN: Don't make it sound as if she doesn't want me.

ELLA: Girls that age -

GWEN: What? You didn't leave till you were 36.

ELLA: And Josie's 42!

GWEN: So?

ELLA: *(sighs)* Count your blessings she didn't leave when Ruth did.

GWEN: She wasn't like Ruth. Not a bit.

ELLA: God, I know that. Good Lord Gwen, give you a locked cell with Jo and a few bloody ornaments and you'd be happy for the next forty years!

GWEN: I don't know why you think of me that way. Anyone'd think wanting to be with family is a crime. *(Pause. She paces to her ornaments and arranges them.)* Do you really have to go?

ELLA: Oh I knew you hadn't had your say on that.

GWEN: We're sisters Ella. Even if I still had George, even if Josie came home - we understand each other.

ELLA: You don't understand me.

GWEN: I do.

ELLA: Oh Lord Gwen, live your own life. You always want to be in someone's shadow. George's, Jo's, mine. You're just like Mum.

GWEN: I've loved you all.

ELLA: Oh don't! I'm going to Katherine's. That's my future.

GWEN: It's not natural to be so far apart.

ELLA: It is.

GWEN: I'll never see you again.

ELLA: We'll come back.

GWEN: What for? Karlly'll come to you for weekends.

ELLA: Fat chance.

GWEN: I don't understand how you can leave him. How can you?

ELLA: He has his own life to lead. If we weren't going he would end up in some pokey... *(GWEN gets up to re-arrange the ornaments again)* He's fed up of us. Always finding fault. He's tickled to death we're going. We've reinstated some respect in him. You always have to work at that with your children. Little thanks you get for it. I don't think he'll miss us at all.

GWEN: She'd never admit it but Josie misses me. I'm sure of that.

ELLA: Bully for you.

(Pause)

GWEN: Ella, don't go. Please.

ELLA: It's all arranged.

GWEN: You can un-arrange it.

ELLA: I don't want to.

GWEN: You'll miss me too.

ELLA: Yes.

GWEN: You will.

ELLA: Why? All I've done is play psychiatrist to you all these years. *(GWEN is shocked)* I've listened to all your silly worries every weekend, all your phone-calls. It's not as if you ever listen to me.

GWEN: *(hurt)* Ella. If I've asked you anything you've clammed up, you know you have. I thought - I never thought. *(too hurt to go on, leaves the ornaments)*

ELLA: *(softening)* Anyway you could come there.

GWEN: *(sits)* You don't want me.

ELLA: For a holiday?

GWEN: *(quietly)* You don't want me Ella.

ELLA: Of course I do. You just haven't the guts to meet me halfway. We can't stay tied together forever.

GWEN: Why not? Why haven't you gone before if you feel like that?

ELLA: I wanted to be close.

GWEN: Did you Ella?

ELLA: I wanted to keep an eye on you. You've always been so - affected by everything. We'd talked of going before but George died and I couldn't leave you like that. Now Jo's left. There'll always be some excuse for this dirge of an existence. Gwen, we're not that old. There's still time for us. And why shouldn't you go to Bingo or classes? Meet people who'd be much better friends to you than I've ever been.

GWEN: You talk as if it means nothing. We're sisters.

ELLA: *(restraining herself)* I'll miss you, of course I will. It'd be easy not to go.

GWEN: It's all fallen apart since

209

Mum died. There's only us.

ELLA: We've shared all our lives. Now I want something different.

GWEN: What?

ELLA: I want a chance somewhere else. New experiences, new people.

GWEN: You're sixty-eight. *(returns to ornaments)*

ELLA: So what?

GWEN: It's so obvious Ella.

ELLA: What is? That I should bury myself alive for your convenience?

GWEN: That your husband's only 55.

ELLA: *(furious)* I've tried to explain but you won't listen will you?*(she grapples with GWEN to get at the ornaments)* You won't listen will you! *(she grabs one and smashes it)*

GWEN: Don't Ella.

ELLA: *(smashing them)* Don't break the cheap junk! Don't disturb the morgue!

(JO enters and is glimpsed in the passage but unseen by the sisters.)

GWEN: Not that one Ella! Ruth bought it ba -

(ELLA smashes it. Seeing GWEN'S expression she flees the room and slams the front door.)

GWEN: Oh Ella.

(She goes to the kitchen. JO appears slightly in the doorway and watches. GWEN returns with dustpan and brush and sweeps up the broken pieces. JO comes into

the room and stands over GWEN)

JO: This is apt isn't it? On your hands and knees over the ghost of Ruth's Past.

GWEN: Shut up Josie.

JO: I can't. I don't have anyone else to banter with do I? Unlike you and Aunt Ella.

GWEN: That's enough.

JO: Do you know, I keep thinking I'll switch on the T.V. one day and there she'll be, smiling and beautifully made-up. Or I'll open the paper and see her there - in an expensive fur at the airport, about to jet off with a celebrity. I encouraged her to go. I wanted her to be happy. You've made me pay for that. I had to be doubly good. You said it killed Dad and I had to pay for that too.

GWEN: I loved Ruth.

JO: You gave. Gave. We didn't even have to think because you'd do that too. You gave us everything but the chance to cope. Do you understand?

(GWEN leaves the dustpan on the floor and clambers to a seat. She is visibly hurt.)

GWEN: Ruth was shallow, vain and pleasure-seeking.

JO: You've got your moral cap on.

GWEN: She's forgotten we exist.

JO: We got all those cards and letters.

GWEN: Four postcards and one letter?

JO: And the phone-calls. All she got was the worry she caused and pleas to come back. Never a word on if she was happy. No wonder she stopped. It'd make the laughing policeman slit his throat.

GWEN: You wasted your affection on her.

JO: How can you say that?

GWEN: She didn't care about you.

JO: That's not true.

GWEN: Alright.

JO: I pushed her into the best world full of life and music. She loved me because I understood. I gave her my life and I'd do it again. Now at least she's happy, savouring every happy musical moment of life. I loved her, I still do.

GWEN: I know.

JO: It's like saying-oh-I don't know!

GWEN: You should listen to me sometimes Josie.

JO: Why? What do you ever say that makes sense eh? All you can talk about is the neighbours and the price of tomatoes.

(She's half out of the door)

GWEN: I saw her.

(It takes JO a second to take this in)

JO: *(delighted)* You saw Ruthie?

GWEN: In 1979.

JO: *(horrified)* What?

GWEN: I never stopped looking for her - you never tried.

JO: *(worked up)* You didn't tell me! All this time and - *(Pause. Triumphantly)* Well then?

GWEN: She's got a house the size of a shoe-box and a mortgage she won't pay off till she's my age. She married a plumber who comes home smelling of drains. They have two delinquent kids and live in Liverpool. I'll give you her address if you like but she doesn't want to see you. I went there one day when you thought I was at Ella's. She blamed me for everything and sent me packing. She didn't react when I told her her father had died. She couldn't care less when I spoke of you. She asked me for money. She looks like a fishwife. *(Pause)* What else do you want to know?

(JO is aware that she's spoken the truth)

JO: How about the meaning of life? *(laughs)*

GWEN: She didn't recognise me.

(JO laughs, and exits)

SCENE THREE:

MAVIS and JO sit facing each other.

JO: *(embarrassed)* I'm sorry about last week. Something came up. You know I get so busy sometimes, I'm still thinking about yesterday when tomorrow comes. But I'll finish the bedroom today. After that though I don't know if - *(sees MAVIS'S expression)* Mavis?

MAVIS: *(flatly)* I don't want you to do any work. You don't have to.

JO: I don't mind.

211

MAVIS: I can't sleep.

JO: You should see the doctor - I don't know why you won't. *(Pause)* Well, I -

MAVIS: No. I don't want you to. Just sit down.

JO: There's no need to be embarrassed about this you know.

MAVIS: I can't sleep at night.

JO: *(squirms)* When the bedroom's finished... *(trails off)*

MAVIS: It doesn't matter.

JO: Mavis? Mavis. I really couldn't come last week. I had so much work. If you had a phone I would've rung. But I didn't say I was coming did I? Not definitely.

MAVIS: I waited in.

JO: It's difficult sometimes.

MAVIS: Yes.

(Pause)

JO: I'm thinking of going away.

MAVIS: If it weren't for you Nancy-

JO: There's more work in another area.

MAVIS: Leave the job dear.

JO: What?

MAVIS: We'll have more time together. I need you now.

JO: Mavis, you're getting mixed up again.

MAVIS: Don't call me by my name - it's disrespectful.

JO: *(strangely repulsed)* Don't do this.

MAVIS: I want you to forgive me. *(JO stands)* Josephine. You didn't know I had a little girl did you? Mine and Robbie's. She's with God now. Aren't you going to visit me anymore?

JO: *(hesitates)* I've been trying to tell you. I'm going away. It'll be very difficult. I'd come if I could, honestly, but well-

MAVIS: You don't have to do any more work. Just half an hour for a chat. Or even ten minutes would do.

JO: I won't be around that often. That's what I'm trying to tell you.

MAVIS: When you can then. I'll always be in.

(They look at each other then JO stares at the floor trying to think of what to say next. She sees MAVIS leaving the room and prepares to escape.)

MAVIS: I've got something for you. Just a minute. Please.

(She exits. JO, uncomfortable, stares around the room. Notices the note isn't pinned to the wall. Goes to see if it's fallen down as MAVIS returns carrying a beautiful red spangled gown of the 20's style.)

JO: No Mavis.

MAVIS: It reminds me. He bought it for me after - I never wore it.

JO: No.

MAVIS: I couldn't throw it out.

(JO sits wearily on the arm of a chair. MAVIS lays the gown over

212

JO'S lap)

MAVIS: It's my goodbye present.

JO: I don't want it.

MAVIS: Please. *(Pause)* I used to be so clean. Changed my clothes twice a day. Dotty... I was so proud. I never asked for help, all my life. I used to help others.

JO: *(strokes the dress, obviously wants it)* Have you found the photos?

MAVIS: I know every single one. Every face and every line. I don't need to look anymore. *(Pause)* I know where they are.

JO: Mavis!

MAVIS: What do I have? Not even self-respect. It's all bartered for company. I can't give away my past as well; that'd be too much to lose. *(defiantly)* No-one shall see my photographs till I'm dead!

JO: *(embarrassed, racks her brains for something to say)* Your note's not on the wall. It must have fallen down. Shall I write you another?

MAVIS: No.

JO: Have you changed your mind? *(looks around)* Where's Suzie? Hiding again?

MAVIS: No Suzie.

JO: Pardon?

MAVIS: I said - no Suzie.

JO: *(realising)* Oh Mavis no.

MAVIS: It was early. She leant on my chest and I stroked her. She hadn't done that for such a long time. "There girl" I said. "can't you sleep either? Never mind." I was thinking I still have Suzie. He's punishing me. Next day, she was like a toy. Too stiff to cuddle. I slept. Let her die on her own. After all these years. *(Pause)* I wrapped her in a scarf. *(indicates)* Out there. I couldn't - all that heavy earth. She's only out there. I want to go and fetch her in. But I can't bring her back can I? Not...

MAVIS is silent. JO watches her, then stands and woodenly exits through back of flat. Lights.

SCENE FOUR:

GWEN is alone on stage, and restless. She wanders around the room, looking at her watch, looking out the window. Eventually she goes to the door and calls.

GWEN: Josie, why don't you come down?

(There is no reply. She returns to the window and stands gazing out. She doesn't hear JO enter. JO wears the red gown of previous scene.)

JO: Yoo-hoo. *(she drapes herself on the door frame)*

GWEN: *(stiffens self-consciously and fusses with the curtain, without turning round)* Your Aunt Ella's a long time.

JO: I know.

(JO comes in and puts on a record and begins dancing.)

GWEN: *(turns)* Where did that dress come from?

213

JO: Mavis. Miss Mavis Russell. Do you like it?

GWEN: Well.. Is it clean?

JO: Shouldn't think so.

GWEN: Who's Mavis Russell?

JO: I used to go and do her flat.

(She stops dancing and switches off the record. GWEN stares)

JO: I met her through my job; one of many. She'd sometimes think I was her dead daughter. *(she looks in mirror)* There was only one room left to clean. If she hadn't interfered. I went out to bury her cat. A stinking glump in a blue silk scarf. Flies. Worms. Maggots. I laughed. There it was - the sum total of all we go through. You end up a stinking lump turning to shit. *(laugh)* I had to laugh. It's funny. *(Laughs again. Pause)* I went back in, picked up my coat, and this dress - I wanted the dress. She just looked at me. Knew I wasn't gonna 'pay'.

GWEN: Josie!

JO: She was begging! I couldn't get out quick enough. "Nancy!" *(Pause)* You'd think the devil was at my heels - not old Mavis and her empty room.

(She laughs. GWEN doesn't know what to say; just stares)

JO: You're not listening.

GWEN: I don't want to.

(GWEN turns away. The bus passes by outside.)

JO: Mum, remember when I was small and we went to Gran's for the night. We shared the small bed and Gran came to kiss us goodnight and tuck us in. I remember the way she looked at you, like you were a little girl.

GWEN: *(hurt by the recollection)* You can be so wicked.

(JO is surprised by her reaction. We hear the key in the lock and ELLA enter.)

GWEN: Ella! Where have you been?

ELLA: *(detached)* I went for a walk. *(removes coat)*

JO: I thought you'd flown back to the safety of Walthamstow.

ELLA: *(hesitates, hangs coat in hall)* Frank's picking me up.

JO: Good old Frank.

ELLA: Yes, well..
(GWEN has turned away and ELLA watches her exit to kitchen. She tries a cheerful manner) Why are you dressed like that?

JO: *(shrugs)* I was bored.

ELLA: Where did you get it?

JO: Perhaps I stole it.

ELLA: *(taking a cigarette from her bag)* I suspected you'd turn into a middle-aged delinquent.

JO: *(stiffens, then)* When did you start smoking?

ELLA: Ages ago. Not often. Did your mother say anything?

JO: Interesting? No. *(suspicious)* What about?

ELLA: Nothing. You know, I have a

214

horrible feeling Gwen isn't getting a rates rebate. Jo?

JO: How should I know?

ELLA: Oh really! You must see to it first thing Monday. Promise me you will. *(JO turns away)* I'd taken it for granted you'd done at least that much for your mother.

JO: I don't operate on the assumption that she's inept at everything.

ELLA: Well I'll sort it out then. See she gets everything she's entitled to while I'm at it.

JO: Great. It'll do your guilty conscience a power of good.

ELLA: It's a shame no-one else around here has one of those. *(Pause)* Oh hell, let's call a truce - I'm not in the mood.

(Pause)

JO: You broke her ornaments.

ELLA: *(ashamed)* I lost my temper. They were awful anyway.

(GWEN shuffles in from the kitchen.)

ELLA: Isn't it strange without the television Gwen? Strange without the background noise. Gwen.

GWEN: When we were girls we used to play games. Your Aunt Ella always won.

ELLA: Not always Gwen.

JO: Shall I put a record on?

ELLA: Do you have any cards?

GWEN: No. *(JO goes to record player)* Oh Josie don't. *(Pause)*

Aren't you going to get changed? I don't know what you look like.

JO: Let's play charades.

ELLA: I thought you had been.

JO: Ha ha. What's the topic?

GWEN: Oh we're not going to play charades.

JO: Why not? Aunt Ella?

ELLA: We might as well.

JO: Alright. Topic. Mum?

GWEN: I don't know. What about place names?

JO: Cities in England. That'll do.

ELLA: Who'll start?

(They begin to get into it and enjoy themselves)

GWEN: You start Ella.

ELLA: Oh dear. Now let me see. Ah good. I've got one. *(stands)* You two sit over there. Ready? Now, this is really difficult. *(mimes)*

JO: One syllable.

(ELLA mimes a strip. Gradually the other two relax and laugh. As she mimes getting into a bath, JO groans.)

GWEN: Bath! It's Bath!

JO: Oh Mum.

ELLA: Your turn Jo. *(she sits)*

JO: Oh no. Er - wait a minute.

(She considers, then stands and mimes.)

ELLA: Two syllables. First syllable.

(JO mimes beautifully the dying swan)

ELLA: Swansea!

GWEN: Is it? How?

ELLA: Swan Lake silly.

GWEN: Oh.

JO: Your go mum.

GWEN: I couldn't.

ELLA: Oh Gwen.

GWEN: Really I couldn't.

ELLA: Come on.

JO: Yes, go on Mum.

GWEN: I can't think of one.

JO: Well try harder.

GWEN: No, you go again Ella.

JO: Oh Mum, you're such a spoilsport!

GWEN: Alright then. *(stands)* Now - one two three syllables.

ELLA: You're not supposed to say Gwen.

(They all laugh)

GWEN: Sorry. *(mimes)*

JO: Three syllables.

ELLA: Third syllable.

(GWEN mimes a diving action with her arms raised above her head)

JO: Dive.

(GWEN shakes her head and mimes the action again. It brings on an angina attack. She crumples to the floor. JO freezes. ELLA is completely shocked, rushes to her aid.)

ELLA: Gwen!

GWEN: *(in some pain, having difficulty breathing)* Get my tablets - from my bag.

ELLA: Where? Where Gwen?

GWEN: Sideboard.

(ELLA runs across the room, rips out the bag, empties contents on carpet, takes tablets to GWEN. JO watches. GWEN puts a tablet under her tongue.)

GWEN: I'll be alright. Let me rest.

(ELLA gets cushions for her head and lies her flat on the floor then rushes out and upstairs. JO, who's been watching turns and mechanically puts on her record. ELLA returns with the quilt, stands momentarily shocked in the doorway, then covers GWEN and makes sure she's comfortable. Then she goes to the record-player and removes the arm, scratching it in her haste. For the first time since GWEN'S attack JO registers concern and reaches out for the record. In her rage ELLA snatches it off the turntable and smashes it. JO stops short, turns and comes downstage. ELLA turns and approaches her, standing a little behind and looking as if she could kill her.)

JO: *(in a low voice)* It's angina.

ELLA: *(forgetting her rage)* How do you know?

216

JO: The doctor told her last week. *(Pause. Flatly)* It's caused by narrowing of the arteries. She told me this morning.

ELLA: You knew!

JO: She didn't want to tell you. Didn't want to spoil your precious chances.

ELLA: *(restraining herself)* You probably brought this on.

JO: Very likely.

(ELLA turns aside)

ELLA: You'll have to move back in as soon as possible.

JO: Why? So you can float away free of responsibility? Anyway, I'm to be let go of, remember?

ELLA: Is it because of this man? Gwen told me. You're not living with him are you?

JO: *(laughs)* I only met him once. I watched him with my big adoring middle-aged eyes and he laughed.

ELLA: You owe it to her. Are you listening?

JO: One doesn't always honour one's debts. *(lightly)* Anyway she's not going to be an invalid you know.

(ELLA simply stares at the back of her head. Suddenly her face contorts and she grabs JO by the hair. They struggle. GWEN stirs. JO throws ELLA off.)

GWEN: Ella! *(she's aware of what's happened)*

ELLA: *(composing herself)* I'm here.

GWEN: Oh Ella.

(ELLA goes to her and strokes her hair.)

ELLA: Why didn't you say anything? Gwen? Do you want to go to bed? Gwen? *(GWEN isn't speaking to her. She tries to get up. ELLA helps her onto the sofa.)* Will you be alright now? *(picks up the cushions and puts them on sofa, folds quilt)* To think Jo knew all this time! I mean, the way she's behaved today, really! *(She looks to GWEN who is still ignoring her. She begins to collect up contents of handbag. Cheerfully)* Isn't it funny, in all these years, this'll be the first time I've stayed here. I mean I'll stay the night of course. Be like when we were girls. I'd pull the blankets to my side and you'd complain. Or have a moody, like now. Do you remember Gwen? Gwen! You're doing this on purpose!

(She slams the bag down on the sideboard and stands with her back to GWEN. We can see the anger drain from her. GWEN watches her but turns her head as ELLA hesitantly comes and sits next to her. She knows ELLA'S miserable and begins to soften.)

ELLA: *(guiltily)* I'm sorry about the ornaments.

(Pause)

GWEN: Do you remember when you threw the saucepan at me?

ELLA: *(lifted)* You told on me for having a boyfriend.

GWEN: Then you ripped up half my clothes.

ELLA: You deserved it.

GWEN: I did not.

ELLA: You were a jealous cat. Dad gave me a double belting. One for the boy and one for your clothes.

GWEN: I was sorry about that.

ELLA: Then Mum had a go at Dad for belting me.

GWEN: She always did come down on your side.

(ELLA reaches out and clasps GWEN'S hand. The bus passes. JO stands discarded and smouldering at the corner of the room.)

ELLA: What was it?

GWEN: What?

ELLA: The mime?

GWEN: Liverpool.

(ELLA laughs and begins to cry)

GWEN: *(pulls her hand away)* Oh soppypuss!

ELLA: *(wipes her eyes)* I won't go.

GWEN: Do you mean it? *(no reply)* Ella.

ELLA: I remember how it got before Katherine married. If I talked to her she looked right through me - oh I know it's silly. *(Pause)* With a slight annoyance as if I were keeping her from more important things, like varnishing her nails or reading a magazine. That hasn't changed much.

GWEN: She wants you to go.

ELLA: Katherine always keeps within the bounds of duty. I'm not saying she doesn't care you know - she does, in her way. *(Pause)* Karlly wants us out. *(Pause)* I'm rambling on. How are you feeling?

GWEN: I'm alright.

(Pause)

ELLA: I don't want to leave you on your own.

GWEN: You've always been the same Ella. You have to know everyone's alright before you do anything for yourself. *(Pause)* Supposing Jo were to come home.

ELLA: There's Frank. He can't bear not having a job. *(Hesitates)* I did consider going there but into our own house. Property's cheaper and with Frank's redundancy and our savings. If we didn't live in the same house you see I'd like it very much. What do you think Gwen?

GWEN: It sounds alright.

ELLA: And it's only a few hours on the train. We'd have lots of room if you'd come for the weekend.

(Pause. They look at JO, who's been listening to it all. She turns and looks at them, adopting a hard casual air.)

ELLA: Well what have you to say for yourself?

GWEN: Don't Ella.

JO: No don't Ella. Be like Mum. She never gets offended. Never gets angry, do you Mum?

ELLA: You callous bitch.

GWEN: Don't interfere Ella.

ELLA: *(stands)* I want to know. Are you moving back here or not?

JO: No.

218

ELLA: Why?

JO: *(laughs miserably)* Do I have to have a reason to call my life my own?

ELLA: You're fierce about this living alone aren't you?

JO: It's nice to have something to be fierce about.

ELLA: And what is it?

GWEN: *(warningly)* Ella.

ELLA: You've launched yourself at forty-two years of age into a greasy bedsitter. What for? Do you still dream a man'll come along? Do you? Still time to have a baby? There's nothing going to happen to you. Nothing has and nothing will.

JO: You've made sure of that.

ELLA: *(amazed)* What?

JO: You both knew about Ruth - all these years - you let me carry on. Regretting. Wasting my life on a stupid dream. What am I now? Nothing! There's nothing left! You don't understand! Nothing left!

(She bangs her fists twice on the sideboard and stands there shaking. GWEN motions the shocked ELLA to leave the room. She does so, quietly.)

GWEN: Josie.

JO: You should've told me!

(Pause)

GWEN: I could've died in this room; you didn't lift a finger.

JO: Because you haven't a speck of guilt or regret for what you've done to me.

GWEN: *(hurt)* Always you. You've got so cold.

JO: I'll tell you what I've got. A few years, maybe five before you'll really need me. Before I come back to this grave.

GWEN: You don't have to come back.

JO: Perhaps nothing will happen. A lot of the time I don't like my greasy bedsitter anymore, but I need those years. To know I had them.

GWEN: You'll have plenty of years on your own when I die.

(The bus rumbles by outside)

JO: It's so safe here. Safe. I'll be safe for a long time. *(Pause)* She called me a middle-aged delinquent. She's right. I've never gone past being a teenager. Stopped growing when Ruth left. Ah, it doesn't matter now.

(Pause)

GWEN: When she left, she turned her back on you as well. That's what you could never forgive me for isn't it? As if you didn't matter at all. *(Pause)* Is this man - ?

JO: I hardly know him. *(Pause)* Sometimes I feel the world is full of women and they all want something from me. The men I see, they're in a separate world where I can't touch them. Sometimes on the bus or the tube, I want to put out my hand, just to see what one feels like.

(Pause)

GWEN: Will you be coming home?

JO: You still don't listen.

(She goes automatically to the record-player but stops remembering the record is destroyed. The irony causes her to laugh one of her sudden laughs.)

GWEN: *(starts)* Don't laugh like that.

JO: *(spins on her with exaggerated laughter)* Ha ha ha ha ha ha ha!

GWEN: Stop it!

JO: Ha ha ha! *(Pause)* Ha! *(Pause. Suddenly furious)* There's nothing left! So I had a few stupid dreams? So what? Now there's nothing but a world of old women tugging on my skirts!

GWEN: You could've left years ago, before we became dependant.

JO: I wish I had.

GWEN: I've waited on you like a servant for all these years. Now I need care and you think you'll blot me out.

JO: *(with false bravado)* Like Ruth. What can you do about it?

GWEN: I didn't mean that. I'm worn down by life Josie. I can take it. But you.

JO: What do you mean?

GWEN: You need me.

JO: *(pronouncing deliberately)* I Want To Get Away From You!

GWEN: If you're going to cope alone you'd better face the truth.

JO: It's the truth that crucifies me you stupid woman!

GWEN: You insisted on my agreement before you moved out. We planned it together. But it's not working and you blame me.

JO: You tried to stop me!

GWEN: Because you always stack the odds up against yourself. That's what's safe, isn't it?

JO: You're mad. You're going senile!

GWEN: You've moulded it to suit. You never really wanted to take any risks.

JO: That's not true!

GWEN: But you had to live up to Ruth.

JO: It wasn't like that.

GWEN: You had to pretend you'd have been like that if only.

JO: No! You're warped. You've smothered me!

GWEN: Your life won't suddenly change.

JO: It has!

GWEN: Accept it.

JO: You're wrong.

GWEN: There's nothing for you out there but loneliness and a hand-to-mouth existence.

JO: No.

GWEN: Make the best of what you have Josie. That way you'll be happy.

JO: I'm not old! I can still get married. It can happen in a day. I just need time. I'll have everything.

GWEN: You never brought your friends home. You never mucked in. You held back and left the limelight to Ruthie because your turn would come, on a sudden when you left. Except holding back is all you ever learnt.

JO: I wanted her to have the attention - I didn't begrudge it. You don't understand. It's different - special for me.

GWEN: Oh Josie, what can I do to make you grow up?

JO: Grow up? I'm not a freak.

GWEN: You can't cope.

(Pause. JO gets up and moves away, stricken by her despair. She laughs.)

JO: You always have to be right don't you?

(Pause)

JO: Do you know, my old school motto was "The only failure is never to have tried". Why is it then that where I've tried the hardest I've failed the most?

GWEN: You're fighting your nature Josie.

(JO laughs)

JO: No - I'm fighting yours Mum.

(She turns to face GWEN. Rushing at her, obscuring GWEN from our view, she puts her hands round her neck as if strangling her, we see GWEN'S arms come down to her side. JO is stock still. She steps back and we see GWEN watching her levelly. The vocals of 'Body And Soul' come softly in. JO clasps GWEN to her body, for a long moment. Then GWEN leads her to the sofa and helps her to lie down. ELLA enters quietly. GWEN puts cushions under JO'S exhausted head. ELLA comes and softly covers JO with the duvet and tucks her in. GWEN strokes JO'S hair. Either side the two women stand guard on JO, as the lights go down, for a moment leaving the window in relief. The lights and music fade softly away.)

BLACKOUT

THE TAKING OF LIBERTY

Cheryl Robson

I had the idea for the play from watching a documentary on the French Revolution made by Alan Ereira in 1989. I contacted the historical consultant on the programme Dr Colin Lucas at Cornell University and he led me to the French source material in the British Library.

The play is based on an account of real events which occurred in Saint Germain-Laval, a small commune near Lyon, in a deeply conservative region of France which rebelled against the Revolution and fought to keep the institutions of the Monarchy and the Church alive. A period of savage repression by the revolutionary forces followed.

In such a rural community, agriculture and religious observance tended to provide the structure for society. With both of these under attack and disempowered - the former by the loss of men to war, poor harvests, fixed price trade limitations and the latter by the dechristianisation rulings, the sense of community broke down and fear and insecurity became all-pervasive.

The play unfolds against this background. The women react to events by a kind of mass hysteria which launches them into conflict with both the men in their commune and the forces of the State. Their need to resist change and cling on to their religious beliefs is wholly understandable (and can be likened to religious adherence in Eastern European states) when you consider that the promises of the Revolution to materially improve their lives had proven hollow and that the revolutionary leaders had shown themselves to be morally and spiritually bankrupt by relying on the guillotine as their only means of containment. In challenging the Revolution, the women themselves undergo a process of transformation in which they discover their power to act, to speak out against their lack of representation and to work towards a more meaningful society.

I visited Saint Germain-Laval in January 1990 and began a first draft of the play. It developed through several drafts under the tuition of Bryony Lavery and Richard Crane at Birmingham University where I've been taking a two-year Masters in Playwriting Studies. It was part-presented at the Allardyce Nicholl Studio in Birmingham and in July 1990 a fuller version was given a rehearsed reading at the Soho Poly Theatre in London, directed by Catherine Arakelian.

In October of that year I gave birth to my second child and before she was a month old I found myself taking her to rehearsals of the play, which had just won the South London Playwriting Competition at the Croydon Warehouse Theatre. Mark Ravenhill, the director helped me to edit and focus the play further and the version that appears here benefits from the ideas and advice of all those who have been involved in developing the piece for production.

CHARACTERS:

The Women

Marie Lebrun	Royalist, mother, captain's wife.
Agathe Bonnefont	A miller, mother of two.
Jeanne Mignéry	Wife of the Mayor, mother of six.
Catherine Vallan	Owner of a cotton-factory. Wife of Henri Chaverondier.
Thérèse de Courtenay	Soldier / prostitute

The Men

(In Feurs)

Javogues	Proconsul for the Loire region.
Lapalus	Commissioner
Jean	a recruit
Envoy	from the Paris National Assembly

(In St. Germain-Laval)

Claude Bonnefont	The Mayor, married to Jeanne.
Henri Chaverondier	Head of the Committee of Surveillance, married to Catherine.
Jacques Bernuizet	Head of the Popular Society, Catherine's lover.
Christophe	a former slave / woodcutter.
Father Tiquet	a priest.

The events of the play are based loosely on historical events in France, from September 1793 until March 1794.

Actors can double roles.
[Suggested doubling.]
Marie/Thérèse.
Javogues/Henri.
Lapalus/Christophe.
Jacques/Father Tiquet/Jean
Claude/Envoy

ACT ONE

SCENE ONE:

The set is strewn with bodies, some hanging in rope nooses.
Music fades up with the lights and AGATHE is discovered walking.

AGATHE: *(to audience)*
  While you've a voice, you can speak
  You can make yourself heard
  And there are always those - who'll listen
  Even when the crowd turns and boos

  While you've a mind, you can think
  You can explore new ideas
  And there are always those - who'll get excited
  Even when the pack hunts you down

  While you're alive, you can dream
  You can stand up and be counted
  And there are always those - who'll respond
  Even when the mob opens fire.

Lights fade.

SCENE TWO:

Winter 1793. The market-place in Saint Germain-Laval. A stone cross on a plinth stands centre stage. JEANNE and CATHERINE sweep up autumn leaves and place them in a brazier. AGATHE enters with a basket. She goes to the cross and removes leaves, dusts it off and places a small sprig of winter flowers at the base. She crosses herself.

CATHERINE: What are you doing?

AGATHE: A few flowers. A bit of colour.

JEANNE: It's not allowed.

AGATHE: When my father-

JEANNE: The priest has sworn an oath Agathe - you'll get him into trouble.

(JEANNE takes the flowers. CATHERINE throws them in the brazier.)

AGATHE: My father would never have sworn to love Robespierre before God.

CATHERINE: Who knows what he would have done?

AGATHE: I know, that's who.

JEANNE: Let's not argue today.

AGATHE: I can't be doing with this - this sweeping of yours. Trying to clean up what can't be cleaned up. Leave them. Leave them to rot where they are.

JEANNE: I like doing it. Getting out of the house of a morning for some reason.

CATHERINE: Not surprised you need to get out, with your lot. I'd be tearing my hair out.

JEANNE: It's fresh today. The rain's stopped. You'll be pleased to hear the baby slept. His cough's nearly gone. Claude came home sober and our eldest has a job in Roanne to go to.

AGATHE: Let's all count our blessings, shall we? Don't mention that we can't even leave a few flowers, without worrying.

JEANNE: Help us with these. You'll

feel better.

(She gives AGATHE the broom. AGATHE holds it but doesn't move. CATHERINE shakes her head and carries on sweeping. She starts on a large pile of leaves and uncovers MARIE sleeping.)

CATHERINE: Will you look at this?

(CATHERINE prods her with the broom and she wakes slightly. MARIE tries to sit up but exhausted, she sinks back. Slowly she tries again and uncovers a baby from her shawl.)

MARIE: Here, take him. Take him, please....one of you. *(The women stare unmoving)* He's a good babe. Not a sound these two days...the milk's dried on me. He doesn't kick. Melted snow's all he eats... he's still alive. Fighting. That means something.

(She cannot hold the child out anymore and gives up. JEANNE goes over tentatively and takes the child. She offers him her own breast. The other women become anxious, look around and then masking MARIE from view AGATHE gives MARIE bread from her basket. While MARIE eats and drinks, JEANNE sings a lullaby to the child in a hushed voice. *)

MARIE: Hide me sisters.

CATHERINE: You know we can't.

MARIE: There's nowhere left for me.

AGATHE: Not here.

MARIE: I've done nothing.

CATHERINE: You married a bloody soldier.

MARIE: An honest man.

AGATHE: A royalist. Those they hunt for sport in the forests.

MARIE: My captain's dead.

CATHERINE: Bollocks!

AGATHE: Then why do they come here turning our houses upside down for him?

MARIE: Lies and much wild talk...go round.

CATHERINE: Most of it spread by the King's friends in Montbrison.

MARIE: I saw Javogues crush Montbrison with his gang of wreckers. Twelve hundred thugs at arms-

JEANNE: Aye, my brother's one of them.

(There is a silence between the women. JEANNE sings gently to the baby. Slowly the sound of marching becomes distinct and the song shrivels on JEANNE'S lips.)

AGATHE: Soldiers.

JEANNE: Go, now.

CATHERINE: She can't.

MARIE: Hide me.

(The women look at each other but say nothing. JEANNE hides the baby beneath her shawl as JAVOGUES, LAPALUS and JEAN, a young soldier enter. JEAN, unfolds a canvas chair for JAVOGUES to sit on and then hands him a flagon of wine from his haversack. JAVOGUES motions to the women and JEAN pushes past to drag MARIE over to him.)

JAVOGUES: The captain's bitch. Here all the time. And the child? Where is it?

(There is a silence. LAPALUS searches the leaves.)

MARIE: Dead....he died.

JAVOGUES: Get up whore. Come here and let me see you. Perhaps there's another infant rebel growing in your belly. You've screwed more priests than I've hairs on my head. Now you'll give us their names.

(He holds her between the legs and then lets go so that she falls back. He laughs. JEAN pretends a grin. LAPALUS helps her up and dusts her down.)

LAPALUS: Madame, your husband-

MARIE: Dead.

JAVOGUES: They're all dead, are they? Well, we'll see if we can't bring the buggers back to life, then.

LAPALUS: Perhaps these citizens can help us?

(He rakes the fire in the brazier furiously with his sword and then brandishes it.)

AGATHE: Give her the chance to answer to her crimes in law.

LAPALUS: The Tribunal sits where we sit. The prisons are packed tight enough.

CATHERINE: When neighbours can defame each other to settle scores, what wonder is it?

JAVOGUES: These women don't seem to understand our purpose. Search the town and bring out every boy you find. Line them up here and shoot them one by one until we have the child. Then we'll get to the father soon enough.

LAPALUS: Can we do that? Should we? Isn't it a little excessive?

(JEAN whispers in JAVOGUES' ear. They wait. JAVOGUES shrugs his shoulders.)

LAPALUS: Madame Lebrun, let me make it clear that you and your child stand accused of aiding and abetting Captain Lebrun in the rebel attack on the revolutionary government of Lyon. Since when, we know you've been hiding out with royalist factions in Roanne, Montbrison and Boën.

MARIE: I've slept in ditches and eaten herbs.

CATHERINE: Gone mad with hunger, poor cow. Begged us to take her in.

LAPALUS: Beware. She is an enemy of the people.

AGATHE: Rubbish! She's half-dead.

JAVOGUES: Sacré mille foutre!

(JAVOGUES smashes the glass flagon. JEAN takes out another from his backpack and hands it to him immediately. The women stare at him, then JEANNE takes the baby and gives it to JAVOGUES.)

JAVOGUES: A minor miracle before our eyes. Raised from the dead it would seem. *(He holds the child up for MARIE to see.)*

MARIE: Its true I loved a man. True I had his child. True I'd kill to see him master here.

JAVOGUES: This won't do. Show

her the list.

(*LAPALUS unrolls a long document which he shows to MARIE. He reads:*)

LAPALUS: Adet, Agoult, Albert, Allarde, Amar, André, Anselme, Artois, Aubry -

MARIE: So many names...

LAPALUS: I fear the pace is slowing. Fewer than four hundred denunciations this month.

MARIE: I don't know these people.

LAPALUS: You're not looking hard enough.

MARIE: (*reads*) Victor Lebrun. You think I'd help you to kill my own man?

JAVOGUES: What better witness could there be? What better proof of loyalty to France?

JEANNE: (*whispers*) And loyalty man to wife?

CATHERINE: Gone out of fashion.

AGATHE: I thought that Paris was all for preserving marriage to counteract free love. I thought that Robespierre wanted wives kept in kitchens. After all, the sacred laws of property would surely crumble if all women ignored their vows and followed their fancies.

LAPALUS: A ghastly prospect. It's true.

JAVOGUES: Shut up. (*JAVOGUES turns to JEAN and whispers. JEAN whispers back.*) We could... cross out the husband's name.

(*LAPALUS crosses through the*

name. They wait.)

MARIE: What harm have these done me?

JAVOGUES: We don't care.

MARIE: But my lies will condemn them?

LAPALUS: We don't want lies lady. Think you to save yourself by lies, then think again. Speak out the names of those you know certain for conspirators.

(*They wait. MARIE stares at the document, frozen. JAVOGUES gets up, takes the child and staggers over to the fire with it where he holds it aloft.*)

JAVOGUES: So, she must stick to God and King. She must suckle her child with hatred of all sans-culottes and she must cherish the traitor's blood that spawned it. (*Pause*) Then we must own her for an enemy of Liberty, incorrigible in her contempt for the principles of equality-

MARIE: Please...

(*LAPALUS goes to her and she whispers that she will sign.*)

LAPALUS: Marat be praised!
(*He gives her the pen. JAVOGUES gives the child to JEAN.*)

MARIE: (*reads*) Amar... Barnave... Belliard... Chabot... Condé... Delaunay... Didot... Elbée... Fauchet... Favart... Florian... Galbaut... Goujon... Hoche... Isnard... Jourdan... Laborde...
(*She stops, staring at the document. LAPALUS stops taking notes. They wait*)
Rob...Robert...Saladin, Simon,

Tallien, Travot, Valady, Ysabeau. *(She sinks to the ground. Slowly she signs the document. LAPALUS waits for her to give him the pen and document. The women talk in hushed tones.)*

CATHERINE: Damned if she signs and lost if she don't.

JEANNE: Poor lamb, she won't forget those names.

AGATHE: I feel faint...

(CATHERINE and JEANNE support AGATHE. Suddenly, MARIE snatches the document and throws it and herself on the brazier. LAPALUS tries to remove her but she clings on. Finally, he pulls her clear. JAVOGUES closes his eyes.)

JAVOGUES: Where are we Jean?

JEAN: West of Lyon, in the mountains.

JAVOGUES: A week away from Paris would you say?

JEAN: Yes.

LAPALUS: What now?

JAVOGUES: She wants to burn, let her burn. And smash this place. Their God, their Cross. All of it.

(He exits. LAPALUS drags MARIE out. JEAN puts the baby on the floor, packs the chair and the wine. The baby starts to cry. He looks uncertain, then packs it in his backpack. He leaves.)

AGATHE: What can we do?

JEANNE: I'm going home.

CATHERINE: Churned my stomach over.

AGATHE: Didn't you hear them?

CATHERINE: Of course I did...So?

AGATHE: What was her name?

CATHERINE: Don't know. Can't remember. Best we forget.

JEANNE: Go home and rest. It's in God's hands.

(They leave. AGATHE stares at the cross, sits beneath it.)

AGATHE: My father put up this cross. He loved God, the Book, the Word. New books now. New words. New world in the shaping. Wind of change rages, brings a flood of rights they say makes us the envy of all Europe. The future is supposed to gleam. But all I see are men who want to trample, slash and tear at things. It makes me wonder, when will paradise break out of the belly of this age of killing?

(CHRISTOPHE enters and listens to AGATHE. He lays down several bundles of wood. He goes over to AGATHE and produces a single flower as if by magic.)

CHRISTOPHE: Stay lucky. Go on take it.

AGATHE: Do I know you?

CHRISTOPHE: I'm Christophe that used to belong to St. Polgues along with everything else round 'ere. Now he's dead and I'm free. Free as the wind and just as cold.

(AGATHE takes the flower and places it at the base of the cross.)

AGATHE: How much for one of those?

CHRISTOPHE: Dry as a bone. A real bargain. You're the miller's wife, ain't yer?

AGATHE: André's no miller. I wish he was.

(She pays him for the wood. He gives her change, she holds out her hand for more, he gives it unwillingly.)

CHRISTOPHE: Dunno anything, me. Don't ask me for truth I won't tell no lies.

AGATHE: That's a relief. Lies are fast becoming the only way of life, you know.

CHRISTOPHE: Who told yer to expect anything else?

AGATHE: It's a habit I'm trying to break.

CHRISTOPHE: I know yer don't need that wood. You've a mountainous pile of it, chopped and stacked from one end of your barn to the other. I don't mind. I wish everyone had your attitude. I'd be a rich man.

(AGATHE goes to the brazier and places the wood inside it, one stick at a time.)

AGATHE: My son wants to join the army. Fight for freedom he says. He's only thirteen.

CHRISTOPHE: You won't stop 'im. I've heard of children dobbin' in their parents - enemies of the people!

(AGATHE stands warming her hands and staring at the fire. She is close to tears. CHRISTOPHE goes over and warms himself too.)

CHRISTOPHE: I know why I'm here in the cold. But you got a home to go to.

AGATHE: Yes.

CHRISTOPHE: Don't want to go there, eh?... Don't want to talk about it, fine... don't mind me.

AGATHE: There was a woman here...

(AGATHE snaps a piece of wood and puts it on the fire. Lights fade.)

SCENE THREE:

Midday. Winter sunlight. The Marketplace at Saint Germain-Laval. A stone cross on a plinth stands centre stage. The sound of hammer blows is heard as lights come up and JACQUES is discovered trying to loosen the cross from the plinth it rests on with hammer and chisel. After a while he gives a thumbs up sign and the cross is hoisted off the plinth and replaced by a statue of a naked woman which is fixed to the plinth with two bolts.

HENRI and CLAUDE enter and stare at the statue. HENRI is carrying a red bonnet and tricolor sash, CLAUDE a red pike. LAPALUS enters and signals to them to begin.

HENRI: Citizens, welcome the symbol of Liberty in our midst. The era of liberation has truly arrived when the trappings of papist oppression give way to the light and humanity of the new age. Your church bells, the gold and silver, the lead from the roof all melted down, transformed into guns and ammunition for the people's army. Your army.

(HENRI places the bonnet and sash on the statue. JACQUES has entered with a stone tablet, with the Declaration of Human Rights engraved on it. CLAUDE and JACQUES argue over which object goes in which hand. Finally, they place the tablet in the right hand and the pike in the left hand. Red paint has rubbed off the pike onto their hands and clothes.)

HENRI: In honour of this occasion we've been deemed worthy of a new name.

LAPALUS: Henceforth till the end of time, we reject the name of Saint Germain-Laval in favour of that noble martyr of the Revolution at Lyon, Chalier. Your commune rises up today from the ashes of roman religious oppression, as Montchalier!

(LAPALUS claps his hands and JACQUES pulls a rope which makes a banner unfold. On which are the words: "Vive la République! Vive Montchalier!"

LAPALUS, JACQUES, HENRI & CLAUDE TOGETHER:

Vive la République!
Vive Montchalier!

(Then they all sing:)

A hymn to Liberty

L'innocence est de retour
Elle triomphe a sa tour
Liberté dans ce beau jour
Viens remplir notre âme
Ennemis des tyrans, commencez vos cantiques
Brûlez l'encens sur son autel
Et que vos mains patriotiques
Courronnent son front immortel.

(LAPALUS kneels and places a wreath at the foot of the liberty statue. Then he kisses JACQUES,

HENRI and CLAUDE. Jaunty, festival music heralds the start of celebrations.)*

LAPALUS: I'd suggest you make a few additions.

HENRI: Speak plainly citizen.

LAPALUS: A tree of Equality's essential.

CLAUDE: A tree?

LAPALUS: And an altar to the country.

JACQUES: *(laughs)* An altar?

LAPALUS: Communes of this kind can demonstrate their loyalty by such items.

HENRI: *(quick)* There's no question of our loyalty here.

LAPALUS: And yet, there are rumours that the royalist rebels were welcomed here.

JACQUES: Rumours and idle gossip.

LAPALUS: We at the Tribunal are keen to know of any rebel sympathisers. It wouldn't harm this commune were you to find some traitors to denounce. Are there no priests-?

CLAUDE: The priest's sworn an oath to the Republic.

LAPALUS: Doesn't he retract this secretly?

JACQUES: How do we know what he really thinks?

LAPALUS: This is why you've a Committee of Surveillance.

HENRI: Of course it is.

LAPALUS: You know, we must rid

ourselves of these impostors.

HENRI: Oh yes. Penetrate deceit that masks contempt for the Revolution.

JACQUES: Denounce our friends and neighbours?

LAPALUS: If need be. Vive la République, citizens.

HENRI/CLAUDE: Vive la Montagne!

(They all stop and look at JACQUES.)

JACQUES: *(reluctantly)* Vive la Liberté!

(LAPALUS leaves. JACQUES exits shaking his head. CLAUDE trails after LAPALUS. HENRI follows but is restrained by CATHERINE, who has entered from behind the statue.)

CATHERINE: We haven't seen you in the cotton-factory today, Henri Chaverondier.

HENRI: Important civic duties must take precedence over dress fabric.

CATHERINE: We'd go around naked if all men took that stance on work.

HENRI: What's more... *(sotto voce)* We've to be extra vigilant, you and I.

CATHERINE: You never see past the end of your nose.

HENRI: Rebel sympathisers are to be rooted out.

CATHERINE: Old men who gossip on street corners?

HENRI: And no question of our loyalty, despite our exiled aristocratic cousins.

CATHERINE: They're your bloody cousins, not mine.

HENRI: Ssh! These are dangerous times, Catherine.

CATHERINE: It's dangerous for me to be here now with a cotton-factory unattended. We'll have no sodding cloth left by the time I get back.

HENRI: Why can't you see-

CATHERINE: I do see. Me - working myself crazy whilst you sit and play politics in the town hall all day.

HENRI: You know what I do all day.

CATHERINE: I don't know. How can I? Women aren't allowed. I come into the square and the first thing I see is this ungodly monstrosity. Never heard a bloody word about it before now, have we?

HENRI: We men must be permitted the time and space to manage the affairs of state without the constant twitterings of midwives and matrons.

CATHERINE: Funny how you need us to help manage your lives, but affairs of state you can manage single-handed.

HENRI: If you'd only try to understand my way of thinking.

CATHERINE: I couldn't bear it. What I do know makes me feel a complete aversion as it is. Why not get to know my way of thinking Henri? It might be a revelation for you.

(HENRI leaves, bumping into JEANNE who stands staring at the statue.)

JEANNE: This thing is grotesque!

CATHERINE: For once I agree with you.

JEANNE: Have you seen what they did to the church? I cried. It'll take years to put right. How could they let them do it? They know how long we spent saving for those stained-glass windows. What does Henri say? He looked vexed.

CATHERINE: He always is these days.

JEANNE: Well it must be a worry for him. Not young, now are you, to be having a baby? Still, you're happy about it, aren't you?

CATHERINE: Happy? When half the bloody village obviously knows about the workings of my body, better than I do myself?

JEANNE: I'm sorry I spoke...I always thought you wanted children and I've tried, you know I have, to get you involved... Every birth, every baptism, every saint day, you've been invited to come and share the joys of family life with me and Claude.

CATHERINE: Watching the way you pander to your drunken husband, then bow and scrape to your feeble offspring isn't really my idea of joy. Not unless you're the kind of person who thinks that drowning puppies is amusing.

(JACQUES enters and stands listening behind the statue.)

JEANNE: Your trouble is you work too hard and you don't know when to stop and cultivate your poor husband. That man needs attending to.

CATHERINE: I know what he needs.

JEANNE: A mother's touch.

CATHERINE: A good fuck. A fuck is what he needs. Any offers Jeanne?

JEANNE: I must've been mad to think you were with child. It's just not possible.

(JEANNE leaves. JACQUES comes out from behind the statue.)

JACQUES: You shouldn't do that to her. It's wicked.

CATHERINE: How did she know, Jacques? I've not told anyone but you.

JACQUES: I haven't told anyone... except my mother.

CATHERINE: Then I've had it. It'll be all over from here to Roanne by now.

JACQUES: Does Henri know?

CATHERINE: God, no. Unless I've gabbed it in my sleep.

JACQUES: Not likely, is it?

CATHERINE: Who knows? The dreams I've been having... visions of little birds and animals-

JACQUES: How is the little man?

(He pats her belly. LAPALUS enters and stands watching.)

CATHERINE: Or little woman.

JACQUES: I don't mind which it is, but boys are less trouble.

(He moves his hand down to her crotch.)

CATHERINE: Not if he's like his

232

father.

(He pulls her closer to him.)

CATHERINE: We'll be seen. (they kiss for a long time) I have to get back.

JACQUES: Mother's gone out.

CATHERINE: She always does.

JACQUES: We've got half an hour.

CATHERINE: If we run.

(They go. LAPALUS comes downstage, makes notes in a small book. HENRI enters left and CLAUDE enters right. He sees HENRI and turns away then sees CLAUDE and turns front.)

CLAUDE: Thought you might like to sample the local hostelry, Commissioner.

LAPALUS: No thanks.

HENRI: Dinner could be arranged at my house.

LAPALUS: No, no. I've eaten. (He waits) Did either of you want to speak with me?

HENRI/CLAUDE: No, no....

LAPALUS: (shuts his notebook abruptly) Then you'll excuse me to take the evening air in solitude.

HENRI: Of course.

CLAUDE: Certainly.

(LAPALUS leaves.)

HENRI: I saw him writing something. Did we offend him?

CLAUDE: No...he's tired. It was a good ceremony.

HENRI: To your credit, Monsieur le Maire.

CLAUDE: Shame they had to smash those windows.

HENRI: Church looks a bloody sight with no bell-tower.

CLAUDE: Graveyard's a terrible mess. And its been closed to burials.

HENRI: This thing gets the blood racing though.

CLAUDE: Watch she doesn't come to life and eat you up, Henri.

HENRI: I wouldn't mind if she did.

CLAUDE: She could eat me up any day.

(They laugh until AGATHE enters)

HENRI: Oh, yes. We need more days like today. Feel you've really achieved something.

AGATHE: Oh yes, a great day for the commune, citizens. Montchalier, your idea Claude?

CLAUDE: No...not exactly. They told us earlier.

AGATHE: You're the mayor and you don't have a say in what they call the place?

CLAUDE: I quite like Montchalier, don't you? And being named after a martyr, that's better than a saint these days.

HENRI: Yes. Most definitely Agathe.

AGATHE: I think you've addled your brains in the Inn. The pair of you.

CLAUDE: I'm dry now. Why don't we go over?

AGATHE: Your hero Chalier. Do you know what he did?

CLAUDE: No. I don't. And does it matter?

AGATHE: He couldn't kill enough people just by shooting them, so he sent to Paris for a guillotine, and when it came he watched as it was erected, piece by piece, hungry for the day he could start chopping at the people of Lyon. But the people of Lyon rose up, and Chalier was the first to see his head roll.

HENRI: A hero.

CLAUDE: A martyr.

AGATHE: A butcher.

CLAUDE: Caution sister, please, before someone hears you.

AGATHE: I want them to hear me. I want us to do something!

HENRI: I'll pretend I didn't hear you.

CLAUDE: Come for a drink and forget about it.

AGATHE: And toast freedom? What a joke, the way you fawn after Master Lapalus hanging on his every pompous word, like the slaves that you are.

(CLAUDE shrugs and goes off with HENRI to the inn. AGATHE sits at the base of the statue. JEANNE enters.)

JEANNE: Shameless, isn't it?

AGATHE: The men won't do anything.

JEANNE: The Count used to like it. Had it in the bedchamber up at the Château.

AGATHE: That's all we need. The men coming out of The Star half-cut and then roused to rutting-

JEANNE: Widows won't be safe in their beds.

AGATHE: Well, it won't last long. We'll find a way to get rid of it.

JEANNE: Where's Claude? He should have told them we didn't want it. How he could stand by and let those soldiers vandalise the church... *(JEANNE goes towards the inn.)* If only they'd pass a law to close the Inn. Then we'd have a mighty revolution.

AGATHE: I'm still trying to live with the one we've got, thanks.

(JEANNE is gone. CHRISTOPHE appears, laughs out loud at the statue.)

AGATHE: We'll be the laughing-stock of the region.

CHRISTOPHE: Is your husband back yet?

AGATHE: None of your business.

CHRISTOPHE: Is it work he's up to in Paris? Or is it somethin' else keep him there so long? Now you need a man to 'elp you.

AGATHE: What?

CHRISTOPHE: It gonna rain. An' me with no roof over me 'ead-

AGATHE: I'm going.

(She leaves. CHRISTOPHE puts down his bundle and starts to

repack it. It starts to rain and the red paint from the pike begins to trickle down the statue's body, collecting at the navel.)

CHRISTOPHE: Lovely lady.
Bleeding heart eh? Not surprised bein' dragged from the big old 'ouse and stuck out 'ere in the midst of this poxy place. Give you a hat and a ribbon, did they? Not much is it? *(He touches the paint and wipes it on his clothes)* I know the feelin'. I was thrown out. Liberated they said. All I've got's these poor clothes. No gratitude for the thirty years loyal service. No. Nothin'.

(HENRI enters with a lantern and an umbrella. CHRISTOPHE hides. HENRI waits nervously. JACQUES enters with a sack of flour.)

HENRI: Where've you been? It's past curfew.

JACQUES: Busy...seeing to something for you as a matter of fact. Blow out the bloody lantern!

HENRI: Could be leftovers from the floor of the mill, like as not. How you manage to get this out of the store without falling foul of Agathe's stock-taking, I'll never know.

JACQUES: Price is fixed so don't start haggling.

HENRI: Bloody law of the maximum is it?

JACQUES: Prices are rocketing, grain's scarce and paper money's only good for wiping your bum.

HENRI: You can't want gold?

JACQUES: No gold, no grain.

HENRI: We'll starve.

JACQUES: Adapt to the new age, Henri. Or don't. What do I care?

(HENRI gets out his purse and counts out gold louis. JACQUES leaves. HENRI picks up the flour. CHRISTOPHE appears from behind the statue.)

HENRI: Who's there?...

CHRISTOPHE: Me.

HENRI: Monsieur Lapalus?...oh, Christophe?

CHRISTOPHE: That's right.

HENRI: Thank God.

CHRISTOPHE: That's what I said when I 'eard two respected members of the local council arguing over the price of a sack of flour. Stolen flour what's more. Buyin' outside of the market, avoidin' the set prices. Payin' in gold...

HENRI: I suppose you want money?

CHRISTOPHE: Assignats, if you don't mind. I wouldn't be caught with a bag of louis. Chopped my old boss for it. Dropped the blade on 'is fat old neck three times, then 'ad to cut it away with a knife. *(HENRI pays him off)* She was 'is. Your lady Liberty. Pride of place before they ransacked the estate.

HENRI: You're not in league with Jacques Bernuizet, are you?

CHRISTOPHE: What if I was? What if I'm not?

HENRI: Oh I hate this...this revolution. When will we get some normality back in Saint Germain-Laval?

CHRISTOPHE: You're running the place.

HENRI: I could help you Christophe.

CHRISTOPHE: Yeh?

HENRI: How would you like to be the manager of a cotton-factory?

CHRISTOPHE: Work for you? No thanks.

HENRI: Have you ever done a day's work? No, of course you haven't.

CHRISTOPHE: I was a slave remember and I know what its like to work for a man like you, thinkin' himself so superior to the rest of us. If I was back in the islands, they'd treat me like a fuckin' king, and I'm savin' for the day I can set sail and get out of this crazy country.

HENRI: My fate in the hands of a vagabond.

CHRISTOPHE: I don't steal off people like you do. I take my axe, walk a day to the forest, chop more wood than I can carry, lug it to market and sell it cheap to old women.

HENRI: It sounds exemplary.

CHRISTOPHE: You'd better watch that one day I don't take my axe, walk down to your factory and chop your thievin' hands off.

HENRI: I'd expect no more from a savage.

CHRISTOPHE: Get out of here!

(He shakes a fist. HENRI leaves with his flour, lantern and umbrella causing him difficulty. CHRISTOPHE picks up his wood and leaves whistling. From the other side CATHERINE and JACQUES enter and stand embracing each other for some time.)

CATHERINE: Poor Henri.

JACQUES: He deserves it.

CATHERINE: First you and then Christophe. I'll pay the price for it all you know. I might have to soothe his poor wrinkled brow.

JACQUES: You told me you never touched him.

CATHERINE: I don't unless he's all het up, like that.

JACQUES: Leave him and live with me.

CATHERINE: On what? The money you make fixing hinges and making locks for trunks?

JACQUES: We could go to Lyon.

CATHERINE: And get massacred in our beds? Don't even think of it. I want my baby here. Raised in comfort, not dragged around from pillar to post with no proper home.

JACQUES: I could get work making guns for the army.

CATHERINE: You're joking.

JACQUES: You could live with my mother.

CATHERINE: I couldn't.

JACQUES: You mean you won't divorce Henri.

CATHERINE: The Pope wouldn't like it.

JACQUES: Fuck the Pope. He's got no say in it.

CATHERINE: He talks to God, Jacques.

JACQUES: So do I but he doesn't answer.

CATHERINE: I'll come over at three tomorrow.

JACQUES: How long will you stay?

CATHERINE: It depends....

JACQUES: On Henri?

CATHERINE: No...on you.

(They embrace. CLAUDE enters with a bottle of cognac, drunk and in a merry mood. JACQUES escapes.)

CLAUDE: Jacques! Was that Jacques you were... er... doing whatever you were doing?

CATHERINE: I don't think so.

CLAUDE: Love that statue. Wish we'd got one sooner.

CATHERINE: Why?

CLAUDE: Want to go straight home to the wife for, well, you know you're a married woman. *(He puts his arm around CATHERINE. She removes it.)* No need to be like that.

CATHERINE: On your way, Claude.

CLAUDE: I've always liked you, Catherine.

CATHERINE: I've always hated you Claude.

CLAUDE: No. You hate Henri. You like me.

CATHERINE: You're pissed.

CLAUDE: You're ravishing.

CATHERINE: You're the mayor. Behave like one.

CLAUDE: Its a terrible strain you know.

CATHERINE: Give it up then.

CLAUDE: I do it for Jeanne. All for Jeanne.

(He lunges at her again. She avoids him and escapes. He sits down beneath the statue, addresses it.) You understand me, don't you? *(He drinks)*

Lights fade.

SCENE FOUR:

Night. JEANNE'S house. On the table lies the rotting corpse of her brother, JEAN-MARIE, an old soldier. Around the table whispering prayers are THÉRÈSE, dressed as a soldier and AGATHE.

JEANNE: Don't tell me this my dead brother lying there is the will of God. Don't tell me that whatever happens, however mad the world turns, it's an act of love from God. Was it love that led the blows that crushed our Jesus, was it love that dared them to defile our graves? Or was it hatred and a world of evil that saw them hurl Madonnas from the windows to shatter into pieces on the streets below? *(Pause.)* I'll grant he wasn't perfect, poor sinner that he was but to die like that his stomach bloated from eating leaves and grass, not even in the field of battle... it makes us mock - we laugh at death and then I know the demons are all dancing.

(They finish praying and immediately start coughing and holding handkerchiefs to their faces. The priest TIQUET enters with an incense burner.)

TIQUET: He's ripe.

AGATHE: Rich.

THÉRÈSE: Been rotting for days.

TIQUET: We'll have to use the common pit.

JEANNE: We can't. I promised him sacred soil next to his dead wife.

TIQUET: Without snow to cover the digging of the grave, I couldn't risk the churchyard.

AGATHE: You can't wait for the snow, Jeanne.

TIQUET: I shouldn't even consider it...with all the denunciations, and that man Lapalus about the place.

JEANNE: Claude wants him out - the children hate the sight of him, wake screaming at night. Hate the stench ...that twisted face...and the floor won't keep dry with his insides dripping out.

AGATHE: Bury him now.

JEANNE: Never liked him. None of you. No. He'll go to God if I've to dig the grave myself.

TIQUET: *(alarmed)* They'd blame me for it. I know they would.

THÉRÈSE: Wish I'd left him where he was. They were digging holes in that field, no problem.

JEANNE: You did right to bring him home.

AGATHE: Do you remember my father told us there's a charnel-house under the church? If we could get into it, he'd be only a few yards from the twins.

TIQUET: And on sacred ground.

JEANNE: Put him in a tomb with hundreds of others he never knew? What sense is there in that?

TIQUET: It's full of his ancestors and yours.

THÉRÈSE: I'll take the old bugger to the pit and have done with it.

JEANNE: You've done enough. I'll see you're paid for it.

THÉRÈSE: I won't take your money, woman until I see my friend there in the ground.

(JEANNE shrugs and gets her shawl. Then she reaches into a wooden box and takes out a large hammer and a chisel, turns and looks once more at her brother.)

JEANNE: Ready.

(TIQUET takes the lantern and they leave. AGATHE stands staring at the body, then goes over and looks at the face even closer.)

THÉRÈSE: I've tried that.

AGATHE: What?

THÉRÈSE: Staring to make him come back. Got to like the old fella then he went and died on me. I was to be a hero bringing home the wounded soldier - now I'm the messenger of death, I'm nobody's friend.

AGATHE: You're with friends here.

THÉRÈSE: Slow to trust strangers, me.

AGATHE: Why's that?

THÉRÈSE: I trusted him. Look at him.

AGATHE: Have you run away from the army?

THÉRÈSE: I was never in the army.

AGATHE: Not really a soldier then?

THÉRÈSE: No.

AGATHE: What then?

THÉRÈSE: I dunno.

AGATHE: Poor man.

THÉRÈSE: *(laughs)* You're wrong.

(AGATHE gives 'him' some food in a bowl.)

AGATHE: Eat...a little.

THÉRÈSE: I can't pay.

AGATHE: You've earned it. *(THÉRÈSE accepts the food and eats but watches AGATHE.)* What happened in Lyon?...

THÉRÈSE: I dunno. I got out.

AGATHE: Tell me... please.

THÉRÈSE: Why?

AGATHE: I want to understand-

THÉRÈSE: What? The fear in people's faces? The way they turn away...the way we all lie and cheat to save ourselves. It's not what you're used to is it?

AGATHE: You don't know me so don't judge me. *(THÉRÈSE carries on eating)* I wanted to know what made the people turn against the revolution? Is that a crime?

THÉRÈSE: I got out I told you... found the people's army camped in a field tending their sick. I offered to bring him home. That's it.

AGATHE: So...what'll you do now?

THÉRÈSE: You tell me.

AGATHE: Lie low until the army moves on and then make for a city where you can be swallowed without trace.

THÉRÈSE: I might just do that.

AGATHE: I won't tell anyone.

(THÉRÈSE kisses AGATHE. AGATHE moves away.)

THÉRÈSE: Have you got any money?

AGATHE: No!

THÉRÈSE: You're married, aren't you?

AGATHE: No. Yes. How do you-?

THÉRÈSE: A heaviness of heart that all wives carry from being slaves to simpletons.

AGATHE: André has no wish to dominate me. He's convinced that women should enter the professions... speak in the Assembly, become elected representatives.

THÉRÈSE: And what does André do about it?

AGATHE: He talks a lot. He's too

busy to-

THÉRÈSE: The worst kind.

AGATHE: My husband's a writer engaged in the study of the universe. Astronomy, cosmology, the birth of stars and planets.

THÉRÈSE: And what about his own bright star? The light's burning out there, I think. *(AGATHE takes the empty bowl away)* Talk to me. I miss my friend. *(She wraps the blanket tight around her, waits)* But then, its safer talking to the dead. They can't denounce you.

AGATHE: He was a bastard.

THÉRÈSE: Men are like that.

AGATHE: Who are you?

(THÉRÈSE holds out her hand. Slowly, AGATHE stretches out her hand to touch THÉRÈSE'S. They hold still for a while.)

THÉRÈSE: I've seen it before. Families. Even children hate.

AGATHE: Mine hate, I know it. He won't let them play in the day because he sleeps. I've to whisper when I get their breakfast. We creep about like mice until the evening. Then the piano's played and the carpet's beaten and the wood's chopped. The eldest wants to kill himself in the army and the little one hides in the attic, dreaming. What life is that for children?

THÉRÈSE: And when you go to bed at night?

AGATHE: I lie aching, with an ocean of room beside me, always empty, never filled. Find I'm staring down into the river sometimes, watching the ice get washed downstream.

(AGATHE turns and stares at the body.)

THÉRÈSE: Let go. Let go of him. This dead man of yours.

AGATHE: What? I don't usually-

THÉRÈSE: I did the same with him. Carried on pulling him on the cart though my back was raw. There was no sound when it happened. No, there was nothing. Dreamed up adventures he might have had...Glory and victory... Comedy and tragedy. Blood and bodies torn asunder by each cannon volley - my soldier passing through unscathed. So...I bring his carcass home and what? He was old and poor and he liked to drink and he let his body waste away, trying to be a soldier for the money.

(THÉRÈSE touches AGATHE. They kiss.)

Lights fade.

SCENE FIVE:

Darkness before the dawn. The village square. JACQUES is carrying sacks of flour when CHRISTOPHE steps out and stops him.

CHRISTOPHE: In a hurry?

JACQUES: Out of my way.

CHRISTOPHE: Been pilfering from Agathe's store, have we?

JACQUES: That's a lie.

(CHRISTOPHE splits open one of the sacks with his axe.)

CHRISTOPHE: Dropped off a passing cart, eh?

JACQUES: I'm warning you-

CHRISTOPHE: Why not take it back?

JACQUES: I'll have you arrested.

CHRISTOPHE: I don't think so.

JACQUES: Look, I'll cut you in, Christophe. There's a lot of money to be made on this.

CHRISTOPHE: And watch the people starve through winter? Then blame Agathe, I suppose.

JACQUES: She's not even there. She's with Jeanne.

CHRISTOPHE: Then you can take those back before she sees they're missing, can't you?

JACQUES: Who are you anyway? You're nothing round here, you're dead.

CHRISTOPHE: And you'd better be quick because your Liberty here's turned nasty. She didn't like what you did to her.

(JACQUES looks up at the statue, goes nearer, touches it.)

JACQUES: You did this, didn't you?

CHRISTOPHE: Not me. Up there.

JACQUES: Shit!

(JACQUES tries running off with the flour but CHRISTOPHE grabs it away from him.)

CHRISTOPHE: I'll take that! Back where it belongs.

(CHRISTOPHE takes two bags and leaves while JACQUES tries to scrape up the spilt flour into the third sack. While he is doing this the ghost of MARIE appears. She is carrying her baby and humming the lullaby we heard JEANNE singing.)

JACQUES: Who's there? (He can see nothing)

MARIE: You saw it all. You let them do it. You kissed their faces. You sang their songs.

JACQUES: Where are you?

MARIE: Can't leave this place. I'm tied to it. To you. To them. To all that let me burn.

JACQUES: There's no such thing. No. You don't exist.

MARIE: But you can hear me.

JACQUES: You don't frighten me.

MARIE: No. I'm not terrifying. I never was but still I burned.

JACQUES: I'm not listening to you!

MARIE: You will. You'll listen. Or else you'll lose everything.

JACQUES: Leave me alone!

MARIE: I didn't choose this.

JACQUES: I looked away when your skin began to bubble. I choked on the smell of roasted flesh. Your hair crackled as it flamed. Your clothes were damp and wouldn't light. I didn't want to care what happened to you. But when I was diving deep into the flesh of another to forget that sight, your face swam up to meet me and I cried.

241

Lights fade.

SCENE SIX:

The church crypt. JEANNE is found demolishing a wall piece by piece by the light of her lantern. She works without stopping. After a while AGATHE enters and tries to interrupt JEANNE'S work.

AGATHE: Jeanne, Jeanne...

JEANNE: I can't stop.

AGATHE: You've got to listen to me.

JEANNE: I've found it. I've seen inside. Look!

(She holds up her lantern to a hole in the wall.)

See the light throws shadows on them. The whiteness of their bones like ghosts. Our people stacked and stored with care. Their limbs and ribs woven together to hold in place for centuries.

AGATHE: Listen. Just stop for a minute, will you? The Liberty's been drenched with rain and the paint's run and stained like blood. The people mock it openly and some call for its destruction.

JEANNE: An omen is it? Or have I woken up the dead tonight?

AGATHE: We can be free of it.

JEANNE: God forgive me if I've disturbed their sleep.

AGATHE: Jeanne, please. Let's go to the square and speak. They can all be swayed. I know they can. The two of us together we can rouse them to get rid of it.

JEANNE: I'm shaking. See my hand. *(she drops her tools)* P'raps I'm here to do the devil's work? For what? For my own selfish needs to have my sinner of a brother turned to God, the way I wanted him?

AGATHE: I need your help, Jeanne. They'll listen to you. They know you for a godly woman.

JEANNE: They never saw me this night. Ripping open tombs.

AGATHE: They're laughing at the statue and making jokes. They're not afraid!

JEANNE: Laughing? It must be magic. Is it light outside?

AGATHE: The sun's been up an hour.

JEANNE: No sign of snowstorms today, I don't suppose?

AGATHE: No...not yet.

JEANNE: Best go home and feed the children. We'll stop off on the way I expect, to see this marvel of a statue and, if the mood takes us, we may say a word or two about it to anyone who'll listen.

AGATHE: They'll listen. I promise you.

JEANNE: Calm down. I've never seen you so excited.

AGATHE: I know...but I can't help it. I don't want to.

They exit.

SCENE SEVEN:

Pale winter day. Lights and music fade up to reveal the statue in the market-place, stained with red paint which has been washed by the rain down its body. One by one men and women enter and stand staring at the statue.

(The language overlaps at times.)

JACQUES: We must clean her.

CLAUDE: Remove this obscenity.

HENRI: Purge these filthy waters that pour from the devil's gateway.

JEANNE: It's a sign.

CATHERINE: Message from God.

AGATHE: Liberty's pike bleeds, her sorrow is so great at the blood of France men spill.

CLAUDE: A curse has come upon our commune.

JACQUES: The curse of the wicked.

HENRI: Root out the wicked ones that brought this curse upon us.

CATHERINE: It's a miracle.

AGATHE: A testament to our devotion.

JEANNE: Pray for forgiveness that the holy cross of Jesus was destroyed here.

JACQUES: Give not the power of thy soul to a woman, lest she enter upon thy strength and thou be confounded.

AGATHE: Who knows the power of thine anger God?

CLAUDE: In an age of Science, such things should never happen.

HENRI: In an age of Science we'll find a way to stop this putrid curse of their sex altogether.

CATHERINE: In an age of Science men will learn to bleed as women do and benefit from a monthly cleansing of their bodies.

JACQUES: Men will never accept an open wound to make a mockery of their bodies.

HENRI: God's sentence hangs over all your sex and His punishment weighs down on you.

JEANNE: It's no punishment to have the force to bring forth children.

CLAUDE: Punish the guilty. Scourge the wicked.

HENRI: All evil comes from the flesh. The flesh of Eve.

JEANNE: It's not our fault.

JACQUES: Then whose fault is it?

AGATHE: You brought her here.

CATHERINE: You painted the pike.

JEANNE: You smashed the cross.

CLAUDE: You prayed for God's intervention.

CATHERINE: And God sent the rain.

JACQUES: The wind brought the rain.

JEANNE: And God sent the wind to bring the rain to mix with the paint and stain the statue red.

AGATHE: Blood red.

JEANNE: Blood of the womb.

CATHERINE: Crying out for the dead.

AGATHE: Murdered in the name of Liberty.

(Silence. Then the men repeat simultaneously.)

HENRI: Cover it up!

JACQUES: Clean it up!

CLAUDE: Hide it away!

(They repeat this as they drift back into the darkness.)

CATHERINE: I had a vision of a statue raised in Babylon. An enormous, dazzling statue, awesome to behold. Its head was pure gold, its chest and arms of silver, its belly and thighs of bronze, its legs of iron, its feet half-iron, half clay. Then a giant rock was hurled at the statue's feet and smashed the iron, the clay, the bronze, the silver and the gold until the shattered pieces were like chaff on a threshing floor...and the wind swept them away without trace, but the rock that struck the statue became a huge mountain that filled the whole earth. This was my dream...

JEANNE: How great are his signs! How mighty his wonders!

AGATHE: He reveals deep and hidden things: He knows what lies in darkness and light dwells with him.

CATHERINE: And God will crush all those kingdoms which do not bow to his dominion, for He will endure from generation to generation.

Lights out.

SCENE EIGHT:

JEANNE'S cottage. THÉRÈSE is asleep. Father TIQUET enters and hauls her up and awake.

TIQUET: I know you. I know your story.

THÉRÈSE: What?

TIQUET: You're not a soldier. Not even a man.

THÉRÈSE: Who says?

TIQUET: We priests are omniscient. Don't you know that? Or don't you go to Church?

THÉRÈSE: What do you want?

TIQUET: I knew the face you see. Never forget a face, not even one from years ago in Paris - and I was there at your trial. Thérèse de Courtenay, the famous whore, got a bit beyond her station though... Dressed in green you were with rubies strung around your neck and down across your naked breasts... you smiled at me. You smiled at all the men as though you owned the courtroom... but the women spat. And you were sent to the Salpêtrière to rot with half of Paris glad, the other half grateful you never gave their names out as your former clients.

THÉRÈSE: What do you want?

TIQUET: To have what they had. The high and mighty you'd perform your tricks for. What made them cry to see you shut away? What were you offering they couldn't get elsewhere?

THÉRÈSE: And then?

TIQUET: Then...nothing. Silence.

THÉRÈSE: I don't believe you.

TIQUET: Did they let you out? Or did you escape?

THÉRÈSE: I was never in Paris.

TIQUET: You were never there. Never in prison. Never in Lyon. Never a virgin.

THÉRÈSE: Get away from me.

TIQUET: This commune's godless now. What do they need with a man of god? They've mutilated the body of Christ and put a bloody whore at the heart of the place. Worship that, they tell me. Do you know how hard it is to be a priest? Your flock bleats for what it can't have. You risk death for even thinking. And they send me the whore of Babylon to test my faith. I'm only a man like any other. My skin sweats, my body's burning in agony-

THÉRÈSE: Get out!

TIQUET: Who can you call? Who'll help you now?

THÉRÈSE: Jeanne will be back-

TIQUET: They're all in the square. Marvelling at the sight of blood from stone. They want me to explain it. They think I know about miracles, you see.
(He moves to grab her but she gets behind the table and tips it and the body on top of him. He scrambles out and prevents her leaving).. the monster has three forms, oh yes. Face of a noble lion...filthy belly of a goat and ...tail of a viper.
(He climbs on top of her and rapes her. Lighting changes to isolate THÉRÈSE'S face.)

THÉRÈSE: At twelve her father sent her to the Marquis, beat her when she failed to like the old man's ways. You can find a way to live with anything, she told herself. And she learned about pain, fantasy and revenge, so when she ran far away from him to Paris she knew her trade. But then she learned another thing: dare to turn a man away, and others beg to be included. The more audaciously she set her value, the more demand there was from dukes and counts and generals... She set up house, employed a maid, ordered a lavish wardrobe of silk, satin and brocade, went to the Opera, the Theatre and Ballet...

(Lights change. The priest climbs off exhausted. He leaves.)

But it was cold in prison. The chains cut my skin... the food was rancid... the hours we wished away... until they came. September the fourth, the Paris mob got in a frenzy, pulled us from our cells to kill. Mutilating some, raping others, they slashed our bodies and drank our blood. Roaring, wild they cut the babes from our wombs and laughed. They didn't care, didn't worry, never mind if they murdered madwomen, whores or orphan girls. We were all women, all dangerous, wicked women.

She gets up and goes out. Lights fade.

SCENE NINE:

The Statue in the Market-Place. Wisps of fog are creeping in. AGATHE and CATHERINE stand frozen momentarily, holding a crowbar and a sledgehammer. JEANNE is kneeling in prayer. As the lights fade up they unfreeze. They chant in unison. Their words are repeated in whispers.

245

THE WOMEN: This place has been defiled by its own people. A curse consumes those who flout the laws and mock the sacred body of Jesus Christ. When statues bleed we know the day of judgement is upon us and the tide of blood will be unstoppable. The fall to sulphurous pits of stinking flesh unceasing where each sinner inhabits an eternal agony of pain.

(The women surround the statue.)

CATHERINE: Are we afraid of it?

AGATHE: It looks almost real tonight.

JEANNE: It's like a lost soul, all alone here.

(They wait. AGATHE pulls the cloth away that has been wrapped around the statue's lower half.)

JEANNE: Perhaps we should just clean it up.

(CATHERINE goes to the statue and knocks loose the bolts on either side of it which hold it onto the plinth. Then AGATHE and CATHERINE try pushing it over but it won't shift. They stand back and look at it.)

JEANNE: Dear God, please let them move it, please let it come down now, please-

CATHERINE: If we had a bit more weight behind it, we might manage, Jeanne.

JEANNE: Alright.

AGATHE: Maybe we could lever it off.

CATHERINE: Yes...that's it.

(AGATHE goes to the statue and climbs up onto the plinth. She places the crowbar at the base of it and with her knees pushes it so that the crowbar can be wedged underneath by CATHERINE. CATHERINE pushes down on the crowbar and AGATHE pushes with her full body weight until the statue topples over. It breaks in half. CATHERINE cheers.)

CATHERINE: Hurrah! At last, the anti-Christ departs!

(JEANNE goes and picks up the Tablet of Human Rights and the red bonnet which she puts in her coat pocket. AGATHE retrieves the pike and picks up the head which she looks at mournfully.)

CATHERINE: It still offends me.

AGATHE: We can't leave it here like this.

CATHERINE: Stand back. I feel the urge to finish it.

JEANNE: What are you doing?

(CATHERINE smashes the statue into smaller pieces as though in a fit of frenzy.)

CATHERINE: Hallelujah! Hallelujah! Hallelujah!

JEANNE: Watch out for bits of flying stone!

CATHERINE: God's given me permission to do this. I'll not be hurt. They'll be reduced to chaff on the threshing-floor and the wind will sweep them away without trace!

AGATHE: What should we do with all these pieces?

JEANNE: Let's take them to the river and wash them clean.

CATHERINE: Or throw them off the roman bridge!

JEANNE: We'll pass the chapel of Our Lady. We can ask for her blessing.

AGATHE: It's almost dark. And the fog's rolling in. Can you find the way to the river?

CATHERINE: I know it blindfold.

AGATHE: I'm not sure....perhaps we should give this back to them.

JEANNE: I'll take them to the town hall. I've got a key.

(She gives JEANNE the pike.)

CATHERINE: Onward! To the river!

(They go and pick up pieces of the statue and go out towards the river. JEANNE remains staring at the empty plinth for a long time as darkness falls. The fog swirls in. The music grows louder. CHRISTOPHE enters with a lantern.)

CHRISTOPHE: Jeanne?

JEANNE: Who's that?

CHRISTOPHE: Its me, Christophe. Father Tiquet sent me. This fog's the perfect cover for moving all the dead into the crypt.

JEANNE: Gone...

CHRISTOPHE: Are you alright? It's very cold out here.

JEANNE: I've got what's left of her here in my pocket....Look.

(She shows him the revolutionary emblems. He takes the pike.)

CHRISTOPHE: What are these? Aren't they from the statue? *(CHRISTOPHE turns and looks for the statue)* Where is she? Has she come to life and run away from this miserable spot? I wouldn't blame her if she did.

JEANNE: We did it.

CHRISTOPHE: What magic have you worked tonight then?

JEANNE: What will I tell Claude?

CHRISTOPHE: Tell him you cast a spell to make the lady vanish, and she did. Do you know a spell to bring her back?

JEANNE: No.

CHRISTOPHE: Gone for good then? Without so much as a message for me...

JEANNE: Claude will lose everything.

CHRISTOPHE: Don't take on so.

JEANNE: You don't know him. You don't know what he's capable of.

CHRISTOPHE: I'll come with you.

JEANNE: No, he'll blame you. Have you locked away.

CHRISTOPHE: Let's go home. They're waiting for us there.

(He takes hold of her arm and she relaxes slightly. They exit. The fog swirls in faster. CLAUDE and HENRI enter with a lantern.)

HENRI: Can't see a damn thing.

CLAUDE: I know the Inn is this way. *(He walks straight into the plinth)* Ow!

HENRI: What is it?

(CLAUDE holds the lantern up but can find no statue. He walks around the plinth.)

HENRI: Well?

CLAUDE: Funny...I think we're somewhere else.

HENRI: What?

CLAUDE: We're not in the market-place after all.

HENRI: Then where the hell are we?

CLAUDE: I don't know. I thought that was Liberty.

HENRI: What is it then? *(HENRI takes the lantern and looks at the plinth and then holds it up but the fog is too thick to see clearly)* Can you see the tree?

CLAUDE: I can't see anything.

HENRI: The tree of equality can't just vanish.

CLAUDE: Are you saying the statue's vanished?

HENRI: I don't know what I'm saying. Isn't that the thing it was sitting on?

CLAUDE: Maybe it's come off.

HENRI: Well look around it.

(They both search the ground around the plinth. CLAUDE finds a small piece of the statue which he holds up to the light.)

CLAUDE: I've got something.

HENRI: What is it?

CLAUDE: I think it's a piece of shoulder. Must have chipped off when it was stolen.

HENRI: Stolen? You mean -

(FATHER TIQUET enters with a cart with a body on it.)

HENRI: Sounds like a cart.

CLAUDE: Let's go.

HENRI: No...we might catch them.

CLAUDE: What if they're armed?

HENRI: Halt! Who goes there? *(They go over and find TIQUET and the cart)* A strange hour to be abroad, father.

TIQUET: Death may come at any time.

CLAUDE: Who's that?

TIQUET: A fever case. Taking him to the pit.

HENRI: Let me see him.

TIQUET: You risk contagion if you touch him.

(HENRI goes and pulls back the covers. The others cover their faces.)

HENRI: Its old Rajat. He's been dead for weeks.

TIQUET: Some families can't bear to part with them.

CLAUDE: Did you see anyone go past?

TIQUET: I can see very little in this weather. Now stand clear. I've a busy night.

(TIQUET moves off.)

HENRI: Suspicious eh?

CLAUDE: You think he could have taken it?

HENRI: He could be in league with them.

CLAUDE: With who?

HENRI: With those who want to see another bloody roman symbol here.

CLAUDE: He seemed quite accepting of the statue when we put it up.

HENRI: A trick to make us think he loves the revolution. Tonight we've seen through the mask.

CLAUDE: Perhaps it was taken by thieves.

HENRI: Or seized by hired brigands working for the aristocrats-

CLAUDE: Who heard that it was taken from a château in the first place.

HENRI: A plot between the priests and the aristocrats most likely. They failed in Lyon and now they try their hand here in Montchalier.

(CHRISTOPHE and THÉRÈSE enter carrying a stretcher with the body of JEAN-MARIE.)

CLAUDE: There's someone there...Its Christophe.

HENRI: That vagabond.

CLAUDE: Who's that with him?

CHRISTOPHE: We're on our way to the common grave to lay your brother to rest Claude.

CLAUDE: Its very good of you. I haven't been home for days because of him.

HENRI: You still here? No hurry to rejoin your company?

(HENRI goes over and looks at the stretcher and THÉRÈSE

CLAUDE: You don't think he's a deserter?

HENRI: Or a spy. What company you from?

THÉRÈSE: The thirty-third.

CLAUDE: That was Jean-Marie's company.

HENRI: Under whose command?

THÉRÈSE: Under General Le Clerc.

CLAUDE: That's right Henri.

HENRI: When do you go back?

THÉRÈSE: Tonight citizen, when my brother's in the ground.

HENRI: Why leave it so late?

THÉRÈSE: The sister's idea.

HENRI: Let me see that man.

(HENRI looks to see if it is in fact JEAN-MARIE. They all turn away from the smell, start coughing.)

CHRISTOPHE: No respect, have you?

CLAUDE: Let them go Henri. It's unbearable.

HENRI: Alright. Get on with it. *(They go out)* Why tonight? Why this sudden passion for burials?

CLAUDE: It's the full moon... perhaps it's the kind of thing they do where he comes from.

HENRI: I thought he came from St. Polgues.

CLAUDE: Before that. He was bought from St. Domingue and you know what strange beliefs those people in the Caribbean have.

HENRI: Are you suggesting that the priest has been converted to some kind of voodoo?

CLAUDE: It could happen.

HENRI: Perhaps we should follow them?

CLAUDE: Why don't we try and find our way to the Star?

HENRI: We're not going to the pub until we find that statue.

CLAUDE: Can't it wait until morning when the fog's cleared?

HENRI: We'll start by searching the houses, questioning people, blocking the roads.

CLAUDE: We can't wake the whole village now. It's after curfew.

HENRI: Will you explain to Monsieur Lapalus how we lost the bloody thing?

CLAUDE: Anyone who wants the wretched thing is doing us a favour, if you ask me-

HENRI: Alright. I'll go to the Chief of Police by myself.

CLAUDE: It might turn up tomorrow. Come on, just one cognac?

(HENRI sighs, gives in. They go towards the inn. The religious chanting fades up again. After a while, TIQUET returns and crosses the stage with an empty cart and then the women return with torches singing.)

Lights down.

End of Act One.

ACT TWO

SCENE ONE:

Meeting in the Town Hall. The sound of the 'Marseillaise' fades up. A banner with an 'eye' and the word 'Vigilance' beneath it. A podium on which LAPALUS steps up to address the people of the commune. CLAUDE and HENRI stand on either side of the podium. LAPALUS raises his arms for silence. The music cuts.

(During the following speech women come on and surround the podium.)

LAPALUS: *(to audience)* Citizens, I'm here today to express my dismay that such an obscenity could have been allowed to occur. The sacrilegious act of this statue's destruction constitutes a crime so serious it threatens us all. Even in the Vendée no-one has dared such an insult to the Revolution. What infamy! This place isn't fit to bear the name of our great Chalier, corrupted by the papists, royalists and other enemies of the revolution who run amok here. I've come here today to save you, to lead you back to justice, to help you with the important task of punishing every

250

man, woman and child who's ever dreamed a dream of discrediting the Revolution.

(There is a silence. HENRI and CLAUDE stare fixedly in front of them.)

CATHERINE: We want to be able to do what they do in Boën.

LAPALUS: *(to CLAUDE)* What do they do in Boën?

(CLAUDE looks at HENRI who shrugs.)

CATHERINE: They have proper services in their churches and they can bury their people in the graveyard with the sacred rites.

LAPALUS: Is this true? *(HENRI shakes his head. CLAUDE nods.)* You do not need the old ways now, when we are transforming the world and all its history.

AGATHE: Why can't we choose what we need and what we don't?

LAPALUS: A most impertinent young woman.

CATHERINE: We don't want you telling us what to think.

AGATHE: Why don't you listen to us for a change?

CATHERINE: We want to vote! We want to vote!

(The women take up this refrain.)

WOMEN: We want to vote! We want to vote!

LAPALUS: Is this a plot against us?

HENRI: I don't think so.

LAPALUS: Who is that woman leading them?

HENRI: That's my wife, citizen.

LAPALUS: Have you no power over your own property?

HENRI: I'll try....Citizens, citizens, please. Please will you let us speak?

AGATHE: When do we get to speak? When will women get the chance to be represented up there?

CATHERINE: How many women sit in the Paris Assembly?

JEANNE: Why can't we pray together like we used to?

(They all nod and murmur together.)

THE WOMEN: That's right. Why can't we?

LAPALUS: Who's that religious fanatic?

CLAUDE: That's my wife, citizen.

LAPALUS: What? Are you all in this conspiracy together? Do I come all this way to find a commune in the grip of the Holy Roman Church?

(CLAUDE and HENRI shake their heads continually, while mumbling denials.)

AGATHE: Why don't you come down here where we can get our hands on you?

LAPALUS: Call out the gendarmes!

JEANNE: We've lost men for your damn war, what do you give us in return?

CATHERINE: We don't want your rules and regulations. Tell Paris to go to hell.

AGATHE: What are you afraid of?

JEANNE: Come down here and talk to us.

LAPALUS: Call out the gendarmes!

JEANNE: You can't make us give up our God.

CATHERINE: You can't make us love Robespierre.

LAPALUS: Order! Order!

(LAPALUS raises his arms, but is ignored.)

JEANNE: That's all we ever hear from you men. Orders, orders.

CATHERINE: We've had enough speeches. We want action.

AGATHE: You'd better change or we'll change things for you.

CATHERINE: You won't stop us. You'll never stop us!

JEANNE: We want to die in our religion.

CATHERINE: Vive la Religion!

THE WOMEN: Vive la Religion! Vive la Religion! Vive la Religion! etc.

(LAPALUS tries taking off his tricolor sash and hat and ceremoniously replacing them to demonstrate his authority.)

LAPALUS: Silence!

(There is a momentary silence and then the women shower LAPALUS with flour bombs. LAPALUS looks distraught. He puffs himself up and

walks with affected dignity offstage, followed by CLAUDE and HENRI. The women cheer. After a while FATHER TIQUET climbs onto the podium. The cheering subsides.)

TIQUET: Pray that the Lord will send an angel to protect the virtuous women of our commune from the dangers now before us. You, who have challenged their corruption, their faith in these false idols, you must be prepared to face the fiery furnace of their fury. Go home my too, too faithful daughters and sleep the sleep of the innocent, for tomorrow, I fear, you'll be mistaken for the guilty. Go home, I beg of you. Go home.

(The women drift back into the darkness during this speech. HENRI enters and shakes TIQUET by the hand, smiling.)

HENRI: Well done, father.

TIQUET: All the kingdoms of the world lost by women. Troy destroyed for Helen, thousands of men slain. Jezebel killed to be queen and men suffered. The Roman Empire crushed by Cleopatra, the worst of women. And now, the world is tormented by their malice!

Lights snap out.

SCENE TWO:

Darkness. JEANNE, AGATHE and THÉRÈSE appear in turn, isolated in circles of light. They are chained. The men do not appear but we hear their voices.

JEANNE: My name is Jeanne Mignéry. I'm guilty as charged. It was my idea and my idea alone to destroy the statue. I couldn't stand to look at it. I hated it. I'm glad I did it and I'd do it again if I had to.

252

CLAUDE: What are you saying Jeanne?

JEANNE: The truth. My voice is shaking.

CLAUDE: But we discussed this.

JEANNE: I'm sorry, no...we never discuss anything. You simply tell me what to do. And I do it. Except for this. This was different. More... enjoyable.

(CLAUDE punches JEANNE in the stomach. She buckles up.)

CLAUDE: Repeat what I told you to.

JEANNE: I'm sorry Claude. I am.

CLAUDE: Tell them you kept the pike safe, and the bonnet and the Tablet of Human Rights - that you took them to the Town Hall - that you weren't involved, that it was all that woman's fault-

JEANNE: It wasn't.

CLAUDE: The priest's signed a statement exonerating you. He says you're the innocent victim of a rebel plot led by this woman you took for a soldier-

JEANNE: Will I be free?

CLAUDE: There are other charges.

JEANNE: I'll hang anyway. Why take her with me?

CLAUDE: If you cooperate-

JEANNE: Sign my name to lies?

CLAUDE: Help me to help you!

JEANNE: My name is Jeanne Mignéry. I'm guilty as charged.

(AGATHE moves into a light.)

AGATHE: We did it! We sent Lapalus packing.

HENRI: You should have listened.

AGATHE: We were strong. We made our voices heard.

HENRI: You made trouble.

AGATHE: Before this, I'd never stayed away from home. I like it.

HENRI: You left your children by themselves while you destroyed the commune's property.

AGATHE: I'm not worried about them. I'm not worried about them or my husband or the rats in the store. I've let them go.

HENRI: You should be bloody shot.

AGATHE: We won't go back now. We'll go on with it.

HENRI: Don't you care what happens to this commune?

AGATHE: Of course we care. That's why we're doing this.

HENRI: I could help you Agathe.

AGATHE: Make them let me go, why don't you?

HENRI: They've only carried out their civic duty. They're not the ones who took the law into their own hands.

AGATHE: Can a piece of rock give me freedom? No. We have to grab at it when we can. Like Eve. Grab for a bite of the apple. Fight for a piece of life.

HENRI: Just give it time. Things are changing faster now than ever before because men and women are working together.

AGATHE: We weren't afraid of him.

He knew it. I saw his eyes.

HENRI: Agathe, please. Use your head. Who'll run the mills? Think of the commune, think of your duties. Think of us men.

(THÉRÈSE moves into a light.)

JACQUES: Do you know that prostitution is a crime against the revolution?

THÉRÈSE: I was put in the Salpêtrière for it.

JACQUES: Why come here?

THÉRÈSE: Thought I'd be safe.

JACQUES: If you loved safety so, why plot rebellion? If you wanted security, why drive these women to such a dazzling action of defiance? No... you're not just any whore but a royal spy come to whip us up for the king's men all sheltering in foreign palaces. Here to pave the way for their invasion, to find supporters and safe houses inside France.

THÉRÈSE: Shit and you know it.

JACQUES: There's testimony from Father Tiquet.

THÉRÈSE: He's full of stories. Heaven and hell for a start. Can you believe you're supposed to be at peace up there, knowing your friends are burning in agony down below? I don't buy it.

JACQUES: You drove them to it. Didn't you?

THÉRÈSE: Nothing to do with me.

JACQUES: You and Agathe ...you were... there was... some sort of intimacy.

THÉRÈSE: I told her to loosen up.

JACQUES: You let them loose. An army of she-devils!

THÉRÈSE: They heard God. I couldn't stop them.

(The lights on the women fade and slowly the lights come up to reveal the men sitting smoking and drinking.)

HENRI: Forget them. They've confessed and will be condemned for it.

CLAUDE: Let them die?

HENRI: We can't save them. It would smack of partiality.

CLAUDE: We can't let them die! We-

HENRI: Watch out for reprisals Claude.

JACQUES: We could write a letter, a petition-

HENRI: It's too late for letters!

(CATHERINE is led on. She has been chained.)

CATHERINE: Dogsbreath! Pissfeatures! Ratsbollocks!

HENRI: We must be formal. We must be objective. Vallan, tell us what part you played in this riotous meeting yesterday.

CATHERINE: Go piss yourselves! You know what happened.

JACQUES: Cathy, we need to know why there were so many people at the meeting? Several workers from your cotton-factory were seen there.

HENRI: The cotton-factory where she's employed. Be careful or I'll have all my goods and property confiscated.

CATHERINE: You bastard? You employ me, do you? I must be owed at least twenty years back pay, if that's the case.

HENRI: Trust me to put the correct legal position.

CATHERINE: Trust you! What am I doing here? Chained like a bloody animal!

CLAUDE: Shut up!

CATHERINE: Look who's come to life. The village idiot.

HENRI: This is your last chance-

CATHERINE: Waving the big stick are we Henri?... Alright, alright...A lot of people heard that in Boën they'd voted to resume religious ceremonies. We thought Lapalus was coming here to take a vote on it.

HENRI: Absurd! Lapalus is known to be vehemently opposed to any such revivials.

CATHERINE: We all got excited, a bit carried away.

CLAUDE: You were possessed! Chanting and ranting and having visions all over the place. It was you, said smash the statue! It was you started shouting at Lapalus about God!

CATHERINE: I wasn't even there that night! When they did the statue in. I was at home. Tell them I was home, Henri.

HENRI: You were home, but not till late.

JACQUES: I can vouch for this woman. Earlier on, she was... visiting my mother.

HENRI: What?

JACQUES: I can vouch for her. Let her go.

HENRI: The charge of incitement to riot still stands so she'll be transferred to Feurs for trial with the others.

CATHERINE: You bloody worm! You shitlicking bastard!

JACQUES: Henri...?

HENRI: Lapalus knows that my wife is involved. He pointed her out and asked me her name.

JACQUES: But...but...

CLAUDE: Certainly can't show any favouritism. Now can we?

JACQUES: But she's pregnant.

HENRI: What?

CLAUDE: Well, if she was, we could-

HENRI: Impossible!

CATHERINE: I know!

HENRI: Wishful thinking.

JACQUES: She's telling you the truth.

HENRI: I know when my wife's lying.

JACQUES: Do you? Do you really?

CLAUDE: Why wouldn't he?

(Silence. JACQUES and CATHERINE glance at each other.)

JACQUES: She was with me that night. She never touched the statue.

HENRI: What?

JACQUES: It's my child she's carrying.

CLAUDE: You mean...

JACQUES: I'm sorry that-

CATHERINE: Sorry? For him?

CLAUDE: We could get a doctor-

HENRI: Its all lies! The lot of it.

JACQUES: I don't want my child born in prison.

CATHERINE: Well, it might not be yours Jacques.

JACQUES: You said you never touched him!

CATHERINE: We're man and wife. He has a right...

JACQUES: You're lying!

HENRI: Surely you know when she's deceiving you?

JACQUES: She's made us both her bloody fools.

(Silence. They all stare at CATHERINE.)

HENRI: Take her out!

(CATHERINE is led out by CLAUDE. The sound of the guillotine starts to fade up.)

HENRI: We must send a deputation to the Tribunal, deploring these outrages. We must distance ourselves from the contemptible crimes of these unnatural women. We must draw up a written document, denouncing every one of them. We must assure the Tribunal that we do everything within our power to hunt down these traitors. They must realise that we sansculottes will never compromise on despotism or liberty!

(CLAUDE returns with a letter which he hands to HENRI.)

CLAUDE: This has come from Feurs tonight.

(HENRI opens it and reads it. CLAUDE takes the letter and passes it to JACQUES.)

CLAUDE: We're forbidden to use the name Montchalier.

JACQUES: Tarnished the martyr's memory have we?

HENRI: You don't see that we're next. First they remove the name, then they'll remove us.

CLAUDE: What have we done?

HENRI: It's us, they'll be chaining to the walls of the prison. It's us, they'll be taking in the tumbrils at dawn. It's our heads that will drop into the basket to the cheers of the waiting crowd.

JACQUES: Can't go back to the saint name now can we?

CLAUDE: Certainly not. They'd be convinced we're in league with the priests if that happened.

HENRI: We need to purify ourselves of this female infection.

CLAUDE: Perhaps another

ceremony? Sing a few hymns, make a few speeches and offer up a new name to the people.

HENRI: *(thinks)* Montpurifiée.

JACQUES: Say again.

HENRI: Montpurifiée!

JACQUES: That's absurd.

CLAUDE: It would demonstrate a fresh beginning to the Tribunal.

HENRI: We could have the ceremony tomorrow!

JACQUES: We're in debt from the last one.

HENRI: Are you questioning your civic duty, citizen?

JACQUES: I'm questioning . the expense.

CLAUDE: We'll have to make it up to Lapalus.

JACQUES: And for that you'll sacrifice the women?

HENRI: They'll receive a fair trial in Feurs.

JACQUES: Feurs is a stepping-stone to the scaffold and you know it.

HENRI: This letter shows they're onto us already.

JACQUES: I won't sign a denunciation. I won't put my name to lies.

HENRI: You won't put your name to lies? Your whole life's been one long deception, hasn't it?

CLAUDE: It's no good if we're divided.

JACQUES: Then it's no good. Don't do it.

HENRI: We've no choice!

JACQUES: Don't you see? The world's turning cautious. We get rid of the priests of doom and we bring in the high-priests of revolution. The power they have to make us cringe, to scuttle for safe holes and never confront the truth of what's really happening.

CLAUDE: My children are crying for their mother.

HENRI: You want them to lose their father as well?

JACQUES: Blame someone else. Blame the royalists. Blame the priests. Blame any criminal you can lay your hands on. Just do it!

(JACQUES exits. HENRI and CLAUDE stare out. CHRISTOPHE enters.)

CHRISTOPHE: Psst! Monsieur le Maire! Over here.

(He gestures to CLAUDE who goes over to him. HENRI cranes to hear what CHRISTOPHE is saying.)

CHRISTOPHE: I wanted you to know there's a conspiracy of thieves in this commune. Stealin' grain from yer sister's store and sellin' it at vast profit to rich customers for gold. I've seen them tradin' after curfew, hagglin' over prices. Got so I 'ad to seize the bags meself and carry 'em back to the store. Do they learn? No. Their greed's beyond reason.

CLAUDE: Why are we whispering?

CHRISTOPHE: These thieves are 'ere. At the top. Among you. And now they're posing as bloody saints and sending women to the slammer. I've 'ad enough of their lies. I want them caught. I want them tried. I want them out of the way for good.

CLAUDE: Calm down Christophe. Who're you talking about?

CHRISTOPHE: Who runs the Jacobin Club?

CLAUDE: Jacques Bernuizet?

CHRISTOPHE: And who's in charge of the Committee of Surveillance?

CLAUDE: No! Its not true. It can't be.

CHRISTOPHE: Out of the way before they do any more harm, Claude. You 'ave to do it.

(They both stare at HENRI.)

HENRI: What is it? What's the matter? Well, say something then. Bloody hell. Have you gone deaf? Tell me! What is it?

The sound of the guillotine crescendoes. Lights fade.

SCENE THREE:

A prison in Feurs. Prison bars or lighting effect. JEANNE lies on the floor, hallucinating, whispering to herself. THÉRÈSE walks up and down trying to beat the cold through exercise.

JEANNE: *(whispers)* Be merciful unto me O Lord for I cry unto Thee daily....from this arid desert plain, I call out, an owl among the ruins....I lie awake and long for dawn, like a bird alone on a roof at night. I can't fly, can't sing, can't sleep, can't....

(She coughs violently and AGATHE gives her a ladle of water from a bucket.)

THÉRÈSE: Go easy there. Its all we've got.

AGATHE: She's much worse today.

THÉRÈSE: If this cold eases she has a chance, if it freezes up again-

JEANNE: *(whispers)* ...Don't cast me out! Don't cast me out!

AGATHE: I begged Claude to send us food and blankets but none have come.

THÉRÈSE: The guards'll be having those. It's what they call their bonus. The sooner we die, the sooner they'll pick us over for gold or lace or handkerchiefs.

AGATHE: I've sold the one I had for food.

(JEANNE begins to crawl around the floor, trying to get up.)

JEANNE: So much ice... growing every night... freezing me.... ice blades between my ribs... ashes in my mouth. My body turned to skin and bones...

THÉRÈSE: She's raving again.

AGATHE: What can we do?

THÉRÈSE: Pray she never knows before her time comes.

AGATHE: When will they take her?

THÉRÈSE: Soon. They show no mercy for the witless.

(AGATHE goes to JEANNE and

holds her.)

AGATHE: We must try and change your dreams little sister, before they take you to a place you can't return from.

JEANNE: Woman was born to serve.... serve the ice, serve the cold, serve the darkness... serve...

AGATHE: You're dreaming Jeanne.

JEANNE: Dreaming?

AGATHE: Visions, nightmares, without substance.

JEANNE: Agathe?...

AGATHE: Were I to dream as you do I'd set sail for brighter shores, for happiness and laughter.

THÉRÈSE: Take me with you.

AGATHE: I'd see myself on a broad soft stretch of sand with such sunshine, you've never seen the like of... bending itself down from azure skies, embracing me with light. Its fingers, pure and white caressing me, entering me and melting me inside it. See me now I'm turning in the light, I glisten against the turquoise sea then rise up and ride on foamy waves to paradise-

(JEANNE starts coughing again. AGATHE goes to fetch water and THÉRÈSE holds JEANNE.)

JEANNE: I can't see the sun! It's gone behind a cloud. Black and full of thunder.

THÉRÈSE: It's nothing but a bit of rain come to cool us down.

(JEANNE drinks.)

JEANNE: Where are we?

THÉRÈSE: An island green and lush with blue-grey mountains at its centre. Name of Saint-Domingue, though the Spanish who live there call it different.

JEANNE: How long have we been here?

THÉRÈSE: Not long, but we can stay.

JEANNE: I'd like to stay here with you, if I can.

THÉRÈSE: You can stay with me, you can stay....

(JEANNE is falling asleep on her.)

THÉRÈSE: Asleep.

AGATHE: Let's lay her down then.

THÉRÈSE: She's been wretching blood.

AGATHE: I wish we had a little soup.

THÉRÈSE: She'd not stomach it.

AGATHE: Then what?

(THÉRÈSE shrugs then sits and stares into space, lost in her thoughts.)

AGATHE: I heard you mention Saint-Domingue. Christophe never stops talking of it.

THÉRÈSE: Christophe's from Saint-Domingue?

AGATHE: He puts every sous towards the price of a passage.

THÉRÈSE: I have to get a message to him.

259

AGATHE: Why?

THÉRÈSE: A plan. For escape.

AGATHE: You think Christophe will risk his neck to get you out of here?

THÉRÈSE: There's money in it if he does.

AGATHE: If that's true-

THÉRÈSE: I lived on Saint-Domingue for a year with a planter named George Delacroix. We were married there. Before he got himself killed trying to talk with slaves who'd heard that all men are born free and equal.

AGATHE: You loved him?

THÉRÈSE: Love? Me? I always count the cost.

AGATHE: You brought Jeanne's brother back for nothing.

THÉRÈSE: No. For me. To say goodbye to my dead man. I used him.

AGATHE: To grieve for the man you loved?

THÉRÈSE: Believe this. When I sailed away from that island I was light as a feather. No ties, no obligations. I'd loved a man, yes, but I'd lost him. I was rich but I walked away. I was free.

AGATHE: Sometimes, we need to put down roots and grow instead of blowing around in every passing breeze.

THÉRÈSE: Come with me to Saint-Domingue.

AGATHE: I can't.

THÉRÈSE: So you'll bend your neck to the blade for their sake?

AGATHE: No.

THÉRÈSE: What will you do?

AGATHE: I'll fight Javogues.

THÉRÈSE: How?

AGATHE: I'll write to him.

THÉRÈSE: Fight or write?

AGATHE: I'll send a petition for an early trial or release. We can't stand another month in prison.

THÉRÈSE: Certainly not.

AGATHE: You're laughing at me?

THÉRÈSE: No, I'm happy. Because we've decided to try and do something. Because we've made a wish come here to keep us warm....

(They embrace for some time then break off and sit staring into space again. CATHERINE is thrown into the cell. She does not get up from the floor. When AGATHE goes to touch her shoulder she flinches.)

AGATHE: We won't hurt you.

CATHERINE: Get away from me.

AGATHE: We have some water.

THÉRÈSE: There's not much left.

(AGATHE goes and gets the bucket and gives CATHERINE a little. She drinks thirstily.)

AGATHE: She's a friend.

CATHERINE: I've no friends.

THÉRÈSE: Do you know her?

AGATHE: It's Catherine. She's the wife of Henri Chaverondier.

CATHERINE: Don't say that name. He wants me dead. He stood and spoke against me.

THÉRÈSE: You've been in court?

CATHERINE: He told Javogues I led the women on. Blamed me, my visions, my love of God. That's why he sends them...sends the guards into us at night. So we can never sleep without watching out for them and then they come and, and they won't stop no matter how we scream.

THÉRÈSE: (whispers) Leave her alone, Agathe.

CATHERINE: Agathe? Is that you?

AGATHE: Yes.

CATHERINE: It's even colder here than in the last place. Everyone died of fever before they brought me here.

AGATHE: Jeanne has fever.

CATHERINE: Jeanne Mignéry? She's here?

THÉRÈSE: She's here.

CATHERINE: I didn't think Jeanne Mignéry was in prison. Couldn't Claude have saved her?

AGATHE: We thought that Jacques might...

CATHERINE: Haven't seen him. He heard I'd lost his baby son - his baby's blood on the prison floor. D'you know one woman tried to lick it up? To lick it up...

THÉRÈSE: It's alright.

(Silence.)

CATHERINE: You're lucky to be kept together.

THÉRÈSE: Agathe is to write a petition.

CATHERINE: Javogues never reads them.

AGATHE: He'll read this one.

CATHERINE: Have you started it?

THÉRÈSE: The small matter of ink and paper.

CATHERINE: You'll have to bribe the guards.

AGATHE: I'll memorise it line by line until we get some....House of Arrest, Feurs, sixth of February, Seventeen hundred and ninety-four.

THÉRÈSE: You'll have to use the revolutionary calendar but I don't know what it is.

CATHERINE: I know it. I heard the date when they put my name on the death list.

AGATHE: Right then... (she inhales) You are exposing the detainees from Saint Germain-Laval-

THÉRÈSE: Montchalier.

CATHERINE: Montpurifiée. That's what they've named it.

AGATHE: Imprisoned for over two months we are mostly reduced to a more terrible state of destitution than it's possible to bear...even in misery. Nor have we had the help we expect-

CATHERINE: ...The help we have a right to from humanity.

261

THÉRÈSE: That's good.

AGATHE: We implore you to be merciful to those whose sole crime is -

THÉRÈSE: Hold on, I've done nothing.

CATHERINE: Ignorance, is our only crime. Ignorance of Javogues' aims in matters of religion.

AGATHE: In view of this unwitting error please end our misery and pain-

THÉRÈSE: Don't beg, they never like it.

CATHERINE: Shall I call Thibaut? The guard.

AGATHE: We've nothing left to sell.

CATHERINE: I know what he wants.

AGATHE: You'd do that?

CATHERINE: How do you think I've stayed alive? Thibaut! Thibaut! Let me out. I want to see you.

(CATHERINE goes out.)

AGATHE: I can't remember any of it.

THÉRÈSE: Yes you can.

AGATHE: My head's so full of shadows.

THÉRÈSE: Then rest.

(She helps AGATHE to go sit down but then gets up and searches the cell inch by inch. AGATHE reaches for JEANNE'S hand and finds that JEANNE is dead.)

AGATHE: What have we done? How

could we be so blind to the world as it is? Blind to real power, dazzled by dreams, we're stupid, ignorant, bigotted believers of what? Nothing. Nothing...

THÉRÈSE: Agathe?

AGATHE: Jeanne's dead.

THÉRÈSE: Are you sure?

AGATHE: Yes.

(THÉRÈSE goes over to JEANNE and shuts her eyes)

THÉRÈSE: It's not your fault.

(AGATHE sits very still.)

AGATHE: What were you doing?

THÉRÈSE: Looking....for a way out.

AGATHE: Find anything?

THÉRÈSE: No...not yet.

AGATHE: How long.... before we just give up?

THÉRÈSE: Never. We never give up.

Lights fade.

SCENE FOUR:

JAVOGUES' house. A brazier into which JEAN is throwing bibles. A cart full of various religious artefacts. JAVOGUES sits reading from a bible aloud.

JAVOGUES: For I know this, that after my departing shall grievous wolves enter in among you, not sparing the flock....

(LAPALUS enters with a bundle of clothes which he drops next to the

brazier.)

JAVOGUES: What are they?

LAPALUS: Priests' habits.

JAVOGUES: Why would I want them?

LAPALUS: Mementoes of our work here. One for every hundred priests we've got rid of.

JAVOGUES: I may keep one.

(He goes and picks up a habit. He holds it up against him. Then he takes an instrument from the cart and gives it to JEAN.)

JEAN: What?

JAVOGUES: Play something suitably religious.

JEAN: It's out of tune.

(JAVOGUES puts the robe on over the top of his clothes.)

LAPALUS: Very good...but are you refractory or an oath-taker?

JAVOGUES: An oath to France when I have sworn an oath to God? I'd not sell my soul dear man for all the tea in the Chinas.

LAPALUS: Then you must come with me father.

JAVOGUES: Why? Do you wish to make confession?

LAPALUS: Oh yes...that's it. I want to tell you all.

JAVOGUES: Very well, I'm listening.

LAPALUS: Forgive me father for I have sinned.

JAVOGUES: Yes.

LAPALUS: I killed a priest yesterday.

JAVOGUES: Yes.

LAPALUS: I shot two the day before.

JAVOGUES: Yes.

LAPALUS: I put six in prison last week.

JAVOGUES: Yes.

LAPALUS: I'm full of bad thoughts on how to get at priests.

(JEAN makes a dissonant noise and stops playing.)

LAPALUS: Only recently I heard of a whole boat full of priests that was taken out into the middle of an icy river and allowed to sink. Eighty-three priests died, regrettably one survived.

JAVOGUES: What solution can you offer to this problem?

LAPALUS: Short of suicide, I'd advise marriage for the clergy.

JAVOGUES: A splendid idea.

LAPALUS: Why father, I've just the girl.

(He goes and takes JEAN'S hand.)

JEAN: Piss off.

LAPALUS: So charming with it.

JAVOGUES: You wouldn't brush me off so easily.

(JAVOGUES makes to chase JEAN. An ENVOY enters and stands

263

watching.)

ENVOY: I've a message for the Proconsul. Is he here?

LAPALUS: Over there.

ENVOY: Where?

JAVOGUES: Here.

ENVOY: I've been charged with delivering this order to you personally Proconsul. You must immediately renounce your position, disband your army and report to Robespierre at the National Assembly.

JAVOGUES: When, did you say? Now?

ENVOY: Without delay.

JAVOGUES: Impossible. Isn't it?

ENVOY: Is that your answer then?

(JAVOGUES walks up and down considering, then turns with passion.)

JAVOGUES: I came here with three aims. Only three aims in my life. I started with a purge of the political societies but everywhere I turned, traditionalists and peacemakers came to moderate my movements. Then the Church, that deadly rhinocerous - could I break its grip on their bodies from birth to death? No. They love the ride in the jaws of hell. And when I say the word 'Equality' they run from me. Only one town brave enough to give me a list of property and goods. They really hate the rich in St. Etienne but elsewhere, they're afraid of them. I can't fuck off now. We haven't even started.

ENVOY: If you're not in Paris within a week you'll be hunted down like any other rebel.

JAVOGUES: Am I talking Greek? He doesn't understand how hard we've tried to bring this region into line. Tell him Lapalus.

LAPALUS: I've often said you should comply with Paris and disband your private army.

(The ENVOY smiles. JAVOGUES takes off his priest's habit and throws it at LAPALUS.)

JAVOGUES: That's true. You never had the stomach for a fight when you could be kissing cunt instead.

ENVOY: Sign this to say you've received the order.

JAVOGUES: Certainly, but won't you stay and partake of our hospitality tonight, citizen?

ENVOY: Monsieur Lapalus and his charming wife have offered to entertain me. I thank you.

(The ENVOY and LAPALUS leave.)

JEAN: You're going to give up? *(JAVOGUES shrugs)* But now's your chance to strike. You've a thousand men who'd as soon march on Paris as kill the English.

JAVOGUES: I must go to the Robespierrists and I must crawl... kiss arse, lick boots, pay for dinners, lend money and fuck old women to save my neck.

JEAN: You can't.

JAVOGUES: I can.

JEAN: You make me puke.

JAVOGUES: When I attack Paris it'll

be planned in secrecy and carried out in shadow.

JEAN: Words, that's all. I'll not follow you.

JAVOGUES: No?

JEAN: I'll kill that bastard. He knew.

JAVOGUES: Oh yes.

JEAN: You've got prisons full of people who hate him. They've denounced him, sacked him, tried to assassinate him.

JAVOGUES: He was useful but never popular.

JEAN: Let them go.

JAVOGUES: A grand farewell gesture. Free all prisoners. Spare the condemned.

JEAN: Yeh.

JAVOGUES: Put distance between old Javogues and the excesses of young Lapalus.

JEAN: They'd murder him.

JAVOGUES: Come with me.

JEAN: Why should I?

JAVOGUES: You see things I don't.

JEAN: Then you'll have to beg me. I'll be Robespierre, you crawl. (*JAVOGUES gets down on his knees and crawls towards JEAN*) And don't you dare raise your eyes from the dirt, you lowly, cringing lapdog.

Lights fade.

SCENE FIVE:

Darkness. A prison in Feurs. AGATHE and THÉRÈSE huddle together, pale and semi-conscious.

THÉRÈSE: I remember a story about you. About Agathe the saint.

AGATHE: I'm no saint.

THÉRÈSE: You don't want to be. Terrible things happened to them. She dared to turn down a man so he sliced off her breasts and threw her in a fire.

AGATHE: Is that why they used her veil to stop a volcano erupting?

THÉRÈSE: Could be. I never knew that.

AGATHE: I believed those stories once.

THÉRÈSE: So did I. Once. Now I believe in me.

AGATHE: Don't believe in anything. Except this place. It's all we'll see before we die.

THÉRÈSE: You can die. I'm getting out.

AGATHE: Yeh, I know. You can do anything you want to.

THÉRÈSE: That's right.

AGATHE: We're going to die in here. Just face up to it!

THÉRÈSE: No way! Was I the one who smashed their statue? Was I the one screaming for a chance to say my prayers? I'll tell them I'm nothing to do with it! I'll tell them I don't give a shit about this country!

AGATHE: You don't give a shit for anything, do you? ...Except yourself.

THÉRÈSE: And you do? Just how many women are dead because of you? How many children are crying for their mothers now because you wanted the world to stop still?

AGATHE: We all wanted it.

THÉRÈSE: I didn't.

AGATHE: Things happened so fast-

THÉRÈSE: Stupid! Stupid woman! You should have loved that statue! Her naked body, her provocative pose, her pouting lips! Yes, she had blood between her thighs, a huge potent woman at the centre of the commune. What better sight?

AGATHE: It wasn't like that.

THÉRÈSE: It was better than looking at a man being tortured to death on two stumps of wood!

AGATHE: My father put up that cross.

THÉRÈSE: So you have to like it? Do you? Can't you think for yourself for once? No. You enjoy letting them push you around. Of course you do! You haven't got the guts for anything else. Never been anywhere. Never seen anything. What do you know about being wide open? About living on the edge, biting, kicking, turning yourself inside out for the hell of it? You know shit. No. You know about grain. About milling bloody grain. About keeping a respectable house. About wiping the dirty bums of your little sons and heirs. What for? Well, what for? For a husband who's off screwing someone else, pretending he's engaged in the holy pursuit of science!

AGATHE: And look at you. A whore who thinks she can go on and on, getting away with it, for ever. No matter how old she gets.

THÉRÈSE: That's right! And I will!

(They turn their backs on each other. AGATHE sits with her head in her hands. THÉRÈSE dozes off to sleep. A pale light signals the entrance of JEANNE'S ghost, cocooned in a large fishing net full of bones and other bits of bodies, which she drags behind her as she walks. Only AGATHE sees her.)

AGATHE: Jeanne!

JEANNE: I've been travelling, back and forth in time. I can't find the way out you see but then I don't know what it looks like.

AGATHE: Why do you keep those?

JEANNE: Thrown away by the world these were. Not of sufficient value. But I collect them. Feet, broken and bound in China, hands, cut off in Persia, eyes, gouged out in Asia, genitals, removed in Africa, ovaries destroyed in Germany, bodies, burned in India, minds, blanked in America. Women's they were. Done for their own good, it seems.

AGATHE: Who'd do such things?

JEANNE: Husbands, sons, brothers, lovers, doctors, lawyers, priests. I say let them be mothers. Let them try it. Let their breasts grow heavy with milk, their skin soft, their hair long, their voices gentle.

AGATHE: They won't change.

JEANNE: You have to make them change.

AGATHE: Me? I can't do anything.

JEANNE: You can. You've a talent for it. I've seen it. When you spoke out and swayed the crowd. You made them listen.

(AGATHE shakes her head and goes back to sitting with her head in her hands. JEANNE disappears and the light changes to flood the prison cell. A man stands silhouetted in the light. He walks forward. AGATHE is dazzled.)

CHRISTOPHE: Walked right in. There's no-one out there.

AGATHE: You came.

CHRISTOPHE: The guards are gone. Place is deserted.

AGATHE: I'm dreaming. Am I?

CHRISTOPHE: I'm here alright. Javogues's been disbarred. Lapalus denounced.

(AGATHE shakes THÉRÈSE awake.)

THÉRÈSE: You've got the boat?

CHRISTOPHE: Waiting at Roanne.

THÉRÈSE: Is the door left open?

CHRISTOPHE: You're free to go. A bloody amnesty.

THÉRÈSE: Free! We're free!

(THÉRÈSE runs around shouting and hugging them. AGATHE remains still.)

THÉRÈSE: Free Agathe.

AGATHE: Yes, we can go. But Jeanne's dead, buried out in the yard, Catherine's gone to Lyon to face her executioner and what of the other women from our commune lying sick or dying in other prisons?

THÉRÈSE: Come with us!

AGATHE: To your island paradise?

THÉRÈSE: Why mock it?

AGATHE: I'd take this hell inside me and ruin heaven within a week.

(There is a silence.)

CHRISTOPHE: Twenty thousand bin taken there as slaves. They knew hell, believe me. But the island itself, the pearl of the Antilles, a person can breathe there. And there's a man, a black prince grown strong picking sugar, come to wipe us clean of the old world's ways.

AGATHE: You're going back to civil war.

THÉRÈSE: Better than staying here with Robespierre butchering any opposition.

AGATHE: I'm going to Lyon.

THÉRÈSE: How? You don't mean to walk there?

AGATHE: There's a chance. I know there is. If I petition the Tribunal in Lyon. They may let Catherine go free and all the others.

CHRISTOPHE: It's a week away and the snow's layin' thick on the roads.

AGATHE: I'll get there.

CHRISTOPHE: They won't listen to you any more than Javogues did.

AGATHE: Things change! Look at us. At least, I'm going to try.

THÉRÈSE: Don't give me that look.

AGATHE: You're going to walk out-

THÉRÈSE: I don't believe you Agathe. You get us all thrown in clink, we nearly die and when by some miracle we get out, you want us to try our damnedest to get locked away again! I want to be free of all this! I want to feel the sun on my skin before I get too old.

AGATHE: You made me see we can't change the world without a fight. It's not about holding on to the past any more. It's not about doing what we've always been told to do. It's about closing the gap between the world we want and the way it is.

THÉRÈSE: Just walk away from it. You feel bad because your friends are out there. In trouble - and you can't help them.

AGATHE: If a woman, a friend, is murdered for what she believes, we're all violated. All stained, all stitched together - a puzzle of knots, not a fine lacework cloth but a blood-drenched rag of a thing dragged from one execution to another.

THÉRÈSE: Just cut yourself loose and fly free.

AGATHE: I can't.

(They stare at each other. THÉRÈSE takes a bag from CHRISTOPHE. She opens it and takes out a loaf of bread which she breaks in two and gives one half to AGATHE. She holds AGATHE to her and then leaves.)

CHRISTOPHE: You make sure they listen good.

AGATHE: I will.

(CHRISTOPHE gives her some money.)

CHRISTOPHE: It's all the money I got. You take it. I want you to.

(AGATHE accepts. CHRISTOPHE leaves.)

AGATHE: Alone. A woman alone. Sounds strange. Never really been so alone before. The guards have gone. Guards I made of home, family, duty, left behind. My life emptied out of me. My old life. The one I followed because it was expected. Can't run back to the safety of father's wishes and husband's convictions and God's commandments now. No, they won't do... I'm going on. To Lyon. To find out. Make my own mistakes.
(She wraps the bread up in her skirt and picks up the bucket of water)
New steps in the snow. Dangerous steps. Nobody ahead and nothing behind. *(She takes a step.)* And what will they see - father, husband, God? They'll see a woman laughing and crying at the same time as she makes her first move. Later, when she starts to speak her words will sparkle in the minds of men and a sigh of pleasure will breathe from the throats of women because their world has finally been named. And I ask you will the woman be alone then?

(Music. Lights change to a blinding whiteness. AGATHE starts walking.)

While you've a voice you can speak
You can make yourself heard
And there are always those - who'll listen

Even when the crowd turns and boos.

While you've a mind you can think
You can explore new ideas
And there are always those - who'll get excited
Even when the pack hunts you down.

While you're alive you can dream
You can stand up and be counted
And there are always those - who'll respond
Even when the mob opens fire.

(The sound of cannon fire. A red flare bursts overhead. Other men and women come on and join in, speaking single lines.)

VOICES: And when the men in suits speak
The whole world trembles
But when they fall quiet
The backroom women know the answers
And when the world spins on its axis
And begs for new directions
The young girl steps up
And gently sets it in motion
And when you and I are free
Do we run away to sea
Or ride the rapids here
All the way to the open water?

They stand motionless.

Lights out.

* Republican Lullaby sung to the tune of the Carmagnole.

Au mouvement d'une chanson
Qui des tyrans fut la leçon
J'aime à bercer à l'unisson
Et mon fils et mon nourrisson
Jadis un pauvre enfant
Craignait un revenant
Avec la Carmagnole
Le coeur lui vient en dormant
Voilà mon nourrisson câlin
Qui rouvre encore un oeil malin
Au lieu de me rendre la main
Veux-tu bien t'endormir soudain
C'est un bon gros garçon
Sans souci, bon luron
Qu'on n'aura pas de peine
A faire au bruit du canon
Qu'on n'aura pas de peine
A faire au bruit du canon
Pour toi, mon fils, d'entre mes bras
Aussitôt que tu sortiras
Sur tes petits pieds délicats
Aussitôt que tu poseras
Petit tambour battant
La Carmagnole aidant
J'espère en bonne mère
Te mettre au pas
J'espère en bonne mère
Tu mettras au pas des soldats

269